LITERATURE
AND INSUBSTANTIALITY
IN LATER EIGHTEENTH-
CENTURY ENGLAND

LITERATURE

AND

INSUBSTANTIALITY

IN LATER EIGHTEENTH-CENTURY ENGLAND

Fredric V. Bogel

WITHDRAWN

PRINCETON UNIVERSITY PRESS

PRINCETON, NEW JERSEY

Copyright © 1984 by Princeton University Press

Published by Princeton University Press, 41 William Street,
Princeton, New Jersey 08540
In the United Kingdom: Princeton University Press,
Guildford, Surrey

All Rights Reserved

Library of Congress Cataloging in Publication Data will be
found on the last printed page of this book

ISBN 0-691-06597-7

Publication of this book has been aided by a grant from
The Andrew W. Mellon Foundation

This book has been composed in Linotron Sabon

Clothbound editions of Princeton University Press books
are printed on acid-free paper, and binding materials are
chosen for strength and durability

Printed in the United States of America by Princeton
University Press, Princeton, New Jersey

FOR FRANK BRADY

AND

IN MEMORY OF W. K. WIMSATT

CONTENTS

PREFACE

This book seeks to make a more convincing case than we now have for the unity of later eighteenth-century English literature and thus for the usefulness of the mid-century mark as a literary watershed. It is an exercise in both synchronic literary history and close analysis, moving between detail and generalization according to the demands of its argument and ranging rather widely over the half century that it treats. My object is neither an exhaustive analysis of any single work nor a series of generalizations uncomplicated by particulars. Rather, I have sought to provide an instance of that useful patterning of major and significant minor works for which we turn to literary history and which constitutes one rough and ready definition of a literary period. As for the question whether literary periods exist, and the host of subsidiary questions inevitably raised in attempting to answer it, I have chosen to embody my own skepticism about periodization—so deep as to be, at times, paralyzing—in the concrete forms of the analysis I undertake rather than in theoretical argument.

I have long believed that the preface to a book ought to provide a crude statement of its argument and a bold outline of its chapters, in the spirit of Spenser's breezy canto-summarizing quatrains. My argument, then, is that English writers in the Age of Sensibility were, to a surprising degree, united by a perception of the impoverishment or insubstantiality of their experience and by their effort both to register and to resist that insubstantiality. In the course of that effort they managed to alter the very terms in which they had assessed their experience and thus to construct a paradigm of valuation capable of disclosing significance and value in the forms of their impoverishment. Such an effort inevitably redefines significance as well as experience, for it generates new modes of valuing as well as new loci of value, and new literary strategies as well as new subjects and themes.

Chapter 1 distinguishes the second half of the eighteenth

century from the first on the basis of an opposition between a concern with being and a concern with knowing. The Age of Sensibility, I argue, is principally an ontological field in which questions of being—of perceived or felt being—take precedence over other kinds of question. When the world is interrogated from this point of view, Chapter 2 argues, it discloses impoverishment of various kinds, modes of insubstantiality. The third chapter, focusing mainly on Samuel Johnson, seeks to demonstrate the ways in which later eighteenth-century writers constructed from their impoverishment a defense of common experience, a rhetoric of substantiality whose power depended on its ability to ascribe meaningfulness and value to that experience without appealing to a transcendent sphere. What that rhetoric does appeal to is the past (Chapter 4) and a newly scrutinized present (Chapter 5), seeking in each a sphere of significance and weight, of substantiality, capable of supplementing the perceived inadequacy of common experience with materials drawn from that very experience. An undertaking like this—supplementation from within rather than from without, so to speak—is inescapably problematic, for it seeks to establish in the here and now an authenticating power that is by definition, or by tradition, discoverable only elsewhere, in a sphere of transcendence or otherness. Chapter 6 explores the ambiguities and redefinitions that result from this effort. It aims as well to provide, in the shorthands of rhetorical pattern and diagram, a conclusion that is less an icon or emblem of my argument as a whole than a series of abstract mnemonics designed to liberate pattern, at times ruthlessly, from a welter of concrete textual materials.

Portions of Chapter 2 and Chapter 4 have been given as lectures at meetings of the Modern Language Association and at Cornell University; an early version of Chapter 2 appeared in *Studies in Burke and His Time* (1973-1974), of Chapter 3 in *Eighteenth-Century Studies* (1979), and of the middle section of Chapter 5 in *Studies in English Literature* (1981). For discussion, criticism, encouragement, and support of many kinds I am happily indebted to John Fyler, Julie Genster, and Janet Gezari. Molly Helms, supported in part by a grant from the Connecticut College Researh Fund, typed the final copy cheerfully and speedily.

One of the many ironies attending this project is that its author's chief supporters were forced so often to compete with it. Let me thank here Lynda, Alexander, and Elizabeth, for their love and patience.

LITERATURE
AND INSUBSTANTIALITY
IN LATER EIGHTEENTH-
CENTURY ENGLAND

· 1 ·

THE TWO CENTERS OF THE
EIGHTEENTH CENTURY

This is a book about the later eighteenth century, but it presupposes a view of the century as a whole that corresponds, in a number of points, to the traditional distinction between the Augustan Age and the Age of Sensibility. At the risk of going over familiar ground, then, this chapter sketches a few large differences between earlier and later eighteenth-century literature in order to frame, or introduce, the more sharply focused argument of the chapters that follow. (In a sense, the present chapter casts into a diachronic idiom some of the results of that largely synchronic argument.)

The distinctions that I wish to urge between the first and second half of the century are not absolute but matters of emphasis. The Augustan Age and the Age of Sensibility are, in this view, not mutually exclusive or discontinuous eras but literary configurations around two centers of gravity that exert pulls on the works of the century. Some works lie very close to one or the other of those centers, some exhibit a strong attraction to neither but enjoy a middling status, and others display some features that lie very near the first, and others that lie very near the second, center of gravity. At what level and on what basis do these centers exert their pull? Style? Structure? Theme? Genre? Mode? World view? Or some combination of these (and others)? We often, and in many cases properly, make such choices pragmatically. We work at the level that allows pattern to appear—at least pattern of a kind that we find interesting and significant—much as we move farther from and closer to a painting if we wish to concentrate on neither its largest patterns nor its minutest details but on a secure connection between a significant number of details and a few meaningful patterns.

The two centers of gravity that organize eighteenth-century

works in this way are more comprehensive and less explicit than literary themes (although they often become themes as well) yet more explicit and less comprehensive than assumptions. They have to do with the kind of thing that is generally at stake in the works of the period, the large concerns of which particular themes and thematic patterns are most readily seen as focused and individualized instances. In the first half of the century what is characteristically at stake is a matter of human knowledge, a concern with the mind's ways and modes of knowing and with the authority of the knowledge it comes to. It is toward this center that Augustan literature largely gravitates. In the second half of the century what is characteristically at stake is not the mind's effort to know but the world's ability to be experienced: the kinds of being—and the force of being—that our world, our experience, other people, and we ourselves are felt to have. It is toward this center, a concern with being, that the literature of the Age of Sensibility largely gravitates. The continuities and exceptions, of course, must be emphasized: the persistence of moral subjects throughout the century, in Johnson as in Pope; or Pope's concern with the substance of the world's being and Sterne's with the labyrinthine comedy of our labors to know. On the whole, though, the Augustan writer's typical concern is epistemological and the later eighteenth-century writer's ontological.

In that useful fiction, a typically Augustan scene, a figure tries to attain secure knowledge of human character and motive, of human nature in general or of himself. In the process he is led (or he fails to be led and thus becomes an object of satire or irony) to a fuller understanding of the complexity of human nature and the intricacies of knowing itself: the obstacles to human knowledge, apparent or unsuspected, and its curious authority—both solid and tentative—when attained. In a typical scene of the later eighteenth century a figure is engaged not in an effort of knowledge but in an act of experiencing, and almost whatever the object of that experiencing, its mode is "ontological": that is, he is experiencing the weight or substance or wholeness or meaningfulness (rather than the meaning) of the world's being, or else he is

4

experiencing the absence of just those qualities. Typically, therefore, he enjoys a plenary experience of being and presence, of the world's ontological adequacy to the demands of mind and heart for being and substance; or (much more often) he experiences just the reverse, a diminishment or thinning out of the world's being, a loss of its ontological potency and presence; and having undergone an experience of the second kind (and perhaps of the first kind as well), he seeks to reinvest his experience, or some aspect of his experience, with the weight and meaningfulness he feels it to lack. At times, he is successful in this effort, though usually not in the way, or to the degree, that he had expected. In each case what is at issue is not chiefly a matter of the mind but of the sensibility, nor of the intelligibility of experience but of its being. Augustan writers repeatedly show us that the complexity of the world may readily elude our systems of knowing; writers of the Age of Sensibility show us that the world, properly known, may amount to less than we had hoped it would.

Human knowledge is often an explicit concern of Augustan literature, most obviously perhaps of Augustan satiric prose and poetry. Intertwined with moral satire in these works is an equally important strain of intellectual satire that operates by exploring or dramatizing failures and abuses of human knowledge, as in Rochester's "Satyr against Reason and Mankind," Swift's *Tale of a Tub* and *Gulliver's Travels*, and Pope's *Dunciad*, especially the fourth book. Knowledge is often a significant theme of nonsatiric Augustan literature as well, or of works in which satire is only a subordinate element. Dryden's *Religio Laici* and *The Hind and the Panther* place human knowledge in the context of Dryden's grand theme, authority, and explore there both its strength and its limits:

> Dim, as the borrow'd beams of Moon and
>   Stars
> To *lonely, weary, wandring* Travellers,
> Is *Reason* to the *Soul*: And as on high,
> Those rowling Fires *discover* but the Sky

> Not light us *here*; So *Reason's* glimmering Ray
> Was lent, not to *assure* our *doubtfull* way,
> But *guide* us upward to a *better Day*.[1]

The first two epistles of Pope's *Essay on Man* also focus sharply on this subject, as do the *Epistles to Several Persons*, most obviously "To Cobham" and "To a Lady." As these examples suggest, in the Restoration and Augustan periods the verse epistle and verse essay (not always fully distinguishable) acquired, in their alliance with the didactic, a new prominence that they were never again to achieve, much as other flourishings of the didactic—and particularly the didactic as it treats questions of human knowledge—coincided with forms of generic experimentation such as Fielding's mixtures of novel and essay form in *Joseph Andrews* and *Tom Jones*.

Among later eighteenth-century writers this thematic emphasis on knowledge is not a common phenomenon, nor do we find much reliance on the verse essay or on the fusing of didactic impulses with forms not traditionally associated with it. The alliance of the didactic with the periodical essay persisted throughout the century, of course, most powerfully in the *Rambler, Idler*, and *Adventurer* essays of Samuel Johnson, but there the emphasis is more often on human desire than on human knowledge, on the fallacies of imagination and hope rather than of reason, and on the inadequacy of experience to imagination and desire:

> It is seldom that we find either men or places such as we expect them. He that has pictured a prospect upon his fancy, will receive little pleasure from his eyes; he that has anticipated the conversation of a wit, will wonder to what prejudice he owes his reputation. Yet it is necessary to hope, tho' hope should always be deluded, for hope itself is happiness, and its frustrations, however frequent, are yet less dreadful than its extinction.[2]

---

[1] John Dryden, *Religio Laici*, in *The Poems and Fables of John Dryden*, ed. James Kinsley (London: Oxford Univ. Press, 1962), p. 282.

[2] Samuel Johnson, *Idler* No. 58, in *"The Idler" and "The Adventurer,"* ed. W. J. Bate, John M. Bullitt, L. F. Powell, vol. 2 of The Yale Edition of

And the didactic element in a work like Cowper's *Task* has little to do with questions of human knowledge or, indeed, with the Horatian verse essay as it appears in Dryden and Pope, the poem's real alliances being rather Vergilian and georgic and its controlling theme the adequacy—even, at times, the visionary bliss—of "secluded domestic life."[3] Outside of the periodical essay and other nonfictional prose (the aesthetic treatise, for example), the later eighteenth century displays neither the same kind nor the same degree of didactic writing as the Augustan Age, and almost nowhere does it reveal anything like a comparable concern with questions of knowledge. Instead of the verse essay or verse epistle treating the theme of knowledge, it characteristically gives us forms that, used as these writers use them, stress the impact and weight of experience on an individual sensibility: forms like autobiography (nonfictional or fictional), biography, journal, epistolary novel, meditation, and ode.[4]

A literary period's characteristic conceptions of reality, no less than its preferences in genre and mode, are imaginative constructions shaped by powerful individual and historical forces, and the eighteenth century's two centers of gravity find expression in two complex images of the experience that its knowing minds and perceiving sensibilities confront. Put simply, significant reality for the Augustans is frequently two-layered, tensional, paradoxical, a holding together of opposed qualities in a union stable yet dynamic—a union, in fact, whose finite but adequate stability often depends on its underlying dynamism, as a boat may float stably on water constantly in motion or a fixed arc of light remain to echo a comet's transient passage:

---

the Works of Samuel Johnson (New Haven and London: Yale Univ. Press, 1963), p. 182.

[3] Donald Davie, *Purity of Diction in English Verse* (London: Routledge and Kegan Paul, 1967), p. 56.

[4] On the genres trypical of the Augustan Age see Rachel Trickett, *The Honest Muse: A Study in Augustan Verse* (Oxford: Clarendon Press, 1967), chap. 2, and Ralph Cohen, "The Augustan Mode in English Poetry," in *Studies in the Eighteenth Century*, ed. R. F. Brissenden (Canberra: Australian National Univ. Press, 1968), pp. 171-192.

> But now secure the painted Vessel glides,
> The Sun-beams trembling on the floating Tydes.
> . . . .
> A sudden Star, it shot thro' liquid Air,
> And drew behind a radiant *Trail* of *Hair*.[5]

Like the paradoxes of Keats's Grecian urn, such an image of reality teases us out of thought. At once an invitation and a challenge to the mind, it underlines both the powers and the limits of our capacity to know, and it gestures toward the considerable intelligibility, as well as the ultimate mystery, of external reality. (In this respect Dryden's belief that while reason can take us far toward an understanding of the truths of religion it must at last yield to the qualitatively different authority of faith is a particular version of the typical Augustan idea of the mind's relation to reality.)[6]

Man himself displays an analogous structure:

> Plac'd on this isthmus of a middle state,
> A being darkly wise, and rudely great:
> With too much knowledge for the Sceptic
>   side,
> With too much weakness for the Stoic's pride,
> He hangs between; in doubt to act, or rest,
> In doubt to deem himself a God, or Beast;
> In doubt his Mind or Body to prefer,
> Born but to die, and reas'ning but to err;
> Alike in ignorance, his reason such,
> Whether he thinks too little, or too much:
> Chaos of Thought and Passion, all confus'd;
> Still by himself abus'd, or disabus'd;
> Created half to rise, and half to fall;
> Great lord of all things, yet a prey to all;

[5] Alexander Pope, "The Rape of the Lock," 2.47-48, 5.127-128.

[6] See Philip Harth, *Contexts of Dryden's Thought* (Chicago: Univ. of Chicago Press, 1968), chaps. 1 and 2. And compare Pope, *An Essay on Man*, 1.187-188: "Shall he alone, whom rational we call,/Be pleas'd with nothing, if not bless'd with all?"

> Sole judge of Truth, in endless Error hurl'd:
> The glory, jest, and riddle of the world!
> (*An Essay on Man*, 2.3-18)

Stable though in dynamic poise, intelligible though mysterious, formulable yet a "Chaos," paradoxical—both glory and jest, and therefore riddle—Augustan man is the counterpart of the world he confronts, as Pope makes clear in this second epistle of *An Essay on Man* (thus, when man finally understands the structure of his own being he can also see his connectedness with the similarly structured cosmos from which he had earlier and proudly separated himself).[7]

The figure confronting such structures of world and self—the dramatic audience or typical consciousness, so to speak, implied by this image of reality—is defined with considerable clarity in the Augustan Age and bears a strong resemblance to the dramatic audience of a poem like *An Essay on Man*. He is primarily a figure engaged in an act of knowledge, an effort of understanding, and he must surmount certain obstacles if that effort is to be successful. The first of these is his own pride and certainty. Armed with assumptions, categories of knowing, and a powerful faith that what he investigates was designed to be investigated, easily comprehended, and both gratifying and flattering to the investigator, this figure must undergo an exemplary humbling, if not a humiliation, for he has mistaken the external world's nature and his own. Then, finding himself a part of what he had sought to comprehend (in both senses), the investigator may begin to revise his assumptions and the terms of his inquiry. If he does so successfully, he will discover the following features of the world and the self that he seeks to know. First (as his humbling ought to have shown him), they are related, as are, in fact, all of the particulars he studies: "All are but parts of one

---

[7] Although (e.g., in *Essay on Man*, 1.149-150, and elsewhere) he must also acknowledge the otherness of that cosmos of which he is merely a part, must therefore, as Wallace Stevens puts it, "see the earth again,/Cleared of its stiff and stubborn, man-locked set" ("Angel Surrounded by Paysans").

stupendous whole." Second, the connections between these particulars are not the links of a complex agglomerative grouping but the subtle interdependencies of a coherent system ("whole"). Third, the whole is not static but rather sustained by energies, tensions, balances, and dynamisms of various kinds; it is not inert but alive, and it enjoys the stability of living process rather than that of mineral inertness. Fourth, the characteristic structure of this whole is therefore tensional, paradoxical, a holding together of opposites: the static and the dynamic, fixity and process, whole and part, centrifugal and centripetal energies, and the like. Fifth, such a radically tensional and paradoxical whole is to a great degree comprehensible yet ultimately mysterious, and this is as true of the observer's own nature as it is of the external world. Thus the act of knowledge that attempts to grasp either is from one point of view inevitably imperfect, from another always incomplete or infinitive ("all our Knowledge is, *OURSELVES TO KNOW*"), and from still another always more or less provisional—not wavering or colored by an easy skepticism (like that of Bacon's jesting Pilate) but marked by a security short of utter certainty and dogmatic thoughtlessness, a security that is always susceptible of revision and correction and which thus, finding its own stability in change and self-correction, mirrors the dynamic stability of the world to be known. (This is why the speaker of *An Essay on Man*, after shattering the dogmatism and self-centeredness of proud man, leaves his posture of thundering sage and, at the close of the fourth epistle, thrusts himself back into the *search* for secure knowledge. Certainty is often a temporary necessity, but it is never a permanent possibility.)[8]

In the Augustan period there is a powerful analogy between its image of reality and its characteristic literary structures, and between its conception of an adequate knower of that reality and the dramatic audience implied by those structures. Knower is to world, then, as dramatic audience is to work. Paradox, tension, *concors discordia*—these pervade the im-

---

[8] See Ralph Cohen, "Augustan Mode," p. 185.

agery and the couplet rhetoric of Augustan poems, as in Denham's famous lines (which also insist on the analogy between world and work):

> O could I flow like thee, and make thy stream
> My great example, as it is my theme.
> Tho' deep, yet clear; tho' gentle, yet not dull;
> Strong, without rage; without o'erflowing,
>   full.

Parallelism, antithesis, chiasmus—one, perhaps, a local effect within a larger structure of the same or a different kind—these define a verse structure mirroring in its tensional difficulty and its demands on the dramatic audience the reality it describes. Nor is it just in the rhetoric of line and couplet or in the imagery of the harmoniously confused that this pattern of tensional and paradoxical doubleness appears. It is also found in the Augustans' typical conception of dramatic audience and in their characteristic form of irony. In each case the movement from the early part of the century to the later involves a dismantling of doubleness, a flattening out of the paradoxical. Insofar as these developments mirror an alteration in the idea of reality, that reality becomes, during the century, more nearly univocal and intelligible but less mysterious and inexhaustible than it had been for the Augustans, and it characteristically challenges us not to know its paradoxical complexity but to endure its largely mystery-less being.

Let us look at dramatic audience a bit more closely. Northrop Frye has argued that the Augustan audience is detached, aesthetically distanced from the work of art it contemplates, while the audience in the Age of Sensibility is closely bound up, psychologically, with the work (or rather with that process of composition, rather than finished product, on which a number of authors in the period choose to focus.)[9] Murray Cohen makes a related point. "The reader of much late-eighteenth-

[9] Northrop Frye, "Towards Defining an Age of Sensibility," in *Eighteenth-Century English Literature: Modern Essays in Criticism*, ed. James L. Clifford (N.Y.: Oxford Univ. Press, 1959), p. 316.

11

century literature," he argues, "is not intended, as was the reader earlier in the century, to negotiate his way through a cleverly interrelated logical (or satirically illogical) process, but to respond to a series of charged expressive scenes or to identify (with) several distinctly affected characters."[10] To the movement from distance to intimacy that Frye sees, Cohen adds a movement from the intellectual to the emotional, from thoughtful "negotiation" to affective response, correctness of knowledge to power of feeling.

Both formulations, however, image these changes as structures of simple succession: A is followed by B, distance by intimacy, thought by feeling. The development of the dramatic audience in the eighteenth century, however, like the development of a number of literary elements, is rather a process in which the components of a double structure, held together in the first half of the century, separate in the second: AB becomes A and B. What Cohen says of later eighteenth-century works, for example, that they "compete . . . for the intensity of readers' responses," that they try to involve us and make a place for us in the text, is indeed true of one kind of work, the kind (like *Tristram Shandy* or *A Sentimental Journey*) that puts the dramatic audience into a position of great intimacy: Boswell's journals, for example, which allow us to share his interior life (even granting us something of the pornography-reader's "involvement"), or Richardson's novels, which make us overhearers of epistolary intimacy, or those sublime odes that allow us to listen in, as it were, on a private and passionate colloquy between poet and Evening or Fear, a moment of lyric privacy.

The other audience-structure characteristic of the later eighteenth century, however, is just the reverse. It places the dramatic audience at a great distance from the scene it depicts, at times far above it, like Troilus "stellified" at the end of Chaucer's poem. In such works we view with something of the detachment of "Observation" at the beginning of *The*

---

[10] Murray Cohen, *Sensible Words: Linguistic Practice in England, 1640-1785* (Baltimore and London: The Johns Hopkins Univ. Press, 1977), p. 105.

Vanity of Human Wishes ("a melancholy and sympathetic omniscience," as Raman Selden puts it)[11] or of Johnson's narrator at the beginning of *Rasselas* (or Voltaire's throughout *Candide*); or from the different yet equally remote perspectives supplied by the speaker of Gray's Eton College ode (an ode on a "Distant Prospect," as the title tells us) and the epitaph section of the *Elegy Written in a Country Churchyard*;[12] or with the massive irony of Gibbon's narrator in the *History*. These are the extremes, and the typical forms, of the dramatic audience in the later eighteenth century. In this period, then, we experience either great intimacy, as in most examples of what Frye calls literature of process, or great detachment, as in most examples of the literature of product. Both kinds of dramatic audience, however, are typical of the Age of Sensibility.

The Augustans, in contrast, rarely offer us such intensities of intimacy or distance because they rarely offer either alone, in a purified form. The typical Augustan dramatic audience (or audience-surrogate) is rather at a qualified and problematic distance, or in a treacherous intimacy. In *The Rape of the Lock*, for example, Belinda is the intimate dramatic audience of her little world and Clarissa its distanced critic, mistress of the sober overview. But the dramatic audience of the poem as a whole must accommodate both of these perspectives to a stable yet self-qualifying view larger and more tentative than either taken alone. *Dunciad* offers even more violent extremes of perspective and far less likelihood of fusing them, for its dramatic audience is from one perspective the intimate of a heroic and tragic satirist yet from another the spectator of a comical follower of Dulness. The case is much the same with what Henry Sams has called Swift's "satire of the second person," which makes of the dramatic audience's distance a

[11] Raman Selden, *English Verse Satire, 1590-1765* (London: George Allen & Unwin, 1978), p. 164.

[12] See Frank Brady, "Structure and Meaning in Gray's *Elegy*," in *From Sensibility to Romanticism*, ed. Frederick W. Hilles and Harold Bloom (N.Y.: Oxford Univ. Press, 1965), pp. 177-189.

trap and of his intimacy an indictment.[13] The point is that in each of these examples, and in Augustan literature generally, the dramatic audience, whether more or less intimate or detached than his counterpart later in the century, is both of these at the same time because the Augustan dramatic audience is a different kind of figure or structure: double rather than single, tensional rather than uniform, problematically rather than univocally related to the utterance of which he is the audience.

That is not to say that the structure of the dramatic audience is always simple in the later eighteenth century, just that its complexity is far less often a matter of the double and equivocal, or of the paradoxical. The later eighteenth-century dramatic speaker, for example, who is related structurally and internally to the dramatic audience, tends to exhibit complexity of a serial and developmental kind, as in the pattern of "satire manqué" that W. J. Bate has described.[14] Here the speaker begins in a classically satiric posture, distanced from the figures he mocks or otherwise disapproves of; but then the satiric mode is abandoned and the satirist's distance is transformed into sympathy for, and connectedness with, those figures. This is a temporal process, however complex it may become: first distance, then sympathy. Far more typical of the Augustans is a simultaneous entertaining of both postures and thus a complexity—in speaker as in audience—of a different sort. The Augustan dramatic speaker often seeks to preserve, as a condition instructive in itself, a certain problematic nearness to and distance from those he addresses or surveys. The speaker in "satire manqué" begins by distancing himself symbolically, as satirists always do, but then collapses that distance, as though the real problem were not a matter of the differences between one kind of person and another but something larger.

[13] Henry W. Sams, "Swift's Satire of the Second Person," *English Literary History* 26 (1959): 36-44.

[14] W. J. Bate, "Johnson and Satire Manqué," in *Eighteenth-Century Studies in Honor of Donald F. Hyde*, ed. W. H. Bond (N.Y.: Grolier Club, 1970), pp. 145-160.

That something larger has to do with the attitudes of eighteenth-century writers toward knowledge and being. Presupposing the solidity of the world, Augustan writers are typically engaged in a questioning of the authority of human knowledge. Such questioning does not often flatly deny that authority, but it does put it in doubt, if only to affirm it more subtly and thoughtfully. Fielding, for example, proceeds by assuming the existence in our minds of categories of thought, or schemata, creating literary equivalents of these (assertions, clearly demarcated levels of style, chapter divisions, neatly thematic parallels, and contrasts of scene or character), and then confronting them with situations or characters or actions not adequately explicable in terms of such categories. This requires that the categories be revised, not rejected, and the revision is doubly instructive for it shows us both a more adequate category and an indispensable process of revision from which no category is exempt (all our schemata, in Piaget's terms, are "corrigible schemata"). In Fielding this pattern of revision is usually a rather secure structure, but it does make the double take a condition of adequate knowledge. We can find something of the same thing in Dryden, Pope, and Swift, although in all three, especially Pope and Swift, and particularly Swift, the structure is often highly equivocal and uncertain and the knowledge arrived at of far less obvious authority than in Fielding. What all these writers are engaged in, though, is the inducement in the dramatic audience of what Kierkegaard (following Hegel) calls "self-estrangement," the undoing of thoughtless immediacy in which we are held by opinions (however correct) and the replacement of that immediacy with an ironic self-awareness that earns its opinions by holding them reflectively, tentatively, and with a full awareness of their corrigibility.[15]

[15] Søren Kierkegaard, *The Concept of Irony*, trans. Lee M. Capel (London: Collins, 1966), pp. 72, 248-249, 340. Socrates, says Kierkegaard, sought knowledge "which estranged the individual from the immediacy in which he has heretofore lived" (pp. 248-249). The point of such estrangement is that "in our joy over the result we have forgotten that a result has no value if it has not actually been acquired. . . . Irony is like the negative way, not the

Presupposing the adequacy of human knowledge, writers in the second half of the century are typically engaged in questioning the solidity of the world's being. For them human knowledge is not particularly uncertain or in need of vigilant scrutiny and correction; it is instead more often useless, either because it cannot help us out of a plight that is ontological rather than epistemological or because it is precisely knowledge itself that threatens to undo the world by seeing through it. It is knowledge which forces the mature to see that "Human life is every where a state in which much is to be endured, and little to be enjoyed," which leads the youthful to "see too far into the system of things to be much in earnest," and which escapes entirely the very young, who therefore see nothing at all, and are happy:

> Yet, ah! why should they know their fate?
> Since sorrow never comes too late,
> And happiness too swiftly flies.
> Thought would destroy their paradise.
> No more: where ignorance is bliss
> 'Tis folly to be wise.[16]

If the Augustans see a certain kind of self-estrangement as necessary to save us from the passivity of mind that is one of Dulness' chief gifts to mankind, many writers in the Age of

---

truth but the way. Everyone who has a result merely as such does not possess it, for he has not the way. When irony appears on the scene it brings the way, though not the way whereby one who imagines himself to have a result comes to possess it, but the way whereby the result forsakes him" (p. 340). This warning applies with great force to the tendency to detach epigrammatic passages (in Pope, Johnson, and others) from the context that shows how they are "held." "Moral lectures and aphorisms," Eric Rothstein has said, ". . . are in a sense the personal form of received ideas" (*Systems of Order and Inquiry in Later Eighteenth-Century Fiction* [Berkeley, Los Angeles, London: Univ. of California Press, 1975], p. 26). When thus isolated, only the passive "receivedness" of such passages remains.

[16] *Rasselas*, chap. 11; *Boswell's London Journal, 1762-1763*, ed. Frederick A. Pottle (London: Heinemann, 1950), p. 77; Thomas Gray, "Ode on a Distant Prospect of Eton College," in *The Poems of Thomas Gray, William Collins, Oliver Goldsmith*, ed. Roger Lonsdale (London: Longmans, 1969), p. 63.

Sensibility discover an inevitable estrangement of the self from substantial experience, an estrangement that knowledge cannot heal and may well cause. They discover a different kind of estrangement as well, a separation of our power to know from our ability to experience and thus, often, from our capacity for happiness and even for action in which we can robustly believe. Thus at the end of *Rasselas* each character forms a wish to be acted upon when the flood waters recede. Yet "of these wishes that they had formed they well knew that none could be obtained." If in the Augustan period knowledge is often uncertain or fragile, in the Age of Sensibility it is more often burdensome, destructive, or simply useless, and what is fragile is the fabric of experience.

This contrast extends to the nature of irony. Irony is, of course, a characteristically eighteenth-century structure, a staple of Dryden, Swift, Gay, and Pope, but also of Johnson, Burke, Gibbon, and even Blake. But Augustan irony usually tells us of the imperfections of our knowledge and of the frailty of what we had taken to be the solid foundations of that knowledge. In contrast, irony in the later part of the century tells us of our imperfect possibilities for happiness and fulfillment in the world, of the world's inadequacy to the demands of mind and heart. When Pope discusses the elusiveness of happiness, such irony as informs his discussion is directed at our inability to see what is within our grasp. For him, happiness, though "still so near us, yet beyond us lies,/O'erlook'd, seen double, by the fool and wise" (*An Essay on Man*, 4.5-6). Indeed happiness is "no where to be found, or ev'ry where" (16), and finding it is a matter of moral and intellectual perception: "Take Nature's path, and mad Opinion's leave,/All states can reach it [i.e., happiness], and all heads conceive" (29-30).

For Johnson, too, we do not see clearly enough, although that is partly because the world itself is a "Clouded Maze" that our emotions—the emotive energies of any man or woman, Johnson's abstractions seem to say—further obscure with "Snares." Thus,

17

> wav'ring Man, betray'd by vent'rous Pride,
> To tread the dreary Paths without a Guide;
> As treach'rous Phantoms in the Mist delude,
> Shuns fancied Ills, or chases airy Good.[17]

Compared to this, Pope's "mighty maze" is a model of per-spicuity. But in Johnson, the obscurity of the world is merely a preliminary problem, for what "Observation" sees beneath that obscurity is a lucid pattern of earthly emptiness, "The Vanity of Human Wishes" and the vacuity of the world's being.[18] "Where then shall Hope and Fear their Objects find?" (343). In Celestial Wisdom, who "makes the Happiness she does not find" (368). As for the world, its apparent governor, fate, "wings with ev'ry Wish th'afflictive Dart,/Each Gift of Nature, and each Grace of Art" (15-16), and the effect of this fatal compromising of blessings is that the pursuit of each merely human good exhibits the same inevitable pattern of expectation and defeat that marks the lives of the candidates for preferment: "They mount, they shine, evaporate, and fall" (76). The ironies of such a vision are turned not against the delusive certainties of false knowledge but the underlying on-tological poverty of the world.

The characteristic vice or human weakness of each half of the century is thus different as well. For the Augustans, as for (and in part because of) Milton, it is pride, and particularly pride as an obstacle to true knowledge of ourselves, of the world, and of our place in the world:

> Of all the Causes which conspire to blind
> Man's erring Judgment, and misguide the Mind,
> What the weak Head with strongest Byass rules,
> Is *Pride*, the *never-failing Vice of Fools*.
> (*An Essay on Criticism*, 201-204)

---

[17] "The Vanity of Human Wishes" (7-10), in *Samuel Johnson: The Complete English Poems*, ed. J. D. Fleeman (N.Y.: St. Martin's Press, 1973), p. 83.
[18] See the interesting essay by D. V. Boyd, "Vanity and Vacuity: A Reading of Johnson's Verse Satires," *English Literary History* 39 (1972): 387-403.

In Pride, in reas'ning Pride, our error lies:
All quit their sphere, and rush into the skies.
(An Essay on Man, 1.123-124)

I here entreat those who have any tincture of this absurd vice [pride] that they will not presume to appear in my sight.
(Gulliver's Travels, ending)

Pride keeps us from seeing our own littleness and the world's immensity, and it thus blinds us to the genuine worth of both self and world. What corresponds to pride in the ontological context of the later eighteenth century is optimism—naive, uncomplicated faith in the ability of experience not just to secure our happiness but also to affirm its own substantiality: to display force, complexity, weight, a sufficiency of being.[19] Optimism thus blinds us to the poverty of the world as pride, for Swift or Pope, blinds us to its orderly abundance. A major dilemma posed by the Literature of Sensibility, of course, is that to divest oneself of such optimism is also to surrender the ontological adequacy of experience.

Voltaire's *Candide* brings together a number of these themes. On one level the book records the undoing of Panglossian optimism; Candide even becomes enamored, for a while, of its opposite as represented by Pococurante: "Oh, what a superior man!... What a great genius this Pococurante is! Nothing can please him."[20] This is the defeat of moral optimism, the discovery that the world one had thought perfectly good is riddled with manifold evil. The sheer rush of horrific events by which the book thrusts this discovery upon us, however,

[19] See, among many Johnsonian texts, *Rambler* No. 196, in *The Rambler*, ed. W. J. Bate and Albrecht B. Strauss, vols. 3, 4, and 5 of The Yale Edition of the Works of Samuel Johnson (New Haven and London: Yale Univ. Press, 1969).

[20] Voltaire, *Candide, or Optimism*, trans. Donald M. Frame (N.Y.: New American Library, 1961), p. 87. On the thematic possibilities, comic and otherwise, of plot and pace in Voltaire, see Erich Auerbach, *Mimesis: The Representation of Reality in Western Literature*, trans. Willard Trask (Princeton: Princeton Univ. Press, 1953), pp. 358-361, and Carey McIntosh, *The Choice of Life: Samuel Johnson and the World of Fiction* (New Haven and London: Yale Univ. Press, 1973), pp. 58-60.

has another consequence as well. For in illustrating the commonplaceness of mindless evil, these events (murders, rapes, disfigurings, treacheries) also desubstantialize the event as such. As a result, individual acts are drained of their ontological weight as well as of their moral significance; things and events lose their capacity to give either pleasure or pain (of which wild amounts are endured with a sometimes comical nonchalance), and they therefore lose their defining or essential character and thus their very potency *as* thing or event. Even certain death is, in several cases, a good deal less certain— and simply less—than it seems (Cunégonde, her brother, Pangloss, and so on). Thus if Pangloss' optimism is absurd because the world refutes it at every moment, Martin's pessimism is no better able to supply happiness or a world of substance and being. And it is questionable whether the cultivation of one's garden is any more efficacious in delivering a world of solid and complex meaningfulness, however effective it might be in curbing our optimism or our sheer speculative energy. To cultivate our garden is, finally, not just to give up optimism and wayward speculation but to abjure—as a dangerous absurdity—the dream of precisely such a world. For optimism tells us not just that the world is ultimately good rather than evil but that it has adequate being as well; *Candide* tells us that both of these beliefs are delusions, efforts to deny the world's physical and moral evil and its irremediable ontological poverty.

That irremediability, of which we find a different form in Johnson, distinguishes a good deal of later eighteenth-century satire from that of the Augustans, who characteristically focus not simply on failures of knowledge and self-knowledge but on the (at least potential) corrigibility of their satiric victims or of the reader to whom those victims are displayed. We can see this large and complex contrast of satiric modes played out with great clarity and some simplification in three versions of a particular kind of epigram, that which sums up the character and life of a satiric figure:

Full sixty years the World has been her Trade,
The wisest Fool much Time has ever made.
("To a Lady," 123-124)

20

His Fall was destin'd to a barren Strand,
A petty Fortress, and a dubious Hand;
He left the Name, at which the World grew pale,
To point a Moral, or adorn a Tale.
          (*The Vanity of Human Wishes*, 219-222)

          Her whole life is an Epigram smack
              smooth & neatly pend
          Platted quite neat to catch applause
              with a sliding noose at the end.
                    (Epigram)[21]

Whatever sympathy we find in Pope's epigram (and there is much sympathy in the portrait of Atossa as a whole, as in those of Flavia, Narcissa, and others in the poem) coexists with a clear distance, and this distance is a measure of the self-knowledge that Atossa might have had but refused, a measure not merely of failure, then, but of the refusal or deflection from oneself of available insight. There is sympathy in Johnson's account of Charles as well, but sympathy of a different kind.[22] In *The Vanity of Human Wishes* people do not gain, as the Friend in "To a Lady" has gained, the insight that can make them virtuous as well as happy. Insofar as insight counts at all in Johnson's poem it tells us that, apart from what heaven can supply, there is nothing. The summary neatness of Johnson's closing couplets, then, does not display the ironic clarity of a pattern that anyone ought to have been able to see (as Atossa ought to have seen the pattern she enacts) but the flatness to which life after life in *The Vanity* is reduced.[23] In this case that reduction is caught in the transformation of individual into type, life into story, person into cautionary example, and even cautionary example in extrapoetic stories (as Charles is an example in the world to which Johnson's poem refers) into cautionary example in *this* story (Charles as example in *The Vanity* itself). In the summarizing

---

[21] William Blake, *The Complete Poems*, ed. Alicia Ostriker (Harmondsworth: Penguin Books, 1977), p. 157.

[22] See Bate, "Satire Manqué," passim.

[23] As are the lives in parts of Crabbe's *The Village* and *The Parish Register*.

epigram we see, not an ironically lucid display of the knowledge a (corrigible) character missed but something like a miniature elegy for the death of substantial experience, its very compression figuring, so to speak, the compressibility—and thus the internal vacuity—of a human life. "It is said by modern philosophers," Johnson tells us in *Rambler* No. 8, "that not only the great globes of matter are thinly scattered through the universe, but the hardest bodies are so porous that, if all matter were compressed to perfect solidity, it might be contained in a cube of a few feet." If a proverb, as Walter Benjamin has said, "is a ruin which stands on the site of an old story and in which a moral twines about a happening like ivy around a wall,"[24] then in Johnson this kind of epigram is similarly a funereal ruin with a moral, standing on the site not of a story but of a character that has "vanish'd out of Substance into Name."[25]

Blake takes this impulse even further. His epigram does not summarize but is the totality of the portrait, and it is the totality of "Her" life as well. Instead of the dwindling of life into literature that we find in Johnson ("Moral," "Tale"), Blake gives us a life whose very mode of existence is precisely that of an epigram. Moreover it is an epigram of a particular kind, a kind that undoes in several ways much of the briskness and point of Pope's and Johnson's couplets. Built in a slack heptameter, avoiding those patterns of internal architecture that lend the eighteenth-century heroic couplet its uncollapsible strength, Blake's flaccid fourteeners align two ghostly paradigms of nonbeing—"life" and "art"—in such a way as to deny any essential tension between them. For Blake "Epigrammatic tautology seems to be a kind of death," as John Hollander has said, and as in Johnson it is principally the death of being rather than of insight.[26]

[24] Walter Benjamin, *Illuminations*, trans. Harry Zohn (N.Y.: Schocken Books, 1969), p. 108.

[25] "Of the Pythagorean Philosophy" (from Ovid, *Met.* 15.636), in *Poems and Fables of John Dryden*, ed. James Kinsley (London: Oxford Univ. Press, 1962), p. 808.

[26] John Hollander, "Blake and the Metrical Contract," in *From Sensibility to Romanticism*, p. 307 (see note 12, above). Blake, of course is no enemy

The conceptual field with which this study is concerned, then, that of the later eighteenth century, is principally an ontological field. The questions posed, the concerns that arise, the themes that achieve prominence, the rhetorical strategies that are deployed, bear most often on the weight or weightlessness, the substantiality or insubstantiality of experience to a perceiving sensibility rather than on its intelligibility to an inquiring mind. The following chapters focus on some of the principal dramas enacted in this field. They attempt to describe the distinguishing features of a remarkable period of English literature and to demonstrate that the middle of the eighteenth century inaugurates a literary era both more coherent and more decisively distinguishable from the era of Dryden and Pope than it has often seemed to be.

---

to the epigrammatic as such (and I suppose few good poets are *pleased* by "epigrammatic tautology"). But when he turns to it, as in the *Proverbs of Hell*, he does so in a dialectical frame of mind, with a strong sense of the more traditional kind of formulation that his revolutionary pith (and vinegar) seeks to overthrow. Hollander's discussion of the "anti-epigram" in Blake is often shrewd, as in the paragraph from which I have just quoted: "The Question Answered" is

> What is it men in women do require?
> The lineaments of gratified desire.
> What is it women do in men require?
> The lineaments of gratified desire.

"The whole Augustan tradition of the two-couplet epigram," says Hollander, "is undermined by the unyielding hammered insistence of the repeated line and the ironic absence of wit. The reader is implicitly rebuked for expecting a logical movement toward the discovery of a conclusion—as if all epigrams were merely circular, just as logical proofs produce only new tautologies—and the form plunges us into the identity without remorse. It is not surprising, then, to find one of Blake's most explicit anti-epigrams couched in a couplet of fourteeners: 'Her whole Life is an Epigram, smart smooth & neatly pen'd,/ Platted quite neat to catch applause with a sliding noose at the end.' Epigrammatic tautology, for Blake, seems to be a kind of death."

23

· 2 ·

THE PERCEPTION OF
INSUBSTANTIALITY

English writers of the half century following Pope's death did not think of themselves as part of a unified literary movement, and the diversity of theme, of style, of tone and structural pattern that the best-known works of the period display suggests that their perception of themselves was, by and large, an accurate one. The cavortings of plot in *Tristram Shandy*; the wry circularities of Johnson's *Rasselas* and *Journey to the Western Islands*; the gradual dilation of *jeu d'esprit* into muted apocalyptic vision in Cowper's *Task*; the juxtaposed perspectives and multiple modes (narrative, dialogue, confession) of Boswell's *London Journal*; the ringing antiphonal pairings of Smart's *Jubilate Agno*—the school that could unite such works as these, that could accommodate Sterne and Smart and Boswell, or Burns and Burke and Chatterton, must exhibit such catholicity of taste as to call into question its very existence as a movement of distinct and definable literary persuasions.

For what the poems and prose works of the later eighteenth century disclose is not so much a shared set of literary assumptions as a common attitude toward human experience: specifically, a pervasive awareness of its insubstantiality. One form of this awareness governs Johnson's greatest poem, "The Vanity of Human Wishes." But the perception of moral insubstantiality that Johnson articulates in that poem is only one aspect of an attitude "less ethical," as one critic puts it, "than ontological": a loss of confidence not simply in the meaningfulness of reality but in its very solidity, an incapacity to experience one's world and oneself as the robust and substantial presences we normally require them to be.[1]

---

[1] D. V. Boyd, "Vanity and Vacuity: A Reading of Johnson's Verse Satires," *English Literary History* 39 (1972): 396. See also page 20 of Georges Poulet, *Studies in Human Time*, trans. Elliott Coleman (Baltimore: The Johns Hop-

This condition, which is closely related to hypochondria as the eighteenth century understood it, is a version of the state of experiential disrepair that R. D. Laing has labeled "ontological insecurity." The ontologically secure person, writes Laing, has "a sense of his presence in the world as a real, alive, whole, and, in a temporal sense, a continuous person. . . . He will encounter all the hazards of life . . . from a centrally firm sense of . . . his integral selfhood and personal identity, of the reliability of natural processes, of the substantiality of natural processes, of the substantiality of others."[2] By contrast, the ontologically insecure person may experience himself as chaotically insubstantial, or temporally discontinuous, or merely two-dimensional and schematic, a kind of humor character. The line between self and other may be indistinct or shifting, and other persons, things, or natural processes may seem as unreliable or insubstantial as the self. At the hypothetical extreme the ontologically insecure person experiences "total loss of relatedness with self and other," a condition that Laing, borrowing the phrase from Blake, calls "chaotic nonentity."

Laing, of course, is not describing the spiritual situation of the later eighteenth century but a pathological state, a schizophrenic manner of experiencing the world and oneself. Yet his terms, specialized and dramatic as they are, can help us to chart less extreme and abnormal modes of consciousness. It is possible, after all, to speak of degrees of mental disturbance, to construct a series of rather fine gradations from the hypothetical state of chaotic nonentity to the equally hypothetical state of perfect psychic integration, without thereby denying or trivializing the special pathos of the genuinely insane. "Perhaps," says Johnson's Imlac, "if we speak with rigorous exactness, no human mind is in its right state." But this

---

kins Univ. Press, 1956), and chapters 1 and 2 of A. D. Nuttall, *A Common Sky: Philosophy and the Literary Imagination* (Berkeley and Los Angeles: Univ. of California Press, 1974).

[2] R. D. Laing, *The Divided Self: An Existential Study in Sanity and Madness* (N.Y.: Pantheon, 1969), p. 39.

opinion does not keep Imlac from distinguishing between the mad astronomer's condition and his own.

Imlac, moreover, makes that distinction by relying on the experience of minds adjudged normal within the world of *Rasselas*, his own among them, and this standard is a perfectly adequate gauge of the astronomer's claim to have "possessed for five years the regulation of the weather and the distribution of the seasons." When a critic is studying the forms of consciousness embodied in a work of literature, however, the standard of normality he brings to that work becomes irrelevant. If the world of *Rasselas*, that is, were one in which men indeed controlled the processes of nature, then Rasselas—and not the astronomer—would be the victim of a delusion; it would not matter at all that Rasselas' conception of possible experience happened to coincide with that of most readers. The same principle applies equally to works that do not conflict so sharply with common-sense notions of reality. When the speaker of *Tristram Shandy* or *The Task* or the *London Journal* experiences the world in a certain way, we must grant him his experience and his world. Indeed, we have no choice but to do so, for we encounter that world only as he has experienced it, only as it is mediated—or constructed—by the consciousness informing the work itself.

Every reader of the *London Journal*, for example, will recall Boswell's recurrent awareness of insubstantiality, whether that awareness is expressed as "a thorough conviction of the vanity of all things," or a vision of "the nothingness of all sublunary enjoyments," or merely as a world-weary journal entry: "Friday 11 February. Nothing worth putting into my journal occurred this day. It passed away imperceptibly, like the whole life of many a human existence."[3] But as critical readers we are not called upon to make a judgment, either to commiserate with the narrator and confirm his perception or to urge on him a more "positive and realistic" attitude toward experi-

[3] James Boswell, *Boswell's London Journal, 1762-1763*, ed. Frederick A. Pottle (London: Heinemann, 1950), pp. 150, 214, 188.

ence. This is his experience. It is, in the only applicable sense of the word, true.

To say that we are not to impose external standards, of course, is not to say that there can be no contrasting perceptions within a work or even within the consciousness of a single character. After paying a reverent farewell visit to Holyroodhouse and Arthur's Seat—"that lofty romantic mountain"—in Edinburgh, Boswell self-consciously reflects: "I am surely much happier in this way than if I just considered Holyroodhouse as so much stone and lime which has been put together in a certain way, and Arthur Seat as so much earth and rock raised above the neighbouring plains."[4] The venerable castle, or so much stone and lime; the lofty romantic mountain, or so much earth and rock—neither description is truer than the other. As Boswell himself recognizes, each is a thoroughly accurate account of the way the world appears, of the way the world is or may be, to a particular consciousness at a particular moment. In the later eighteenth century, for Boswell as for many others, that world is pervaded by insubstantiality.

The political and the aesthetic theories of Edmund Burke, for example, work to resist that insubstantiality by participating in what might be called a quest for otherness, an effort to establish the solidity and presentness of the world external to the mind. Like the speaker of Yeats's "Meru," Burke believed that the human intellect leads man "ravening, raging, and uprooting" through the centuries. In his own time, particularly in the events and theories of the French Revolution, he saw it threatening to reduce the real world to the "nakedness and solitude of metaphysical abstraction."[5] Thus his insistence on the circumstantial and organic nature of human institutions, and on the chastening vastness and vagueness of the sublime image, are different aspects of a single effort to

[4] Ibid., pp. 41-42.
[5] Edmund Burke, *Reflections on the Revolution in France*, ed. Conor Cruise O'Brien (Baltimore: Penguin Books, 1969), p. 90.

tame that reductive intellect and summon back into substantial existence the world it had reduced.

This concern with an external reality substantial enough to resist the energies of mind also connects the sublime with the picturesque, for the effect of the picturesque, according to its theorist Uvedale Price, "is curiosity. . . . It is the coquetry of nature."[6] This coquetry of the picturesque object does not astonish as does the Burkean sublime. Rather, its irregularity and roughness, its variety and sudden discontinuities gradually lead the mind toward a full perception of what is observed and thus toward a willingness to grant it "interest," to acknowledge its solid and various actuality. In another sphere the quest for substantiality lies behind the sublime and other forms of what Karl Barth has called the eighteenth century's "pursuit of the mysterious,"[7] a pursuit in which even Samuel Johnson, despite his contempt for the sublime, took an active part by virtue of his enduring interest in such phenomena as ghosts and second sight.

Insubstantiality threatened not only the fabric of the external world but the wholeness and continuity of the self as well. There is Johnson's anguished perception of the "vacuities of being" that result from indolence or guilt; Boswell's recurrent feeling that his experience and identity are discontinuous or decaying, that he must reconstruct and reformulate himself; Cowper's gentler assessment in *The Task* (4.282-298) of those moments of discontinuity when "the understanding takes repose/In indolent vacuity of thought," his confession—foreshadowing the note of torpid vacancy that Coleridge captures in "Frost at Midnight"—of "a soul that does not always think";[8] and of course, earlier in the century there is Hume's compar-

---

[6] Uvedale Price, *An Essay on the Picturesque* (London, 1796), p. 105. I am indebted to the fine discussions of the picturesque by Martin Price in *To the Palace of Wisdom: Studies in Order and Energy from Dryden to Blake* (Garden City, N.Y.: Doubleday, 1964), pp. 375-388, and "The Picturesque Moment," in *From Sensibility to Romanticism*, ed. Frederick W. Hilles and Harold Bloom (N.Y.: Oxford Univ. Press, 1965), pp. 259-292.

[7] Karl Barth, *Protestant Thought: From Rousseau to Ritschl*, trans. Brian Cozens (N.Y.: Harper, 1959), p. 13.

[8] William Cowper, *Poetical Works*, ed. H. S. Milford, 4th ed. (London: Oxford Univ. Press, 1967), pp. 188-189.

ison of the mind to "a kind of theatre, where several perceptions successively make their appearance; pass, re-pass, glide away, and mingle in an infinite variety of postures and situations." But the theater itself, Hume reminds us, the subsistent identity, is nowhere to be found.[9] Such a perception could, of course, be liberating: "I have discovered," writes Boswell, "that we may be in some degree whatever character we choose."[10] But it could rarely escape being a source of anxiety. Where to choose? Who, precisely, is doing the choosing?

Finally, the awareness of insubstantiality could enter into the very structure and texture of a work. Indeed, the work of art could itself constitute a lesson in substantiality, offering resistance to the reductive mind, insisting upon its own difficult otherness. To those readers "who find themselves ill at ease, unless they are let into the whole secret from first to last, of every thing which concerns" them, or whose "vile pruriency for fresh adventures in all things" devours narrative and experience alike, Tristram Shandy opposes the complexity and opaqueness of his narrative. "All I contend for," he challenges, "is the utter impossibility for some volumes, that you, or the most penetrating spirit upon earth, should know how this matter really stands."

Nor is Tristram himself, gleefully penetrating spirit that he is, exempt from a certain longing for a world less transparent, a world more substantial. At Lyons, drawn almost irresistibly to objects whose very opaqueness constitutes much of their magnetic power, he plans to see first the "wonderful mechanism" of Lippius' clock and the "thirty volumes of the general history of *China*." And he reflects: "Now I know almost as little of the *Chinese* language, as I do of the mechanism of *Lippius*'s clock-work; so, why these should have jostled themselves into the first two articles of my list—I leave to the curious as a problem of Nature."[11]

[9] David Hume, *A Treatise of Human Nature*, ed. Ernest C. Mossner (Baltimore: Penguin, 1969), p. 301.

[10] Boswell, *London Journal*, p. 47.

[11] Laurence Sterne, *The Life and Opinions of Tristram Shandy, Gentleman*, ed. James Aiken Work (N.Y.: Odyssey, 1940), pp. 7, 57, 49.

As it informs the literature of the later eighteenth century, insubstantiality is a phenomenological concept, an aspect of lived experience rather than of "things in themselves." Thus *ontological*, as Laing and others use the term, refers not to the supposed constitution of objective reality abstracted from human experience of it (the classical sense of the word) but to the kind of being the world is felt to have, the character it presents to human consciousness. It seems scarcely an accident, however, that the experience of insubstantiality should acquire such importance in English literature at precisely the time when one major current of philosophic speculation had virtually succeeded in removing the concept of substance from the vocabulary of philosophy. Substance is, of course, that which makes a thing a thing rather than a mere aggregate of qualities. Etymologically it is what "stands beneath" the qualities of things and supports them, providing a stable and abiding core of ontological presence, a centrality of being that unites qualities into distinct entities, whether material or spiritual. "When we say *what* a thing is," remarks Aristotle, "we do not say 'white' or 'hot' or 'three cubits long,' but 'a man' or 'a god'" (*Met.* 7[Z].1).

The history of British philosophic thinking about substance has been recounted often and well, and despite its real complexity it is not necessary to venture very far into what that casually philosophic gentleman, Lord Bolingbroke, called "the tedious and impertinent subtilties of ontology" to trace its outlines.[12] From Locke's discrimination of primary from secondary qualities, to Berkeley's assertion that primary qualities, no less then secondary, reside in the perceiving mind rather than the perceived object, and that material substance therefore does not exist, to Hume's further denial of spiritual substance (of which Berkeley had asserted we have a "notion") and thus of the basis of personal identity, the history is one of the slow but inevitable decline of the concept.

At the moment, then, when philosophers seemed to be banishing from reality its traditional ontological center, the idea

[12] *The Works of Lord Bolingbroke*, 4 vols. (Phila.: Carey and Hart, 1841), 3:164.

of substance, the imaginative writers of the later eighteenth century were creating a literature permeated by the experience of insubstantiality. That experience, it is important to remember, could be exultant as well as anxious, since the destruction of old categories and metaphors is inevitably liberating to some, while to others, as inevitably, it is a source of profound unease. The "vacuities of being" that so threatened Johnson were for Sterne, at least much of the time, invitations to freedom and imagination, fresh blank canvases on which to depict his ebullient Shandean cosmos. "In short," announces Tristram in Book 7 of *Tristram Shandy*, "by seizing every handle, of what size or shape soever, which chance held out to me in this journey—I turned my *plain* into a *city*."

Whatever the character of their response, English writers of the later eighteenth century were part of a profound shift of sensibility in the course of which new ways of experiencing their world and themselves came into being. The analogy that can suggest the scope rather than the precise nature of this shift is not with the critique of substance developed by British empirical philosophers but with the medieval notion of the radical contingency of created things: their dependence—for continuance as for creation—on the creative potency of God. "His hidden power," writes St. Augustine,

> pervading all things with its undefilable presence, gives being to every thing that exists on every level, in so far as it has being; for, were it not for his action, a thing would not only not be like this or like that, but it could not be at all. . . . And if he were to take away his constructive energy, so to speak, from objects, they will no more be than they were before they were created.[13]

Augustine, of course, is demonstrating the sustaining power of God at least as much as he is reminding us of the dependency of the created world. But as one critic, Georges Poulet, has argued, the "psychological nothingness" that appears in eighteenth-century French writers is rooted in an experience

[13] St. Augustine, *The City of God*, trans. Gerald G. Walsh et al. (Garden City, N.Y.: Doubleday, 1958), 7.25 (p. 266).

analogous to that which Augustine only hypothetically envisions:

> To the eighteenth century, . . . existence seems constantly being saved from nonbeing. . . . [But] this continued existence is no longer continued by an act of divine creation. The preservation of the universe and of the creature no longer is directly conceived as the immediate effect of the creative action. The latter is relegated to a remote past, to that far off, almost fabulous moment, the primal moment of created things. From the present moment God the creator and preserver is absent.[14]

This is no doubt too sweeping and too dramatically put, yet the character of the experience it describes, the reorganization of reality in the minds of many later eighteenth-century writers, English as well as French, can be amply documented from the literature of the period.

For what medieval writers took to be the heart of the matter, and what the later eighteenth century knew as an aspect of present, lived experience rather than an article of belief about the origin of things, was the utter nothingness from which all was originally created. For many medieval Christians this account of the creation simply testified to the unimaginable power of the Creator. Aquinas could answer the argument that all that comes from nothing can return to nothing ("omme quod est ex nihilo, vertibile est in nihilum") by asserting that it is not in the creature but in the Creator that the power to return the creature to nothingness resides. But for others, like St. Bonaventure, this *vertibilitas* of the created world could be understood more ominously, could be taken to suggest, as Etienne Gilson puts it, that "since it has been created from nothing, the world harbors in itself a sort of inner tendency to revert to its primordial nothingness."[15]

Of course as Carlyle's Teufelsdröckh remarks, "the Mythus of the Christian Religion looks not in the eighteenth century

---

[14] Poulet, *Studies*, p. 19.
[15] Etienne Gilson, *The Elements of Christian Philosophy* (N.Y.: Doubleday, 1960), p. 215.

as it did in the eighth." Neither the external world nor the self is literally threatened with the annihilation of being that Augustine or Bonaventure imagine. In the later eighteenth century, rather, this metaphysical possibility is both translated into the realm of subjective experience and to a certain degree made actual. Both world and self repeatedly suffer an analogous reversion to nothingness, a felt loss of their sustaining being and substantiality, a decay of their presence to the experiencing consciousness. The nothingness they manifest is not that which preceded the moment of creation but an aspect of things as they are presently experienced, a phenomenological nothingness. In its effects on a number of later eighteenth-century writers, however, it is scarcely less potent than a vision of the primal void.

For Teufelsdröckh's warning, salutary as it is, is nevertheless only half the truth. To describe the connection between the medieval notion of *vertibilitas* and the phenomenological reversion of things to nothingness in the eighteenth century is to describe continuity as well as change, a process of "displacement," to adapt Northrop Frye's term, in which a single structure of experience is translated into a new context and acquires there a new import. To forget that displacement is a double movement of continuity and change or, to alter the figure, a spiral rather than a circle or a straight line, is to simplify not only the later eighteenth century but the movement of literary and intellectual history as well.

Such simplifications usually emphasize continuity at the expense of change, as in the following formulations of the eighteenth-century intellectual climate:

> [T]he underlying preconceptions of eighteenth-century thought were still, allowance made for certain important alterations in the bias, essentially the same as those of the thirteenth century. . . . [T]he *Philosophes* demolished the Heavenly City of St. Augustine only to rebuild it with more up-to-date materials.[16]

---

[16] Carl L. Becker, *The Heavenly City of the Eighteenth-Century Philosophers* (New Haven and London: Yale Univ. Press, 1932), p. 31.

[I]t is evident, as one makes one's way through the writings of the standard authors of Enlightened England, that their view of man and his place in the universe and his destiny is essentially that of such earlier Christian writers as Spenser and Milton, Donne and Herbert, rather than that of Voltaire and Diderot.[17]

For the first writer, the *philosophes* simply revived the assumptions of the thirteenth century. Voltaire becomes a man of faith, Enlightenment criticism of enthusiasm becomes itself an enthusiasm, Posterity assumes the function of God, and so forth. But Voltaire's faith is not Aquinas', an enthusiastic critique of enthusiasm is not an enthusiastic critique of skepticism, and the immortality that Posterity is capable of conferring is rather different from that which traditional Christianity promises to its elect. Similarly, for the second writer, the ethic to which eighteenth-century English writers subscribed was a happy union of Augustinian Christianity and British empiricism, an ethic that stressed the dangers of pride, of our tendency to substitute egocentric fantasy for accurate perception of the world, and of our readiness to be taken in by words and concepts divorced from real experience. But the student so naive as to ask what is eighteenth-century about the eighteenth century is not much helped by such a general and unexceptionable ethic, nor by the curious disclaimer that it would be "nonsensical" to view this ethic "as something peculiar to the English writers of the seventeenth and eighteenth centuries," although "it could perhaps be argued that the English climate of opinion of the eighteenth century was peculiarly favorable to such an ethic."[18]

What is wanting from both of these formulations is an awareness of the existential context of belief, of that entire mode of experiencing that is to belief and conscious thought what a key is to a musical phrase: the determinant of its special character and timbre, the force investing a system of abstract

---

[17] Donald Greene, *The Age of Exuberance: Backgrounds to Eighteenth-Century English Literature* (N.Y.: Random House, 1970), p. 93.
[18] Ibid., pp. 109-110.

relationships with unique and concrete being. Sterne, for example, was an orthodox—if singular—clergyman; but even if the orthodoxy he professed was Augustinian, even if the "ethic" we might extract from his novels and sermons could be shown to clash in no significant way with that of Spenser or Milton or Augustine himself, his mode of experience was not Augustine's. Indeed, the argument that claims to demonstrate the Augustinianism of *Tristram Shandy* must either misread that novel or define Augustinianism so broadly as to make it difficult, in any age and clime, to locate non-Augustinians.[19] There are, to be sure, similarities and meaningful analogies between Augustine and Sterne, as between the attitudes of other writers in periods widely separated in time. Indeed, a perception of the insubstantiality of experience is itself the exclusive property of neither medieval Christianity, twentieth-century Existentialism, nor later eighteenth-century English literature. But the significance of such attitudes and perceptions will be different in each age as the peculiar pressures of an era give to common experience its special and characteristic tone.

The metaphors and structural devices that writers use to describe substantial experience are often patterns of reconciled opposites, patterns that permit multiplicity and complexity to flourish but not to shade over into mere chaotic diversity. The concept of *concordia discors* is one such pattern, and the literature of the later eighteenth century, as Earl Wasserman has argued, reveals the progressive inability of this concept to organize experience in significant ways.[20] The metaphor of order and chaos, however, is only one of two crucial metaphors contained within the notion of *concordia discors*. The other is a metaphor of substance and insubstantiality. For the breakdown of *concordia discors* signals a loss not simply of

[19] For a fuller account of the contrasts between the *Confessions* and *Tristram Shandy*, see Chap. 4, pp. 159-161.
[20] Earl R. Wasserman, *The Subtler Language* (Baltimore: The Johns Hopkins Univ. Press, 1959), chap. 5.

certain traditional principles of order but also of that paradoxical nexus at the heart of things which seems to be bound up with our capacity for substantial experience, or at least with the imagery we draw upon to describe such experience. Paradox, as Rosalie L. Colie has pointed out, "attempts to give the appearance of ontological wholeness."[21] It gestures toward a fullness of being, a region of truth more solid and whole—more substantial—than nonparadoxical language is usually called upon to render. Kierkegaard makes this point when he virtually equates the paradoxical with the unknowable, the wholly "other," but insists as well that it is a genuine category rather than a mere concession, "an ontological definition which expresses the relation between an existing cognitive spirit and eternal truth."[22]

By the time of the Augustans the paradoxes that Renaissance writers loved to explicate do not disappear, but they require rediscovery and preservation more than explication. Augustan literature strives to preserve a paradoxical substantiality that continually threatens to break down: to simplify itself in one or another direction, or to degenerate to mere alternation and mere pairing. The poetry of Pope, for example, frequently articulates a pattern of *concordia discors*, but it also dramatizes the poet's struggle to maintain or recover it, and this effort is as much a part of the meaning of his poetry as the more static pattern of "reconcil'd extremes." In *An Epistle to Dr. Arbuthnot*, Pope makes exemplary forays into extreme stances of various sorts: the satirist's disengagement from the world, and the aspiring poet's entrance into literary society; the hero's vision of goals for which the world is well lost ("For thee, fair Virtue! welcome ev'n the *last!*") and the ordinary mortal's involvement in the business of living ("With lenient Arts extend a Mother's breath"). But he must finally unite these extremes in the tensional relationship that consti-

---

[21] Rosalie L. Colie, *Paradoxia Epidemica: The Renaissance Tradition of Paradox* (Princeton: Princeton Univ. Press, 1966), p. 518.

[22] *The Journals of Kierkegaard*, trans. Alexander Dru (N.Y.: Harper, 1959), pp. 117-118.

tutes his identity, and his effort to do so is the defining movement of the poem.

In contrast, the greatest writers of the latter half of the century have abandoned, or lost, or freed themselves from an understanding of paradoxical substantiality. More central than substantial paradox to the literary expression of this period are figures whose ontological import, in practice, tends in quite the opposite direction, figures like dilemma and contradiction. "Marriage has many pains," says the Princess Nekayah in *Rasselas*, "but celibacy has no pleasures." Such patterns may govern thematic as well as rhetorical structure, as they do, for example, in Johnson's *Journey to the Western Islands*, which portrays the Highlanders caught between ancient pastoral barbarity and modern commercial meanness. The two terms in such cases do not gesture toward a central reconciling substance but deny the possibility of its existence. If a middle term appears at all, it is most often what Thomas Vaughan calls a middle "between both Extreames, and not that which actually unites the whole together."[23]

Where that substance is human nature itself, the individual is confronted with choices that are unavoidable yet destructive of his substantial reality. Rasselas, for example, falls from a state of unthinking ease but almost immediately plunges into self-conscious posturing, as though a point midway between innocence and inauthenticity were not a possibility in his world. He utters his newly felt sentiments of discomfort in the Happy Valley "with a plaintive voice, yet with a look that discovered him to feel some complacence in his own perspicacity and to receive some solace of the miseries of life from consciousness of the delicacy with which he felt and the eloquence with which he bewailed them."[24] The same pattern appears on the verbal level in certain eighteenth-century forms of periphrastic

[23] Thomas Vaughan, *Anthroposophia Theomagica* (1650), pp. 38-39. Quoted in Jonathan Swift, *A Tale of a Tub*, etc., ed. A. C. Guthkelch and D. Nichol Smith, 2d ed. (Oxford: Clarendon Press, 1958), p. 150, n. 3.

[24] Samuel Johnson, *The History of Rasselas, Prince of Abissinia*, ed. Geoffrey Tillotson and Brian Jenkins (London: Oxford Univ. Press, 1971), chap. 2. Subsequent references will be given by chapter number in the text.

naming that seem, as W. K. Wimsatt puts it, "to have a hole in their center."[25] In answering, that is, to both terms of a phrase like "scaly breed" or "fleecy kind," the substantive fish and sheep may seem to disappear.

Dilemma and contradiction are only special cases of a pervasive pattern of doubleness. The literature of the later eighteenth century repeatedly presents us with pairs of disjunct choices, or situations, or conditions, or modes of being, both terms of which must somehow be met although no reconciling third term is possible. The terms are juxtaposed, as they are for the Augustans, but in the latter part of the century they are usually joined by no vital center, no organic nexus. The structure of *Jubilate Agno* illustrates this pattern, for Smart's idiosyncratic yoking of homely detail and sacramental superstructure, whatever its debt to Hebrew antiphon, is a distinctly late-eighteenth-century form of binary mania:

> Let Noah rejoice with Hibris who is from a wild boar
>   and a tame sow.
> For I bless God for the immortal soul of Mr Pigg of
>   DOWNHAM in NORFOLK.[26]

Such structures may intimate connection, but they insist at least as much on the gulf dividing the two terms and on the precariousness or absence of the center that might have joined them. This is of course as much a pattern of meaning as of structure. The precarious disjunction of orders of being, the need to suffer it and the effort to heal it—these are Smart's major themes. As he writes in another fragment of *Jubilate Agno* (C, 18, 23, 25): "For Christ being A and Ω is all the intermediate letters without doubt," but "the Devil is two being without God. . . . For he is called the Duce . . . on that account."

---

[25] W. K. Wimsatt, "The Substantive Level," in *The Verbal Icon: Studies in The Meaning of Poetry* (N.Y.: Noonday, 1962), p. 143. The entire essay (pp. 133-151) is relevant to my argument.

[26] Christopher Smart, *Jubilate Agno*, ed. W. H. Bond (London: Rupert Hart-Davis, 1954), pp. 58-59 (Fragment B1, 116). Subsequent references will appear by fragment and line number in the text.

A very different but analogous pattern of doubleness informs the web of role playing and posturing that Boswell weaves around himself in the *London Journal*. Boswell's role playing is not simply a flight from himself or a transformation of that self into successive roles; his real goal is an unattainable consciousness of depth, complexity, and substantiality of identity. It is this substantial harmony of impulses that he attempts to counterfeit with the simultaneous doubleness of self and role. A telling commentary on Boswell's own situation is provided by his account of a dispute between Thomas Sheridan, the actor and elocutionist, and "a Captain Maud of the Blues." Sheridan, recalls Boswell, "said that an actor ought to forget himself and the audience entirely, and be quite the real character. . . . This Mr. Maud opposed as wrong; because an actor in that case would not play so well, as he would not be enough master of himself." And, Boswell concludes, "I think he was right."[27]

This effort to replace a substantial center with patterns of simple doubleness is one structural characteristic of the period. Another, equally pervasive, might be called the elaboration of singleness: the appearance, in oddly purified form, of structures and impulses more often found in tensional union with complementary structures and opposing impulses. This pattern appears at the verbal level, but it also governs narrative movement, most clearly, perhaps, in the areas of plot and pace. Whether the physical action of epic warriors or the psychic progress of a first-person narrator, plot is a combination of forward thrust and local elaboration, of movement toward an end and openness to what is encountered on the way. The special tone of a number of later eighteenth-century works, however, derives in large part from their nearly exclusive dependence on one or the other of these impulses.

At one extreme is the plot of a work like Johnson's *Rasselas*, the epigraph to which might well have been, "in my beginning is my end." The first paragraph of Johnson's fable is declaimed by a speaker who seems to have passed beyond the need for

<hr/>

[27] Boswell, *London Journal*, p. 109.

the kind of plot that is an analogue to discursive knowledge. Conclusions, for him, are not discovered on quests but permitted to emerge from within us even at the outset of our progresses of error. As a result, plot as action in *Rasselas* is continually being measured against an ideal of plot as deductive sequence, the contrast reminding us that the rambling quest of the royal party is the slow way to the knowledge that is their goal. The clauses of that thunderous and periodic opening paragraph, like the exploits of Rasselas and his friends, are merely an exemplary postponement of a conclusion more efficiently reached without them.

At the other extreme there are triumphs of local elaboration with a necessary attenuation of directed movement, the sort of thing that makes Collins sound occasionally like a lecturer who has lost his place and is filling time until he finds it again. The opening of the "Ode to Evening" is a good example:

> If aught of oaten stop or pastoral song
> May hope, chaste Eve, to soothe thy modest ear,
>   Like thy own solemn springs,
>   Thy springs and dying gales,
> O nymph reserved, while now the bright-haired sun
> Sits in yon western tent, whose cloudy skirts,
>   With brede ethereal wove,
>   O'erhang his wavy bed;
> Now air is hushed, save where the weak-eyed bat
> With short shrill shriek flits by on leathern wing,
>   Or where the beetle winds
>   His small but sullen horn,
> As oft he rises midst the twilight path,
> Against the pilgrim borne in heedless hum:
>   (1-14)[28]

Then, at last, "Now teach me" (15). If Collins' lengthy beginning perpetually postpones coming to the point, it is also

---

[28] *The Poems of Thomas Gray, William Collins, Oliver Goldsmith,* ed. Roger Lonsdale (London: Longmans, 1969), pp. 463-464. Subsequent references to all three poets are to this edition and will be cited by line number in the text.

40

possible to suggest that genuine beginnings are themselves scarcely available. The uniform style of Gray's slow-starting Elegist, for example, implies that one point is as significant or insignificant as another, that there is no real point to come to:

> The Curfew tolls the knell of parting day,
> The lowing herd winds slowly o'er the lea,
> The plowman homeward plods his weary
>   way,
> And leaves the world to darkness and to me.

"Only in its last line," remarks Thomas R. Edwards, "does the first stanza even minimally escape the drugged iteration of disjunct declarative statements. . . . The poem only barely manages to begin, only just overcomes the inertia of the mood." In the "Elegy," Edwards adds, "Gray found a beautiful poetic equivalent for emotional poverty."[29] Gray's "Elegy" is only one of a number of later eighteenth-century works that communicate such emotional poverty, or what I would call a perception of insubstantiality, by means of a psychic plot that approaches perilously near to the static.

What is striking about both kinds of plot is that either, taken alone, threatens to result in immobility. The teleological impatience of Johnson's narrator, the dissolving in local observations of Collins' or Gray's speakers, each seems to undermine significant progress, significant action. Both impulses have a common source in a mode of knowledge that is destructive of substantial experience. If Johnson's narrator knows only too soon "how it all comes out," so in another sense does Gray's Elegist: "The paths of glory lead but to the grave." And so does the speaker of the "Ode on a Distant Prospect of Eton College":

> Alas, regardless of their doom,
> The little victims play!

[29] Thomas R. Edwards, *Imagination and Power: A Study of Poetry on Public Themes* (N.Y.: Oxford Univ. Press, 1971), pp. 121, 123.

No sense have they of ills to come,
Nor care beyond today:
. . . .
Thought would destroy their paradise.
(51-54, 98)

It is knowledge that sees through experience to nothingness, reducing time to a medium of mere addition, or inevitability, or aimlessness, and plot to a mere string of episodes, or a virtual deductive sequence, or a rambling progress difficult to distinguish from stasis.

Indeed, while the destructiveness of insight is reflected in the literary structures of this period, it is an important theme as well. It lies, for example, behind that peculiarly eighteenth-century form of the tragic that begins with a recognition of insubstantiality and consists largely in attempting to live with the consequences of that recognition, as though the *anagnorisis* occurred in the very first scene of the first act. "I see too far into the system of things," admits the young Boswell, "to be much in earnest." And the middle-aged Boswell, describing the hypochondriac temperament that he knew at first hand, sounds a similar note: "His corrosive imagination destroys to his own view all that he contemplates."[30] The young Pope had begun in much the same way: "I begin where most people end, with a full conviction of the emptiness of all sorts of ambition, and the unsatisfactory nature of all human pleasures."[31] But in Pope's case this was merely a beginning, to be imaginatively resisted and then incorporated into a larger and paradoxical vision of both the vanity and the possibility of earthly existence. What Boswell and certain other writers of the later eighteenth century experience only fitfully, however, is "that love of life," as Johnson puts it, "which is necessary

[30] Boswell, *London Journal*, p. 77; James Boswell, *The Hypochondriack*, ed. Margery Bailey, 2 vols. (Stanford: Stanford Univ. Press, 1928), 2: 44 (No. 39).

[31] Pope to Steele, 15 July 1712. In *The Correspondence of Alexander Pope*, ed. George Sherburn, 6 vols. (Oxford: Clarendon Press, 1956), 1: 148.

to the vigorous prosecution of any undertaking."[32] Thus it is Boswell, and not Pope or Swift or Fielding, who writes: "I am rather passive than active in life. ... I may say, I act passively. That is, not with my whole heart, and thinking this or that of real consequence."[33]

It is the strength of writers of the later eighteenth century to verge on extremes like these, dramatizing their dangers and their attractions much more fully than the Augustans had but usually controlling them to such a degree, at least, as to make of them significant structures of meaning. If the royal party in *Rasselas* take the slow way to their goal, they also take the only way that is open to them. Temporality, wandering, the tedious and piecemeal discovery of what ought always to have been known—these are not at last merely ridiculed or wholly despised by Johnson's narrator. Rather, as W. J. Bate has argued, *Rasselas* "embodies the fading of satire into a more profound analysis of human experience."[34] In an analogous way, Collins' "Ode to Evening" and Gray's "Elegy" finally permit the emergence of genuine voices from the uncertain and torpid "silence" with which they begin. Nor, to take two other examples nearly at random, does the "in vain" that closes Gray's "Sonnet" on the death of Richard West quite signify an absence of progress from the "In vain" that opens it, or the vision of "hope's delusive mine" that begins Johnson's elegy on Dr. Levet quite reduce to insignificance Levet's exemplary "toil of ev'ry day."

Johnson's corrosive and reductive vision was countered by a powerful sense of the self-defeating absurdity of reductiveness. "Think nothing gain'd," cries Charles XII in "The Vanity of Human Wishes," "till nought remain." Johnson also fash-

---

[32] Samuel Johnson, *Rambler* No. 59, in *The Rambler*, ed. W. J. Bate and Albrecht B. Strauss, vols. 3, 4, and 5 of The Yale Edition of the Works of Samuel Johnson (New Haven and London: Yale Univ. Press, 1969), 3: 315.

[33] Boswell, *London Journal*, p. 77.

[34] W. J. Bate, "Johnson and Satire Manqué," in *Eighteenth-Century Studies in Honor of Donald F. Hyde*, ed. W. H. Bond (N.Y.: Grolier Club, 1970), p. 157.

ioned a prose style that invested reductive abstractions with such weight and power as to make them reasonable substitutes for the substantiality that vision had driven out. "He made a kind of poetry of abstraction," W. K. Wimsatt remarks. "Out of emptiness he conjured weight, out of the collapsible he made structures."[35] And as Wimsatt's language suggests, Johnson's achievement is as much ontological as stylistic. How much merely individual responsibility for this conjuring Johnson would have admitted to is of course a question that the very nature of his style makes it impossible to answer. At the opposite extreme Sterne claims full responsibility for investing the insubstantial with significance, much as he glories in the digressiveness of a Collins or turns the dawdling of a Gray into an occasion for self-conscious pathos. As Yorick asserts in *A Sentimental Journey*:

> I pity the man who can travel from *Dan* to *Beersheba*, and cry, 'Tis all barren—and so it is; and so is all the world to him who will not cultivate the fruits it offers. I declare . . . that was I in a desert, I would find out wherewith in it to call forth my affections—If I could not do better, I would fasten them upon some sweet myrtle, or seek some melancholy cypress to connect myself to—I would court their shade, and greet them kindly for their protection—I would cut my name upon them, and swear they were the loveliest trees throughout the desert.[36]

Johnson and Sterne have often been seen as antithetical anachronisms, one all conservative nostalgia, the other all precocious existentialism. But despite their differences, temperamental as well as literary, they stand at the center of their age. They are united by the strength of their responses to the insubstantial world in which they found themselves and by their effort to create literary structures that would express

[35] W. K. Wimsatt, *The Prose Style of Samuel Johnson* (New Haven: Yale Univ. Press, 1941), p. 96. See also the remarks on pages 55-56 and page 60.
[36] Laurence Sterne, *A Sentimental Journey Through France and Italy by Mr. Yorick*, ed. Ian Jack (London: Oxford Univ. Press, 1968), p. 28.

those responses. Like Smart, like Boswell, like Collins and Gray and the others, they articulate a perception of the insubstantial while engaging upon a quest for substantiality as Johnson defined it in his *Dictionary*: "The state of real existence."[37]

If we can see Pope and the Augustans holding together impulses that separate later in the century, we may be obliged to adjust the argument of Northrop Frye in his important essay, "Towards Defining an Age of Sensibility."[38] What Frye calls prose literature of product, for example, is characterized by the fact that "the suspense is thrown forward until it reaches the end, and is based on our confidence that the author knows what is coming next." By this definition, however, *Rasselas* is such an extreme development of literature of product as also to constitute a kind of joke at its expense. The narrator knows what is coming next—but so should we all. On the other hand, it is hard to see why the present-tense meditation that makes up most of *An Epistle to Dr. Arbuthnot*, though it is rarely vatic and may never demand of us a "primitive response," does not testify to its kinship with the poetry of process, although other features also connect it with the poetry of product.

I would suggest that the main line of development in the eighteenth century is less a movement from a literature of product to a literature of process than a movement from a fusion of these modes to purified forms of each. For underlying Frye's terms, "product" and "process," are two intersecting dimensions of human experience. On the one hand, there is the insistence on design, on the a priori, on being. On the other, there is the exploration of temporality, of empirical

[37] Samuel Johnson, *A Dictionary of the English Language*, 2d ed. (London, 1756), s.v. "substantiality."

[38] Northrop Frye, "Towards Defining an Age of Sensibility," in *Eighteenth-Century English Literature: Modern Essays in Criticism*, ed. James L. Clifford (N.Y.: Oxford Univ. Press, 1959), pp. 311-318.

discovery, of becoming. The poetry of Pope, and Augustan literature generally, strives to exist at the intersection of these two dimensions, an intersection from which Johnson and Sterne, with the greatest writers of the later eighteenth century, take their characteristic and distinct directions.

· 3 ·

THE RHETORIC OF
SUBSTANTIALITY

The challenge posed by insubstantiality to the solidity of perceived experience is a challenge not just to perception but also to a traditional system of values and a traditional rhetoric of valuing. To meet that challenge, rather than simply register it, it is necessary to fashion a rhetoric capable of delivering a new, at least a newly valued, image of reality: a rhetoric of substantiality. In the Age of Sensibility the principal goal of that rhetoric is a reclamation of common experience. Literary and historical scholarship have already done much to suggest that the eighteenth century was an age of experience, an age marked, in Lionel Trilling's words, by an "increasing concern with the actual, with the substance of life in all its ordinariness and lack of elevation."[1] The latter half of the century in particular was a time in which artists sought to reclaim aesthetically "low" subjects and aesthetic theorists to provide a reasoned justification for that effort, a justification that might rely less on established canons of beauty or proportion than on a concern with the quality of the observer's response, psychological and even physical, to natural and artistic forms. "By looking into physical causes," says Burke, "our minds are opened and enlarged."[2] Minds were opened and enlarged as well by attention to those "physical causes" that constituted the world of technology and to which the writers of the *Encyclopédie* devoted so many hours of research and columns of print. Diderot was said to have scale models of machines

[1] Lionel Trilling, *Sincerity and Authenticity* (Cambridge, Mass.: Harvard Univ. Press, 1973), p. 89. On the philosophic backgrounds of literary realism see Ian Watt, *The Rise of the Novel* (1957; reprint ed., Berkeley and Los Angeles: Univ. of California Press, 1964), esp. chap. 1.

[2] Edmund Burke, *A Philosophical Enquiry into the Origin of Our Ideas of the Sublime and Beautiful*, ed. James T. Boulton (Notre Dame and London: Univ. of Notre Dame Press, 1968), p. 5.

for knitting stockings and for making cut velvet and to practice dismantling and reassembling them.[3] It was a time, too, of almost unparalleled concern with the everyday workings of the mind, of a self-scrutiny so intense as frequently to issue in an effort of self-creation, and of a narrative stance that in Boswell, in Rousseau, and in Sterne's Tristram considered nothing autobiographical alien to it. That this remarkable attention to ordinary experience could also nourish a system of morality—or, better, a moral stance—was demonstrated by Samuel Johnson. Rejecting abstract theories of conduct as well as romantic conceptions of moral choice ("Once to every man and nation comes the moment to decide"), Johnson attempted to ground the moral life in common human experience, "the great test of truth," and to assert the dignity of quotidian habit, of continued adequacy to the demands of common life: "The modest wants of ev'ry day," he wrote in his elegy on Dr. Levet, "The toil of ev'ry day supplied."[4]

Yet if Johnson was a confirmed dweller in experience, finding "the full tide of human existence" at Charing Cross and the full power of Gray's "Elegy" in "sentiments to which every bosom returns an echo," that was not his only home. For while he may have had "the Enlightenment style" of critical analysis and respect for the truths of experience, he also bemoaned his having lived, in that Enlightenment, "to see things all as bad as they can be"; he despised most of the *philosophes* and their closest British counterpart, David Hume; and he seemed to a number of his contemporaries as to many modern readers to live precisely out of the common life of his time rather than in it—politically, morally, theologically, even stylistically.[5] It is difficult, in short, to subsume all of Johnson

---

[3] Arthur M. Wilson, *Diderot: The Testing Years, 1713-1759* (N.Y.: Oxford Univ. Press, 1957), pp. 199-200.

[4] On habit, which for Johnson still held some of the force of the medieval *habitus*, see his *Dictionary* (6th ed., 1785), s.v. "habit." Definition number 4 is "custom; inveterate use," but the quotation from Locke that serves as the third definition is more telling: "*Habit* is a power or ability in man of doing any thing, when it has been acquired by frequent doing the same thing."

[5] Peter Gay, *The Enlightenment: An Interpretation*, vol. 1, *The Rise of Modern Paganism* (N.Y.: Knopf, 1966), p. 21.

under the rubric "common experience," and it is at least as difficult to make sense in these terms of such contemporary literary phenomena as the forgeries of Macpherson, or the bardic utterances of Gray and Collins, or the splendidly sacramental imaginings of Christopher Smart.

Critics of Johnson have been alert to the difficulties of classification that he poses. While recognizing his deep commitment to common experience, they have recognized as well his remarkable detachment from it, a detachment that it is one of Boswell's chief purposes in the *Life* to convey.[6] In a brief essay titled "Dr. Johnson and the Literature of Experience," for example, Ian Watt draws attention to Johnson's fondness for those literary forms—"the diary, the letter, the memoir, the prayer"—that seem closest to the inscribed utterance of everyday life, forms "to which we can give the name of the literature of experience." Watt then turns to the special mixture of engagement and detachment in Johnson's attitude toward experience, observing that "his great capacity for cheerfulness kept breaking in on his conviction of human inadequacy."[7] Watt's formulation, which is virtually a commonplace of modern critical appreciation of Johnson, is from a rhetorical point of view also a commonplace. For it is one instance of a widespread tendency to describe Johnson's characteristic stance toward the world—his existential posture—by means of an oblique or compressed rather than a simple antithesis, an antithesis that telescopes two sets of antithetical terms. Watt does not oppose cheerfulness to cheerlessness or

6 William C. Dowling, "The Boswellian Hero," *Studies in Scottish Literature* 10 (1972): 80. Before meeting Johnson, Boswell had imagined "a state of solemn elevated abstraction, in which I supposed him to live in the immense metropolis of London" (James Boswell, *The Life of Samuel Johnson*, ed. G. B. Hill, rev. L. F. Powell, 6 vols. [Oxford: Clarendon Press, 1934-1964], 1: 384).

7 Ian Watt, "Dr. Johnson and the Literature of Experience," in *Johnsonian Studies*, ed. Magdi Wahba (Cairo: Société orientale de publicité, 1962), pp. 15, 17. Watt alludes, of course, to Oliver Edwards' remark: "You are a philosopher, Dr. Johnson. I have tried too in my time to be a philosopher; but, I don't know how, cheerfulness was always breaking in" (Boswell, *Life*, 3: 305).

a conviction of human adequacy to a conviction of human inadequacy; he opposes the positive term of the first antithesis to the negative term of the second.

One effect of this rhetorical practice is to portray Johnson's mind as instinctively antithetical within a given scheme or on a given axis and at the same time instinctively drawn to acknowledge the competing claims of two distinct schemes or axes or value systems—ultimately, I would insist, of two distinct ways of apprehending reality. Whether critics have intended so much, or exactly this, by their oblique antitheses I do not know, but the figure itself occurs with striking frequency and points to what I take to be an equally striking feature of Johnson's thought. The complex tensions it suggests, moreover, are not merely the idiosyncrasies of a divided personality, or a last-ditch Augustan, or a Sir Thomas Browne born a century too late: for all the singularity of Johnson's opinions and style his are to a great extent the tensions of his age. That age, I want to argue, may indeed be termed an age of experience, but if the phrase is to suggest anything like the real nature of Johnson's literary achievement or that of his contemporaries it must be allowed both greater significance and greater precision than we are usually required to grant it in common discourse.

The emergence in the later eighteenth century of a new attitude toward commonplace reality is not an isolated phenomenon. Its larger literary and intellectual context is that critique of the religious and mythopoeic imagination known to its champions and its disinterested students as the Enlightenment and to its foes as the Rise of Skepticism or, alternatively, the Decline of Faith. The choice of labels need not detain us long, for it is not necessary to enter into the debate whether the later eighteenth century was, all things considered, a success. Yet the writers of the period were themselves divided over the significance and worth of the times in which they lived, and their attitudes toward the age are an integral part of its meaning. Many, in England especially, were more than skeptical

toward the skepticism of the *philosophes* and toward that
social upheaval that was thought to embody the *philosophes'*
principles, the French Revolution. Nevertheless, the current
of skepticism and critical energy that is traditionally identified
with the Enlightenment was not confined to the Continent.
Johnson himself admitted that his own religious faith was not
easily won or naively held, that "every thing which Hume has
advanced against Christianity had passed through my mind
long before he wrote."[8] And for all their differences, from
Johnson's faith as from each other, the skeptical irony of a
Gibbon and the comfortable piety of a Boswell—"For my
own part, Madam," he tells Louisa, "I look upon the adoration of the Supreme Being as one of the greatest enjoyments
we have"[9]—are unmistakable signs that, in England as in
Europe, the luminous order that had once embraced the world
was fast becoming a glimmer at the edge of experience. Few,
perhaps, were as willing as Hume "to live with uncertainty,
with no supernatural justifications, no complete explanations,
no promise of permanent stability, with guides of merely prob-
able validity," as Peter Gay puts it.[10] But in adopting such a
stance Hume was less an exception to the British thought of
his time than the figure in whom certain tendencies of that
thought found their purest and most complete expression.

The age, of course, had its ardent believers as well as its
cool or passionate skeptics, believers, moreover, who made
God's relationship to their world and to themselves a central
literary theme. Yet even these writers exhibit the strain that
the religious imagination underwent in the later eighteenth
century, a strain that signals the emergence of the modern
period and places a poet like Christopher Smart in the spiritual
company of Keats or Whitman or Yeats, or even Sylvia Plath,
sooner than in that of Herbert or Milton.[11] Smart's brilliantly
forced disclosure of the sacramental significance of things, his

[8] Boswell, *Life*, 1: 444.
[9] James Boswell, *Boswell's London Journal, 1762-1763*, ed. Frederick A.
Pottle (London: Heinemann, 1950), p. 101.
[10] Gay, *The Rise of Modern Paganism*, pp. 418-419.
[11] See, in particular, Plath's "Black Rook in Rainy Weather."

imaginative compelling of the deity's appearance, creates finally an uneasy tension rather than a stable union. "Resistance is not of GOD," he writes in *Jubilate Agno*, "but he—hath built his works upon it," and much the same thing could be said of Smart himself.[12] The two worlds in which his poetry participates, the natural and the supernatural, are forever straining against the force that holds them together.

From one point of view Smart's elaborate exegesis of the world is a strategy designed to reconcile uncommon belief with common perception, to assert the sacramental character of reality in a climate of skepticism by subordinating the ordinary appearances of things to their sacred inwardness. Indeed, the special tone of Smart's poetry derives, to a great extent, from his treating the hidden and elaborate in the accents of a man describing the obvious and elementary: "For there is Water above the visible surface in a spiritualizing state, which cannot be seen but by application of a CAPILLARY TUBE./For the ASCENT of VAPOURS is the return of thanksgiving from all humid bodies" (B1, 207-208). Yet even though for Smart "flowers are musical in ocular harmony" and "the names and number of animals are as the names and number of the stars" (B2, 508; B1, 42), the world does not offer a simple revelation of God's creative power but a system of elaborate correspondences and intricately contrived connections, connections that, in their resolute idiosyncrasy and persistent embrace of the commonplace, look forward to Plath's theophanic rook, table, and chair more directly than they recall Davies' orchestra or Milton's "starry dance." For this is a world that must be teased into significance by a remarkable play of wit, a world whose spiritual meaning is not immediate and plain but covert and cryptic. Every stone may hold its sermon, but that sermon will edify only those who, like Smart, have mastered its extraordinary idiom.

The characteristic tensions that mark the religious expres-

---

[12] All citations from Smart are to *Jubilate Agno*, ed. W. H. Bond (London: Rupert Hart-Davis, 1954). References to fragment and line will appear in the text. This quotation is from B1, 162.

sion of the later eighteenth century are not generated by a crisis of belief, in the usual understanding of that phrase, nor can they be understood by reference to so treacherous a term as "secularization," even when the latter is conceived as "a subtle shift of attention" rather than a wholesale plunge into atheism and materialism.[13] Secularization and faltering belief there certainly were, but faith and devotion too. The difficulty is that while firmness of faith and intensity of devotion may do much, in any age, they do not necessarily offer an antidote to what one writer has called "the thinning of reality's texture, the feelings of non-existence"[14] that have become a common-place—often a cliché—of modern experience and that first achieved the status of a sizable cultural phenomenon in the eighteenth century. Faith, belief, metaphysical argument and conviction—these work to convince us of the existence and attributes of God, or indeed of man and the world, but they cannot prescribe the manner in which we shall experience them. They cannot ensure that what we believe to exist we shall also feel to be present.

The literature of the later eighteenth century insists, though often implicitly, on just such a distinction. The model of con-sciousness that it presents requires that we distinguish between two dimensions of experience, two axes on which to plot the significance of that experience. On the one hand, we determine that things exist and the kind of existence they have. We more or less believe in or doubt them, find them true or false, phys-ical or spiritual, apples or angels. Insofar as we are concerned with their ultimate nature, with the spiritual bases of reality, we may call this axis metaphysical. On the other hand, we become aware of the quantity of being things seem to possess. We note how substantially they present themselves, how force-

---

[13] Gay, *The Rise of Modern Paganism*, p. 338.

[14] Richard A. Lanham, "Theory of the LOGOI: The speeches in Classical and Renaissance Narrative," in *To Tell a Story: Narrative Theory and Prac-tice* (Univ. of California, Los Angeles: William Andrews Clark Memorial Library, 1973), p. 97. See also Georges Poulet on "psychological nothingness" in *Studies in Human Time*, trans. Elliott Coleman (Baltimore: The Johns Hopkins Univ. Press, 1956), p. 20.

fully or variously or richly they impinge on consciousness, how present to us they are. This is not, of course, a simple distinction between rational and emotive, or objective and subjective responses to experience, but more like that between form and force, or truth and substance, or between an empirical and a phenomenological apprehension of reality.

In creating a literature that gave new prominence to the dimension of the substantial in the extended or phenomenological sense, as an aspect of one's way of experiencing the world, later eighteenth-century writers gave new body and color to the very notion of experience as such. This is not to say that at some point near the middle of the eighteenth century substantiality, or even experience, began to exist. The dimension of the substantial is pretty clearly a permanent category of human consciousness; it did not spring forth *ex nihilo* at the death of Pope, nor does its continued survival seem anything but assured. What has always existed, however, is not always visible. It is in the eighteenth century that the substantial begins not to exist but to emerge as a distinct category, to disentangle itself from those other aspects of consciousness that had hitherto performed its function and dispersed its identity. (Similarly, it is only in the late seventeenth century that "wit" becomes a distinct term for the combined forces of verbal agility, aptness at similitude, and intellectual penetration.) The experience of the substantial and the insubstantial, moreover, appeared long before a special terminology to describe it. Johnson often resorts to metaphors of fullness and vacancy, or of presence and absence; Boswell to the language of Stoic and Christian commonplace ("nothingness," for example, and "vanity," which—like Johnson—he uses with a strong sense of its root, *vanus*); Burke to the imagery of the obscure and the clear, and the themes of the circumstantial and the rational; Sterne, Rousseau, and others to the vocabulary of the passions. In each case, however, what is being described is the substantial or "ontological" character that experience presents to the individual consciousness.

What is that character? What are we doing when we say that an experience or a thing, an idea or a person—even oneself—is substantial? First, we are using the word to designate a kind of middle ground between two somewhat simpler meanings: the metaphysical (substance as a certain something that supports qualities) and the purely physical (flour is a white powdery substance). This middle ground is most familiar in phrases like "a man of substance," and Johnson captures its middling status when, under a single definition of "substantial" in his *Dictionary*, he writes both "moderately wealthy" and "responsible." Such an association of matter and meaningfulness, of existence and worth, is quite irrational from a strictly logical point of view, yet it is wholly consistent with the way we use the language of substantiality: as a simultaneous assertion that a thing exists and that it has a certain kind of existential worth, though not necessarily that it is beautiful or good. It exists, and it is in some sense satisfying or adequate to the perceiving consciousness. As Hemingway's laconic heroes say of a caught fish or a campsite, "It was very satisfactory."

In seeking to designate or describe this elusive quality, therefore, we most commonly resort not to aesthetic or moral terminology (beauty or goodness) but to material metaphors that are also terms of approval, acknowledging both the existence of certain qualities and their "interestingness": metaphors of fullness, wholeness, weight, solidity, density, texture, complexity, sometimes of opacity and three-dimensionality, or of intensity. Such a vocabulary allows us to acknowledge meaningfulness and value without incurring metaphysical obligations. The insistence on material metaphors is a kind of protest that we are not attributing a soul or an essence, a first cause or a final, to that which we describe. At the same time the clear note of approval, which forces us to take each material term in a sense other than the literal, serves notice that neither are we talking about pounds avoirdupois or specific gravity or the red end of the visible spectrum.

The rhetoric of substantiality, in short, permits us to designate aspects of common experience and to ascribe value to them without claiming either that that value is merely a subjective imposition or that it derives from a sphere—whether moral, aesthetic, or metaphysical—distinct from common experience itself. It offers a way, at times an uneasy way, of reaffirming intrinsic value when the very notion of the intrinsic seems to carry with it an unacceptable burden of metaphysical lumber (essence, substance, and the like). In this sense the rhetoric of substantiality helped eighteenth-century writers both to express and to bring into being the sphere of what Trilling calls "the substance of life in all its ordinariness and lack of elevation," and thus it may properly be termed a rhetoric of experience as well. And it is in this special sense, finally, that we may term the later eighteenth century an age of experience. Not that it laid bare the veritable *Ding an sich*, experience itself (whatever that would mean), but that it developed a new set of literary and perceptual conventions, a new rhetoric in the largest sense, with which to call into being that literary and cultural construct, common experience.

It is far from an axiom, however, that the emergence, the coming to prominence, of ordinary, unelevated life engenders delight in the heart of man. It seems to have done so for Hume, for some of the *philosophes*, for Gibbon and for Franklin. But Sterne, while powerfully committed to the sphere of common experience, is at times uneasy with it, and a writer like Boswell is uneasier still. For the rhetoric of substantiality is also, inevitably, a rhetoric of insubstantiality, and the reality that it discloses may as readily appear mean, impoverished, or nonexistent as solid, various, and actual, particularly to a mind religiously disposed or metaphysically inclined. Indeed, in many of the writings of this period we can see the metaphysical and the substantial exacting distinct and at times incompatible allegiances. In *Jubilate Agno*, for example, Smart is arguing neither that God exists nor that He is good (these are Smart's metaphysical presuppositions) but that He is present, that the physical world reveals not simply the wisdom of God in the Creation but the manifest and substantial presentness of divine being:

For EARTH which is an intelligence hath a voice and
a propensity to speak in all her parts.

For flowers are peculiarly the poetry of Christ.

For the Electrical fire is the spiritual substance, which
God sends from heaven to sustain the bodies both
of man and beast.

(BI, 234; B2, 506, 764)

This is the thrust of Smart's argument, and it is also the locus
of its greatest strain, for the poet suffers not from religious
doubt but from a virtually unappeasable ontological hunger
that neither faith nor reason can satisfy. Somewhat like the
speaker in Frost's "To Earthward" Smart longs to feel the
very impress of being, the substance and pressure of reality;
yet the elaborately explanatory mode of the poem constantly
affirms the poet's distance from that divine reality whose immediacy he strives to demonstrate, affirms a separation instead
of a union. It is this effort to invest the metaphysical with
substantial import, to demonstrate the virtual identity of heaven
and earth, that chiefly distinguishes Smart from more conventional physico-theological writers of the eighteenth century.[15] For the defining mark of the works that set Smart apart
from such writers, as from himself as a writer of conventional
religious verse, is not the originality of their doctrine or ideas
but the freshness and fullness with which they render a special
way of experiencing.

Like Smart, Johnson acknowledges that the distinction between the divine and the earthly spheres corresponds (whether
by nature or convention) to that between the metaphysical
and the substantial modes of apprehension. But while Smart
seeks to overcome these distinctions, Johnson, at least much
of the time, resolutely insists on them. In the first place Johnson habitually presents the heavenly and earthly orders as

[15] For a slightly different interpretation of Smart and of his relation to the
physico-theologians see David B. Morris, *The Religious Sublime: Christian
Poetry and Critical Tradition in Eighteenth-Century England* (Lexington:
Univ. of Kentucky Press, 1972), p. 171.

distinct, though not wholly discontinuous. The moment of death may be the moment of our translation from one realm to another, but while we are alive we live on earth. The penultimate chapter of *Rasselas*, in which the little party contemplates the mysteries of the soul and Nekayah hopes "hereafter to think only on the choice of eternity," is a chapter, so to speak, in parentheses. It is an obscure window from this world to the next, and it is not the business of life to stand gazing through it: "They then hastened out of the caverns, and, under the protection of their guard, returned to Cairo." It is such a window, too, that opens from "the busy Scenes of crouded Life," in the last lines of "The Vanity of Human Wishes," onto a heavenly realm that is properly the object of men's prayers rather than their knowledge and from which we must seek the strength to endure earthly existence and not the means to escape it. Nowhere does Johnson endorse the belief that heaven shall exist on earth before the last day or that we may somehow escape worldly trials while yet we live in the world.

The secular version of those beliefs produces, respectively, utopian and pastoral fantasy, one version of the latter appearing in the chapter of *Rasselas* devoted to the hermit, who comes to realize that "the life of a solitary man will be certainly miserable, but not certainly devout." Yet Johnson had undertaken a more extensive and equally skeptical study of the desire "to remove from all apparent evil" some twenty years earlier in "London: A Poem." Thales, who is "Resolv'd at length, from Vice and London far, /To breathe in distant Fields a purer Air" (5-6), is a younger version of the hermit, as yet unchastened by fifteen years of solitude.[16] Identifying vice with the city rather than with human perversity, he correspondingly idealizes the country, expecting to find there not just "a purer Air" or an escape from the symbolic center of Walpole's administration but a veritable *locus amoenus*:

[16] All citations from Johnson's poetry are to Samuel Johnson, *The Complete English Poems*, ed. J. D. Fleeman (Harmondsworth, Eng.: Penguin, 1971), and will be cited by page number in the text.

There ev'ry Bush with Nature's Music rings,
There ev'ry Breeze bears Health upon its Wings;
On all thy Hours Security shall smile,
And bless thine Evening Walk and Morning Toil.
                    (220-223; cf. 43-50, 170-173)

Elsewhere, oppressed by the uniform corruption of "these degen'rate Days" (35), he finds in the past the Golden Age for which he longs, whether in the reigns of Elizabeth (25-28) or Edward III (99-100), or in the "Blest Age" of Alfred (248-253). The poem's narrator shares Thales' admiration for Elizabethan England, commends his decision to leave London (though he has few illusions about life in pastoral seclusion, where "all whom Hunger spares, with Age decay" [12]), acknowledges the urban chaos that so outrages his friend—but chooses to remain in the city. He stands to Thales much as Imlac stands to the little party in *Rasselas*: in a position of greater experience that includes, but also diffuses and goes beyond, their narrower and intenser energies.

   Johnson's preference for the city over the country is as much moral as geographical. The "nooks obscure" that Cowper envisioned or the "secret Cell" imagined by Thales might be the necessary environment of those constitutionally unfit for experience. But to most people, as Johnson saw it, the world at large, and a city like London preeminently, afforded not only a multiplicity of objects sufficient to fill one's consciousness and supply its vacuity with the sentiment of being but also the greatest possible opportunity for the exercise of virtue in all its modes. In contrast, enclosure and isolation are limiting. There is no Eden in the fallen world, and any substitute provides at best a "blissful captivity" like that of the Happy Valley in *Rasselas*. A similar thematic significance attaches to the imagery of enclosed spaces in the *Journey to the Western Islands*. The barriers that keep others out, Johnson shows, may also keep us in; the flourishing walled orchards that occasionally dot the Hebrides have as their demonic counterpart the cave in which Macleod choked his enemies with smoke

THE RHETORIC OF SUBSTANTIALITY

"and left them lying dead by families as they stood."[17] Johnson is always aware of the ambiguity of enclosure, physical or spiritual, of the ease with which a *hortus conclusus* may become a cul de sac.

In "London," it is Thales' tone as he prepares to depart which reveals the toll that spiritual isolation has already taken, for his hermetic intransigence is another of Johnson's images of captivity. Thales' self-pity, his self-inflation, his strident and simplistic condemnation of the city of London and of modern England itself—these stand in sharp contrast to the more reflective and judicious lines with which the narrator opens the poem:

> Tho' Grief and Fondness in my Breast rebel,
> When injur'd Thales bids the Town farewell,
> Yet still my calmer Thoughts his Choice commend,
> I praise the Hermit, but regret the Friend.

Thales has no "calmer Thoughts" like these and none of the narrator's judicious self-division. In the body of the poem he never acknowledges, as Pope does even in the harshly satiric *Dunciad* and *Epilogue to the Satires*, that he is generically akin to those he attacks, that he too is a fallible man in a fallen world. Rather, he enjoys conceiving of himself as a figure of "surly Virtue" (145), a "Foe to Vice" (261), condemned by his fearless integrity to "Live unregarded, unlamented die" (82)—a line that might be described as masochiastic.

Thales' image of himself, in short, is the counterpart of his conception of rural retirement: both are powerfully idealized and contrast sharply with the imperfect world from which he tries to dissociate himself. This idealization, like the sweeping generality of his satire, suggests that Thales seeks "an alternative," as D. V. Boyd puts it, "not only to the corruptions

---

[17] Samuel Johnson, *A Journey to the Western Islands of Scotland*, ed. Mary Lascelles, vol. 9 of The Yale Edition of the Works of Samuel Johnson (New Haven and London: Yale Univ. Press, 1971), p. 69.

of London life, but also to the limitations of the human lot."[18] There is virtue in such a stance, but there is also, for Johnson, narrowness, pride, and—insofar as we believe that an earthly "alternative" exists—a potentially disastrous confusion of this world with our imaginings of the next. "Imagination," Arieh Sachs remarks, "sets up Heavenly Cities on earth."[19] The result is not simply to reduce heaven to our own conceptions of it but also to obscure the earth. Johnson frequently enough inveighs against the first sort of error, reminding us that we see but darkly. Yet he also insists that utopian schemes presuppose a creature other than man and that dreams of perfect bliss are likely to divert us from both a realistic perception of human nature and the real performance of our human duties.

If Johnson resolutely keeps the heavenly and earthly realms distinct, then, he does so not simply to subordinate earth to heaven but also to value each in the manner appropriate to it. Despite his belief that human existence is a state more to be endured than enjoyed and his contention that "no man would choose to lead over again the life which he had experienced," Johnson lived not just as a man awaiting release from hope's delusive mine but as one who also felt "that love of life which is necessary to the vigorous prosecution of any undertaking."[20] This is not a matter of mere alternations of mood but of that allegiance to both the metaphysical and the substantial modes of consciousness that the oblique antitheses I have mentioned suggest so economically. Johnson knew as well as anyone in his age what common experience may seem to amount to when it is viewed under the aspect of eternity, in terms of its ultimate metaphysical import. His guilt, his

[18] D. V. Boyd, "Vanity and Vacuity: A Reading of Johnson's Verse Satires," *English Literary History* 39 (1972): 395.

[19] Arieh Sachs, *Passionate Intelligence: Imagination and Reason in the Work of Samuel Johnson* (Baltimore: The Johns Hopkins Univ. Press, 1967), pp. xii-xiii.

[20] Boswell, *Life*, 4: 301; *Rambler* No. 59, in Samuel Johnson, *The Rambler*, ed. W. J. Bate and Albrecht B. Strauss, vols. 3, 4, and 5 of The Yale Edition of the Works of Samuel Johnson (New Haven and London: Yale Univ. Press, 1969), 3: 315.

indolence, his anguished perception of vacuity—these are all aspects of the inadequacy that such a vision yielded.[21] But unlike Thales—perhaps because he had seen that insubstantiality more vividly and authentically than Thales, had seen, in fact, not merely the disappointments of experience but its ultimate contingency and *necessary* inadequacy—he also knew that experience has its own kind of value and consciousness its own mode of apprehending that value.

This is why he can sometimes assert, as Robert Shackleton puts it, "that established opinions must be enforced because they are established and not because they are true," or that Boswell need not worry about arguing a legal cause that he "knows" to be bad because "you do not know it to be good or bad till the Judge determines it."[22] Johnson, at such moments, is neither overvaluing human beings and their institutions nor cynically setting convention and conformity above truth. He is insisting that there is a kind of truth besides the metaphysical and that it must be respected for what it is; limited and imperfect, yet real, and what we have. It is not an absolute truth existing anterior to the reasonings and judgments of men, as Boswell supposes in this exchange, but precisely the truth that arises from those reasonings and judgments. Similarly, Johnson's idea of poetic generality is not, as Lionel Basney puts it, "a Platonic ideal or moralistic truth, but a Lockean complex idea." It does not exist anterior to the particulars of a poem, like a disembodied essence requiring to be mediated to the reader's consciousness; it is rather a wholeness, a "quality of organized specificity and integrated detail," that arises from those particulars.[23] This suggests, of

[21] Trilling, *Sincerity and Authenticity*, p. 160; R. D. Laing, *The Divided Self: An Existential Study in Sanity and Madness* (N.Y.: Pantheon, 1969), pp. 40-64.

[22] Robert Shackleton, "Johnson and the Enlightenment," in *Johnson, Boswell, and Their Circle* (Oxford: Clarendon Press, 1965), p. 82; Boswell, *Life*, 2: 47.

[23] Lionel Basney, " 'Lucidus Ordo': Johnson and Generality," *Eighteenth-Century Studies* 5 (1971): 45. See also pp. 53-54, and Jean H. Hagstrum, *Samuel Johnson's Literary Criticism* (Minneapolis: Univ. of Minnesota Press, 1952), pp. 87-89.

course, that in their discussion of legal truth it is not Johnson but Boswell who "hankers after the absolute," in George Eliot's phrase, and who seeks to regulate human institutions and human actions by principles stabler than they. Judging experience by standards drawn from experience itself, Johnson refuses to claim a certainty to which he can have no real access and, as Donald J. Greene says, "rigidly excludes theological and supernatural considerations of every kind from his conception of the way government [and, I would add, much else] comes into being and operates."[24]

Nevertheless, the image of Johnson as an intellectual "absolutist"—a declaimer of principles, a seeker after large general truths, a quester for certainty in a time of doubt—is not merely a popular distortion or a Victorian myth or a Boswellian falsification. For while Johnson's scrupulous separation of heaven and earth, his reluctance to view "the real state of sublunary nature" through metaphysical categories alone, leads him to an apprehension of common experience in terms more appropriate to it, it does not prevent him from seeking within that experience principles as well as phenomena, categories as well as the categorizable, "the stability of truth" as well as a "multiplicity of agreeable consciousness." And it is the special triumph of his rhetoric and style to present those principles so as to suggest that they are, in some sense, the experiential counterparts of metaphysical absolutes.

His treatment of the concept of "general nature" is a good example of this strategy. General nature is not, as Johnson conceives it, a metaphysical entity, a kind of Adamic essence imparted by each generation to its progeny or a Platonic Form of which individual men and women are more or less accurate copies. Nor does this lack of metaphysical status mean that there is no such thing as general nature, merely numerous particular individuals. Rather, it is an "empirical" concept, of sorts, derived from the testimony of human history, the evidence of literature and other cultural witnesses, and—let

[24] Donald J. Greene, *The Politics of Samuel Johnson* (New Haven: Yale Univ. Press, 1960), p. 244.

63

us acknowledge—the particular cast of mind that we recognize as Johnson's, though hardly Johnson's alone. Yet it will not quite do to call "general nature" an empirical generalization, not because Johnson failed to conduct a rigorous survey or to tabulate data derived from questionnaires but because the concept signifies, for him, an object of value as well as an object of knowledge. His belief that such a thing as general nature exists is inseparable from his belief that it is, in a special sense, a good thing. "Nothing can please many, and please long," he writes in the *Preface to Shakespeare*, "but just representations of general nature," which permit the mind to repose on "the stability of truth." It is not merely a fact but a virtue that Shakespeare's power was the "power of nature," that he was "the poet of nature." If "the work of a correct and regular writer is a garden accurately formed and diligently planted," that of Shakespeare is "a forest, in which oaks extend their branches, and pines tower in the air, interspersed sometimes with weeds and brambles, and sometimes giving shelter to myrtles and to roses; filling the eye with awful pomp, and gratifying the mind with endless diversity." Those correct and regular writers "display cabinets of precious rarities, minutely finished, wrought into shape, and polished unto brightness," but Shakespeare "opens a mine which contains gold and diamonds in unexhaustible plenty, though clouded by incrustations, debased by impurities, and mingled with a mass of meaner minerals." It is a robust and difficult beauty that Johnson describes here, as, given his praise of Shakespeare's art, it must be. For that art expresses a difficult reality, neither "beautiful" nor good" in any simple sense. "The real state of sublunary nature . . . partakes of good and evil, joy and sorrow, mingled with endless variety of proportion and innumerable modes of combination."[25]

[25] The quotations are, in order, from the "Preface to Shakespeare," in *Johnson on Shakespeare*, ed. Arthur Sherbo, vols. 7 and 8 of The Yale Edition of the Works of Samuel Johnson (New Haven and London: Yale Univ. Press, 1968), 7: 61, 62, 73, 62, 84, 66. As Johnson well knew, of course, he was hardly the first to praise Shakespeare's "nature." Yet to appreciate the degree to which he conceived this nature in terms of its substantiality we need only

It is clear that for Johnson Shakespeare's art and the world of human experience that it mirrors are not chiefly beautiful or good but solid, various, textured, weighty, complex—in a word, substantial. Yet Johnson does not always treat general nature in these terms. Elsewhere he makes use of a rhetoric that stresses precisely uniformity, generality, universality, a rhetoric which suggests that general nature is less a richly substantial and complex whole—a forest or a mine—than a unitary principle, an abstract and almost a metaphysical entity. Consider the following brief anthology of remarks on general nature, in and out of art, and on concepts roughly synonymous with it:

Human nature is always the same.

Reason and nature are uniform and inflexible.

Great thoughts are always general, and consist in positions not limited by exceptions, and in descriptions not descending to minuteness.

He [the poet] must consider right and wrong in their abstracted and invariable state; he must disregard present laws and opinions, and rise to general and transcendental truths, which will always be the same.

Truth indeed is always truth, and reason is always reason; they have an intrinsic and unalterable value, and constitute that intellectual gold which defies destruction.[26]

From this point of view "the real state of sublunary nature" does not so much exhibit "awful pomp" and "endless diversity" or "good and evil, joy and sorrow, mingled with endless

---

compare the relevant passages from his *Preface* with those (chiefly, the opening and closing pages) from Pope's *Preface* of 1725.

[26] The quotations are, in order, from Samuel Johnson, *Adventurer* No. 99, in *"The Idler" and "The Adventurer,"* ed. W. J. Bate, John M. Bullitt, L. F. Powell, vol. 2 of The Yale Edition of the Works of Samuel Johnson (New Haven and London: Yale Univ. Press, 1963), p. 431; *Rambler* No. 125 (4: 301); "Life of Cowley," in *Lives of the English Poets*, ed. G. B. Hill (1905; reprint ed., N. Y.: Octagon, 1967), 1: 21; *Rasselas*, chap. 10; "Life of Cowley," 1: 59.

variety of proportion and innumerable modes of combination," as, in Jean Hagstrum's words, "the permanence and immutability of human nature" and thus "a system of moral and psychological universals."[27]

The status of these universals, however, is inescapably problematic, in large part because Johnson, in passages like these, treats the experiential in terms of a rhetoric of metaphysics, yet nowhere does he unequivocally ascribe metaphysical import to what is not explicitly theological. He reconstitutes the a priori or metaphysically derived category "general nature" (or "human nature" or "experience") as an empirical or "substantial" concept, the lived and observed nature of real life; but at times he surrounds this concept with intimations of absoluteness and nearly succeeds in converting it into that fertile absurdity or oblique antithesis, an empirical universal. (We might recall here Kant's contemporary and still disputed notion of a *synthetic a priori* statement.) If, as Arieh Sachs argues, "Reason, through experience, learns to concentrate upon true absolutes—the ultimate truths of religion—where Imagination treats the relative and contingent as if they were absolutes," then we must grant that reason and imagination were not always so distinct for Johnson as the act of capitalizing them may suggest.[28]

There is strain in such an effort as Johnson's, an effort that is the precise obverse of Smart's insistence—equally strained and equally splendid—that the metaphysical may be invested with substantial import. At the level of logic it is the strain of treating "the relative and contingent as if [or almost as if] they were absolutes." At the level of verbal style it is the strain of treating the adjectival and grammatically contingent—at least, the nonsubstantive—as though it were substantive. If Johnson is interested "in the classes to which things belong," writes W. K. Wimsatt, "the aspects which unify groups of objects, he becomes at moments even more interested in these aspects as things in themselves, as metaphysical realities."

[27] Hagstrum, *Samuel Johnson's Literary Criticism*, p. 71. See also p. 14.
[28] Sachs, *Passionate Intelligence*, p. xii.

Indeed, "he made a kind of poetry of abstraction; out of emptiness he conjured weight, out of the collapsible he made structures."[29] These structures, however, are never unequivocally metaphysical any more than words like "fugacity" or "labefactation" are unequivocally nounal. Grammatically, of course, there is no question of their status: they are nouns. But they come to us trailing clouds of the verbal (*fugere*) and adjectival (*Eheu fugaces, Postume, Postume*). They are nouns much as the Crystal Palace is an exhibition building or as Mae West is a woman, calling attention by their hyperbolic assertiveness to the energy devoted to making them what they are, announcing their nature as insistently as they exemplify it. And, inevitably, displaying the brave precariousness of will and artifice as well.

There is, at least in Johnson's case, a special kind of integrity in such a display, the integrity of acknowledged overstatement rather than that of cautious precision. Johnson's version of this integrity, and of the historic propensities that underlie it, is perhaps less familiar to us than its counterparts in Boswell or Sterne or Rousseau. But neither his prose style nor his rhetorical posture nor the special status of his quasi-metaphysical statements about common experience can be understood without reference to that knowing self-dramatization which permitted him to play the role of Dr. Samuel Johnson, Arbiter of Absolutes, while acknowledging that it was, in part, a role. For all their differences we may say of Johnson what Martin Price says of Sterne, that his peculiar tone "comes of his readiness to say too much and his alertness to see that it is too much."[30]

---

[29] W. K. Wimsatt, Jr., *The Prose Style of Samuel Johnson* (New Haven: Yale Univ. Press, 1941), pp. 55-56, 96.

[30] Martin Price, *To the Palace of Wisdom: Studies in Order and Energy from Dryden to Blake* (Garden City, N.Y.: Doubleday, 1964), p. 337. I have tried to explain the two views of nature in Johnson's *Preface* in a different way than Murray Krieger in his "Fiction, Nature, and Literary Kinds in Johnson's Criticism of Shakespeare," *Eighteenth-Century Studies* 4 (1970-1971): 184-198.

I have dwelt on Johnson and, to a lesser degree, on Smart because their writings point with special clarity to the large role that the substantial dimension of experience played in the literature and thought of the later eighteenth century. They are, of course, difficult and highly idiosyncratic writers, as different from each other as they are from the majority of their contemporaries. Yet their very distance from what we commonly think of as the mainstream of the Enlightenment only serves to set in relief the degree to which they participated in one of its most characteristic modes of consciousness. It is my aim not to reduce them to the status of, as college course descriptions put it, "Representative Writers of the Later Eighteenth Century" but to resist the view of them as merely craggy and singular anomalies, a view expressed in the kind of literary history text that is organized by themes or topics but dwells overmuch on Smart's insanity and gives "Dr. Johnson" a chapter to himself. Not every effort to discern unity or connection need be construed as a ruthless forcing of individuals into the trivial seemliness of the *Zeitgeist*, and the concept of substantiality is in any case almost distressingly roomy.[31] As much a category of apprehension as a theme, it permits us to organize literary works across as well as along thematic lines. It provides, for example, an additional context in which to consider the role of the factual in later eighteenth-century literature, a phenomenon that appears in relatively pure form in Boswell's remarkably unremarkable "Dialogues at Child's," extends through those genres that Watt terms "the literature of experience," and enlarges into the various flourishings of the biographical and autobiographical impulses in Boswell, Franklin, Gibbon, Rousseau, and even Sterne's Tristram.[32] As this last example implies, it is a short—and from a critical

[31] For a strong and lucid attack on the validity—and the Hegelian underpinnings—of cultural history see E. H. Gombrich, *In Search of Cultural History* (Oxford: Clarendon Press, 1969).

[32] See Frank Brady, "Fact and Factuality in Literature," in *Directions in Literary Criticism: Contemporary Approaches to Literature*, ed. Stanley Weintraub and Philip Young (University Park and London: Penn State Univ. Press, 1973), pp. 95, 105.

viewpoint, a nonexistent—step from the factual to the factual seeming, the effort to render the texture of common experience without regard to literal truth. If we think here of descriptive detail in Crabbe or in a post-Augustan satirist like Churchill, we may also want to recall the way in which Richardson's epistolary immediacy serves to register the "feel" of an event or conflict in the letter writer's or recipient's sensibility as well as its significance in a developing narrative. (F. A. Pottle long ago remarked on Boswell's debt, in the *London Journal*, to the Richardsonian notion of "writing to the moment.") Finally, it is not too farfetched, I think, to connect this novelistic and autobiographical exploration of the contours of sensibility with the attention of critical theorists, in particular the associationists and theorists of the picturesque, not just to psychological "laws" but to the manner in which we experience literary or pictorial works, to what might now be called the phenomenology of reading or viewing: the attempt to describe what we experience exactly as we experience it and often simply *because* we experience it.

In an essentially comic writer like Sterne the effort to depict ordinary experience shades readily into the impulse to celebrate it. In *Tristram Shandy* the account of Corporal Trim's sermon-reading posture is at once an effort of accurate observation and a tribute to the plenitude and expressive power of the visual and gestural in everyday life. Similarly, the treatment of pleasure in Burns, especially sexual pleasure, is as much an insistence on the intrinsic worth of experience as it is an exaltation of the erotic. Burns's repeated juxtaposition of sexual openness and clerical rigidity, the latter frequently tinged with hypocrisy or self-deception, is only in part a satiric strategy. For the institutional and repressive are countered not simply by whisky drinking and houghmagandie but by an ethic of worldly experience, coherent though unsystematic, that stresses liberty, authenticity, tenderness, self-awareness, and common sense. From this point of view ordinary life provides not only substantial pleasures and pains but also adequate indications of the way it is to be lived. Burns is of course not a moralist in the usual sense of the word, but neither is he a mere hedonist, for he conceives of the capacity for honest pleasure as a sign of human adequacy to the substantiality of experience.

At the opposite end of the spectrum are those writers for whom common experience is precisely insubstantial and whose works either express that perception of insubstantiality or project a vision—bardic, oracular, sublime—of a world more intensely present, more substantial and imposing. Such a vision presupposes the inadequacy of ordinary life, and this inadequacy is frequently imaged as the result of a fall from a more heroic, robust, and imaginative past, as in Gray, Collins, Macpherson, and others. What I would stress here is that this sense of present inadequacy is neither an isolated nor an exclusively poetic phenomenon. The feeling of poetic belatedness, for example, of writing after—and in the shadow of—Milton or Spenser or Homer, is assuredly part of it, but the very susceptibility to such anxieties is itself a symptom of the larger cultural phenomenon I have tried to outline. The wistful celebration of a heroic past, moreover, is at least as likely to follow from discontent with the present as to generate it. The Gaelic bards and Spenserian songsters that we find in some later eighteenth-century literature are, like Goldsmith's Rural Virtues and Boswell's notions of feudal bliss, part of the familiar furniture of the myth of the Golden Age and not the exclusive property of a burdened Gray and an anxious Collins.[33] Such evocations of a visionary past, in the consciously heightened style of the sublime ode, are precisely analogous to Johnson's superb compelling of common experience into a rhetoric of absolutes: in each case the writer gestures toward a reality—whether romantic or metaphysical—beyond ordinary experience, and in each case the very sweep and extravagance of the gesture reserve, so to speak, the commitment it announces.

[33] In this paragraph I allude to W. J. Bate, *The Burden of the Past and the English Poet* (Cambridge, Mass.: Belknap Press, 1970), and Harold Bloom, *The Anxiety of Influence: A Theory of Poetry* N.Y.: Oxford Univ. Press, 1973).

The heightened perception of common experience in the later eighteenth century, then, was neither restricted to the Continental Enlightenment nor avoided by those who in many ways deplored what they perceived. At a deeper level than the division of thinkers into those who welcomed and those who resisted the notion of ordinary life as, if not the source, at least the end and test of itself, the period is marked by the very emergence of, in effect, a newly isolated category of consciousness. What is remarkable is not that Hume or Franklin or the *philosophes* appealed so often to common experience and seemed to insist that there was little or nothing else to appeal to, but that a figure like Johnson, to whom the implications of such a view were profoundly disturbing, conducted his campaign of defiant resistance with little more than the materials of that very experience. To be sure, he subjected those materials to the extraordinary pressure of a rhetoric and a style designed, as it were, to express the metaphysical, the abstract, the categorical and absolute. Except when he spoke or wrote of religious matters, however, his language chiefly expressed the substance of common life, "the real state of sublunary nature." His is at least as much the voice of his time as of an earlier, for he did battle with his own age in the very terms which that age, to his distress, espoused.

Johnson's, then, is a special case, but a special case of a general condition, not an exception to it. He wrote in a time when human experience, progressively less reliant on metaphysical or transcendent authentication, was itself becoming the source of the terms in which it was to be considered: a time when the sphere of experience itself was invested with new value, new explanatory power, and heightened interest. Thus the older conception of the later eighteenth century as a proto-Romantic age of feeling was not a simple error but an incomplete truth. For the point is not that writers in the latter part of the century began suddenly to feel but that certain emotions, and the emotional life as a whole, came to be credited and valued precisely—in some cases, solely—because they were an undeniable element of human experience. The same argument, at least in part, applies to the appearance

THE RHETORIC OF SUBSTANTIALITY

of new kinds of subject matter in literature and the visual arts. For it is not simply new subjects that the age introduces but a new respect for experience. And if the treatment of new subjects can teach us to value the experience from which they derive, the initial investing of the sphere of experience with value may also liberate the treatment of new subjects.

The claim, at least the wish, to confront experience "on its own terms" is of course a recurrent one, hardly confined to the later eighteenth century. Indeed, it is not Johnson or Boswell or Sterne but Wordsworth who proposes to muse "On Man, on Nature, and on Human Life" and to express that musing in "words/Which speak of nothing more than what we are." Yet despite his attempt to bring the language of poetry closer to that of common speech and to focus on figures and incidents in many ways unheroic, Wordsworth's major poetry is distinctly a creation of the Romantic era rather than of the Enlightenment. For he replaces an older conception of the metaphysical import of common experience with a newer, and he is not chiefly concerned with what we may call the intrinsic qualities of human experience. He may have, as Earl Wasserman claims, "invested with value the very act of experience,"[34] but even in this narrow sense of "experience" (the equivalent of "perception") it is clear that the value with which he invested it did not derive from experience or perception themselves but from their metaphysical foundations. Despite his contrasting of his own poetical venture with that of Milton and his use of highly general terms to indicate his subjects ("On Man, on Nature, and on Human Life"), Wordsworth's special greatness does not mainly consist in a widening of the range of experience that poetry depicts or in a new perception of "the substance of life in all its ordinariness and lack of elevation." That achievement, which Wordsworth does not accomplish but presupposes, was largely the work of the generation of writers that immediately preceded him. My argument may seem to suggest that those writers require yet

[34] Earl R. Wasserman, "The English Romantics: The Grounds of Knowledge," *Studies in Romanticism* 4, no. 1 (1964): 24.

another label for their era: The Age of Experience, or, more guardedly, An Age of Experience. One would, of course, have to specify the particular sense of "experience" implied in order to avoid the suggestion that Chaucer and Shakespeare, Dickens and Joyce, wrote about a different subject altogether. But the choice of a label is not especially important compared to the achievement it designates. For in this period a number of writers of remarkable and diverse powers seemed to see common experience plain—seemed unable, at times, not so to see it—and their writings reveal both the special nakedness that such a vision imposes and their special strengths in attempting to meet its challenge.

· 4 ·

PAST AND POEM:
WORLDS OF FINE FABLING

"In a dark time," says Theodore Roethke, "the eye begins to see." What it sees, if it is the eye of a poet like Roethke or Smart, is a radiant and disturbing prospect, "All natural shapes blazing unnatural light."[1] This is the characteristic visionary undertaking: to look hard at the world of everyday reality until its surface of accustomed appearances dissolves, revealing the realm of truth or being it had obscured. Such an undertaking is a search for meaning, at least for meaningfulness, and the visionary quest is only one of the forms it may take. What is required is a region of experience both distinct from common reality (though in some sense available to it) and more meaningful than that reality (though not necessarily transcendent). In our own age the unconscious as described by Freud is one such region; science, particularly to the nonscientist, is another; and semiotics, particularly its linguistic and anthropological forms, is at times a third. Carl Becker has argued that in the later eighteenth century the idea of Posterity—the future—served this function, eliciting from "philosophers and revolutionary leaders a highly emotional, an essentially religious, response."[2]

Yet, in Enlightenment England at least, the future was far from being the blissfully soteriological realm—a kind of earthly New Jerusalem—that Becker depicts. As a sphere that had (by definition) not yet come into being the future was likely to seem a potentially dangerous object of speculation that only the presumptuous would claim to know as a reality. For Johnson it was a typical "vain imagination," a fantasy, however

---

[1] Theodore Roethke, "In a Dark Time," in *The Collected Poems of Theodore Roethke* (Garden City, N.Y.: Doubleday, 1966), p. 239.

[2] Carl L. Becker, *The Heavenly City of the Eighteenth-Century Philosophers* (New Haven and London: Yale Univ. Press, 1932), p. 142.

necessary; and for Burke, it was a fantasy bred of revolutionary gnosis and spawning political and moral disaster. Even when knowledge of the future was not treated as a proud dream, it was far from being a source of comfort. In Gray "the dreadful powers/That read futurity," whether those powers are human or superhuman, almost uniformly discover doom and destruction: "The ministers of human fate,/And black Misfortune's baleful train," or "the painful family of Death."[3] And while Johnson, investigating second sight in the Hebrides, reports that "good seems to have the same proportion in those visionary scenes, as it obtains in real life," he also notes that "the impression is sudden, and the effect often painful," that "those who profess to feel it, do not boast of it as a privilege, nor are considered by others as advantageously distinguished," and that "there is now a 'second sighted' gentleman in the Highlands, who complains of the terrors to which he is exposed."[4]

It was not chiefly in the future nor in a genuinely visionary interpretation of the present that later eighteenth-century English writers sought meaningfulness and substantiality. They turned, rather, to the past viewed as a repository of fact and dream, myth and legend, and to the present viewed as an extraordinarily rich conjunction of common reality and human modes of apprehending that reality. Perhaps, says the narrator of Nabokov's *Transparent Things*,

perhaps if the future existed, concretely and individually,
as something that could be discerned by a better brain,

[3] Thomas Gray, "Agrippina, a Tragedy" (pp. 64-65); "Ode on a Distant Prospect of Eton College" (pp. 56-57, 83); in *The Poems of Thomas Gray, William Collins, Oliver Goldsmith*, ed. Roger Lonsdale (London: Longmans, 1969), pp. 35, 60, 62. All citations of the poetry of Gray, Collins, and Goldsmith are from this edition and will be acknowledged by line number in the text.

[4] Samuel Johnson, *A Journey to the Western Islands of Scotland*, ed. Mary Lascelles, vol. 9 of The Yale Edition of the Works of Samuel Johnson (New Haven and London: Yale Univ. Press, 1971), pp. 108, 107, 110. Subsequent references are to this edition and will be acknowledged by page number in the text.

the past would not be so seductive. .... But the future
has no such reality (as the pictured past and the perceived
present possess); the future is but a figure of speech, a
specter of thought.[5]

It is with the "pictured past," the past as it was reconstructed,
imaged, and above all used by English writers in the second
half of the eighteenth century, that this chapter is concerned.

"The seeds of excellence," writes Goldsmith in *An Enquiry
into the Present State of Polite Learning in Europe*, "are sown
in every age, and it is wholly owing to a wrong direction in
the passions or pursuits of mankind, that they have not received the proper cultivation."[6] In attributing the decay of
excellence in the arts at mid-century (1759) to faulty cultivation (inadequate patronage and public acclaim, overzealous
and mechanical criticism, and other causes) rather than to an
absence of "the seeds of excellency" themselves, Goldsmith
was adopting a moderate position. But his central point, that
there had indeed been a decline in the literary arts, was a
conviction shared by many of his contemporaries. "The spate
of critical writing that suddenly begins in the middle of the
eighteenth century in England," writes W. J. Bate, was an
attempt "to reground the entire thinking about poetry in the
light of one overwhelming fact: the obviously superior originality, and the at least apparently greater immediacy and
universality of subject and appeal, of the poetry of earlier
periods."[7]

What was at stake, of course, was not simply a certain idea
of poetry but also a certain idea of experience, experience
neither diffusely comprehensive nor narrowly intense but solid,

[5] Vladimir Nabokov, *Transparent Things* (N.Y.: McGraw-Hill, 1972), p.
1.

[6] Oliver Goldsmith, *An Enquiry into the Present State of Polite Learning
in Europe*, in *The Works of Oliver Goldsmith*, ed. Peter Cunningham, 4 vols.
(Boston: Little, Brown, 1854), 2: 7.

[7] W. J. Bate, *The Burden of the Past and the English Poet* (Cambridge,
Mass.: Belknap Press, 1970), p. 48.

meaningful, complex, robust, and coherent, experience (as Ecclesiastes, Longinus, and Johnson tell us) adequate to the mind's need to be filled. If the present could not supply such experience, perhaps it was to be found in an earlier age, in a Heroic Past or an Age of Romance. After all, writes Carlyle, "no age ever seemed the Age of Romance to *itself*."[8] Yet what, and where, was that past? How could it be gotten at and in what sort of relation to it did eighteenth-century writers imagine themselves to stand? These are problems that do not much trouble the simple-mindedly nostalgic, but they were taken very seriously by the poets and prose writers contemporary with Goldsmith, many of whom sought not simply to discover that earlier Age of Romance but to tap its energies and participate in its substantiality.

Yet even discovering it was difficult enough. "The most ancient times (except what is preserved of them in the scriptures)," Bacon had written in the preface to *The Wisdom of the Ancients*,

> are buried in oblivion and silence: to that silence succeeded the fables of the poets: to those fables the written records which have come down to us. Thus between the hidden depths of antiquity and the days of tradition and evidence that followed there is drawn a veil, as it were, of fables, which come in and occupy the middle region that separates what has perished from what survives.[9]

What, then, can "history" mean? Can it be anything but fable and legend? And even with the best of intentions and the most painstaking efforts of research, could one really discover the past *wie es eigentlich gewesen ist*, as Ranke was to assert, subordinating oneself wholly to its otherness, or—at the opposite extreme—ought one to consider history merely as "phi-

---

[8] Thomas Carlyle, *The Diamond Necklace*, in *Critical and Miscellaneous Essays*, 7 vols. (London: Chapman and Hall, 1869), 5: 133. Quoted in Arthur Johnston, *Enchanted Ground: The Study of Medieval Romance in the Eighteenth Century* (London: Athlone Press, 1964), p. 217.

[9] *Selected Writings of Francis Bacon*, ed. Hugh G. Dick (N.Y.: The Modern Library, 1955), p. 403.

losophy teaching by examples," in Bolingbroke's words? Was historical thought an act of memory and cognition that discovered what had been, or was memory itself, here as elsewhere, a fabricator of necessary fictions, "the medium of the must-have-been," as Julian Jaynes puts it.[10]

The question of the continuity of past with present was central, for the goal was not simply historical knowledge but imaginative and experiential nourishment, and a number of Enlightenment writers were able to experience something of that continuity. Guided by his feelings, Rousseau could not only recall his own past but re-experience it in the very act of recollection; Tristram Shandy, like Henry James a century and a half later, was virtually overwhelmed by the discovery that "to knock at the door of the past was in a word to see it open to me quite wide—to see the world within begin to 'compose' with a grace of its own round the primary figure, see it people itself vividly and insistently."[11] This is the present conceived as growing organically out of the past, a present that is, in Leibniz' rhythmically cheerful phrase, "chargé du passé et gros de l'avenir." Such continuity is least flawed, perhaps, in certain kinds of autobiographical reminiscence, where the past that is now recalled has earlier been fully lived. The growing interest in children, in the later eighteenth century, expresses a concern with this kind of continuity, as does Johnson's reiterated alarm during his Hebridean tour at the scarcity of trees in the Highlands.[12]

What Johnson seeks, with Yeats's "haughtier-headed Burke, who thought the state a tree," is something like the rich continuity that Cowper finds in the subject of "Yardley Oak."[13]

[10] Julian Jaynes, *The Origin of Consciousness in the Breakdown of the Bicameral Mind* (Boston: Houghton Mifflin, 1976), p. 30.

[11] Henry James, *A Small Boy and Others* (N.Y.: Charles Scribner's Sons, 1913), p. 2.

[12] See Murray Cohen, *Sensible Words: Linguistic Practice in England, 1640-1785* (Baltimore and London: The Johns Hopkins Univ. Press, 1977), p. 125.

[13] William Cowper, *Poetical Works*, ed. H. S. Milford, 4th ed. (London: Oxford Univ. Press, 1967), pp. 410-414. All citations from Cowper's poetry, except where noted, are from this edition and will be acknowledged by line number in the text.

Here is a past that once held within it the energies of the present and future. The oak is an organic whole that has passed "through all the stages . . . of treeship" and that even in decay is not merely a *memento mori* but an emblem of persistent, multiform, and continuous life:

> Yet life still lingers in thee, and puts forth
> Proof not contemptible of what she can,
> Even where death predominates. The spring
> Thee finds not less alive to her sweet force
> Than yonder upstarts of the neighbour wood,
> So much thy juniors, who their birth receiv'd
> Half a millennium since the date of thine.
>
> (130-136)

The oak's present energies spring from its rootedness in the past, from that "root sincere" whose "stout spurs and knotted fangs, . . . crook'd into a thousand whimsies, clasp/The stubborn soil, and hold thee still erect" (116-119).

Similarly, in Book VI of *The Task* the sound of village bells "opens all the cells/Where mem'ry slept," and, says Cowper, "in a few short moments I retrace . . . the windings of my way through many years" (1-18). Syntactically as well, present dissolves into past and then re-emerges (1-58). If this is a psychological phenomenon, it is nevertheless grounded, for Cowper, in the very nature of the created world, for God is the present sustainer as well as the original creator of the world: "The Lord of all, himself through all diffus'd,/Sustains, and is the life of all that lives" (221-222). Thus it is that natural beauty prompts the observer "with remembrance of a present God"; for "His presence, who made all so fair, perceiv'd,/Makes all still fairer" (252-254). Even the first sin, which set man against beast in fear and defiance (371-378), seems half undone in the woody shades that the poet loves to frequent (305-320), and this mild recapturing of an Edenic harmony prepares for the apocalyptic vision later in Book VI. There Cowper not only offers a vision of redeemed nature as though it were already present—"Behold the measure of the promise fill'd" (798)—but he also treats that future-made-present as a recovery of past perfection: "Thus heav'n-ward all things tend. For all were once/Perfect, and all must be at length restor'd" (818-819). An imagined future recovery of past harmony has been made present.

Cowper's faith in continuity, in time as a redemptive medium allowing the present to thrive on the energies of the past and hold within itself the force of the future, and particularly in the past conceived as a reservoir of available energies rather than a burden or a shadowy and ambiguous province or a mere vacuity, is far from common in the later eighteenth century, and some of Cowper's own poems offer a more troubling image of what may be accomplished by the slow growth of time. The glaciers in his late poem "On the Ice Islands," for example, seem at first to be the product of forces much like those that lent Yardley oak its mighty substance and vitality:

> By slow degrees uprose the wondrous pile,
> And long-successive ages roll'd the while;
> Till, ceaseless in its growth, it claim'd to stand
> Tall as its rival mountains on the land.
> (39-42)

But then, "supplanted yet/By pressure of its own enormous weight,/It left the shelving beach" (45-47) and now threatens to float southward to "a softer air" and its own destruction. However one may wish to allegorize the poem, its view of time, of growth, and of continuity is a kind of demonic inversion of what we find in Book VI of *The Task* or in "Yardley Oak." Here, slow accretion has become murderous: the "giant bulk/Of girth enormous," emblem of the slow time that lent the oak its dignity, has become a massy burden impelling the ice islands toward a suicidal independence.[14]

The past may also survive into the present without developing, without changing its nature. In such a case we have not fruitful continuity but mere stagnant continuance, gro-

---

[14] With the ice islands "self-launched," solitary, and floating toward their own doom, compare Cowper's "The Castaway": "We perish'd, each alone." The poems were written within a few days of each other.

80

tesque and startling persistence. In an abandoned vault at St. Andrews Johnson and Boswell encounter

> an old woman, who claimed the right of abode there, as the widow of a man whose ancestors had possessed the same gloomy mansion [the house that had stood over the vault] for no less than four generations. The right, however it began, was considered as established by legal prescription, and the old woman lives undisturbed.[15]

Like the legal prescription that permits her to live there ("custom continued until it has the force of law"),[16] the woman herself has become rigidified by the pressure of time. Neither flourishing nor defunct, she denies the observing mind both gratification and relief, and her condition therefore mimics that of the University of St. Andrews itself. "Had the university," says Johnson, "been destroyed two centuries ago, we should not have regretted it; but to see it pining in decay and struggling for life, fills the mind with mournful images and ineffectual wishes" (9).

Neither the aged Mrs. Bruce nor the declining university was what Johnson sought in Scotland and the Hebrides. "He was reckoning," as Mary Lascelles puts it, "on a fold in the web of time: the opportunity to observe living people still tracing a pattern of life elsewhere extinct."[17] What he discovered, however, was that the principal attribute of that "system of antiquated life" which constitutes the authentic past is its elusiveness. "Men skilled in architecture," says Johnson at the monastery of Aberbrothick, "might do what we did not attempt: They might probably form an exact ground-plot of this venerable edifice. They may from some parts yet standing conjecture its general form, and perhaps by comparing it with other buildings of the same kind and the same age, attain an idea very near to truth" (11). For most of their journey, in fact, this is the utmost that Johnson and Boswell

---

[15] Johnson, *Journey*, p. 8.

[16] Samuel Johnson, *A Dictionary of the English Language*, 4th ed. (1773), quoted in Johnson, *Journey*, p. 8, n. 4.

[17] Johnson, *Journey*, p. xix.

can do: pore over "fragments of magnificence" and attempt to reconstruct from them a vanished past.

If the continuity of past with present can prove destructive as well as enabling, then, it may also prove tenuous and uncertain. As Johnson describes himself and Boswell clambering among the ruins of the old castle at Auchinleck, he also notes that "here, in the ages of tumult and rapine, the laird was surprised and killed by the neighbouring chief, who perhaps might have extinguished the family, had he not in a few days been seized and hanged" (162). The Boswell family has escaped extinction, but much else in the Highlands seems to have succumbed to it. Almost from the beginning the optimistic notion that a journey through space (to Scotland; to the mountainous country) can also be a journey through time is undermined by Johnson's vigilant skepticism. "Mountainous countries commonly contain the original, at least the oldest race of inhabitants" (43), he concedes, but "that the primitive manners are continued where the primitive language is spoken, no nation will desire me to suppose" (44). For one thing, in countries "where there is hardly the use of letters, what is once out of sight is lost for ever" (65), and thus "edifices, either standing or ruined, are the chief records of an illiterate nation" (73). Even the genealogies of clans, once carefully preserved by the Highlanders, are now less certain, for the Highlanders are "losing their distinction, and hastening to mingle with the general community" (47). The recital of those genealogies, in fact, "has never subsisted within time of memory" (112).

But when were the primitive manners available for inspection? Martin Martin, says Johnson, who "lived in the last century, when the chiefs of the clans had lost little of their original influence," might have recorded those manners adequately, but he did not, and "what he has neglected cannot now be performed" (64-65). Yet even in Martin's time, it seems, the chiefs had lost at least some of their "original influence," and one wonders when they had not. The *Journey* itself, after all, opens with a forgotten origin: "I had desired to visit the Hebrides, or Western Islands of Scotland, so long,

that I scarcely remember how the wish was originally excited."
And the decay of memory, Johnson later reminds us, requires
no great time in which to begin:

> An observer deeply impressed by any remarkable spec-
> tacle, does not suppose, that the traces will soon vanish
> from his mind. . . . [But] he who has not made the ex-
> periment, or who is not accustomed to require rigorous
> accuracy from himself, will scarcely believe how much a
> few hours take from certainty of knowledge, and dis-
> tinctness of imagery; how the succession of objects will
> be broken, how separate parts will be confused, and how
> many particular features and discriminations will be com-
> pressed and conglobated into one gross and general idea.
> (146-147)

Like the sand raised so profusely by a tempest that "an estate
was overwhelmed and lost" (18; cf. 125), time buries the
particulars of the past beneath its featureless uniformity.[18]
Whether or not that original past ever existed outside the
imagination of the curious traveler, Johnson and Boswell "came
thither too late to see what we expected, a people of peculiar
appearance, and a system of antiquated life." Indeed, "a longer
journey than to the Highlands must be taken by him whose
curiosity pants for savage virtues and barbarous grandeur"
(57, 58).

As the stylistic mockery of those last phrases suggests, the
need for a heroic or primitive past may be more certain than
its object. "In Sky," Johnson remarks, "as in every other place,
there is an ambition of exalting whatever has survived memory, to some important use, and referring it to very remote
ages" (72), and this mythologizing of the past colors the accounts of past times on which the travelers were forced to
depend for information. Indeed, it is "vain to inquire" even
whether the traditional *senachi* was "a historian, whose office
was to tell truth, or a story-teller" (112), and such indeter-

[18] In Johnson, as in Shakespeare, the temporal implications of "tempest"
are important.

minacy is at the heart of historical knowledge in the Highlands
and perhaps elsewhere. Yet if "the fables of the poets," as
Bacon said, succeed to the silence of antiquity, not all poets
are equally acceptable. "If we know little of the ancient Highlanders, let us not fill the vacuity with Ossian" (119). For it
is possible if not to recover those "primitive manners" at least
to experience a modern version of the delight a feudal wanderer must have felt upon passing from "the gloom of woods,
or the ruggedness of moors, to seats of plenty, gaiety, and
magnificence." Johnson himself experiences this when he enters upon "the hospitality and elegance of Raasay or Dunvegan" (77).[19]

He might, for all his thoroughness, have experienced still
more. One of the most curious passages in the *Journey* is the
brief account of the Catholic islands of Egg and Canna. "If
we had travelled with more leisure," writes Johnson,

> it had not been fit to have neglected the Popish islands.
> Popery is favourable to ceremony; and among ignorant
> nations, ceremony is the only preservative of tradition.
> Since Protestantism was extended to the savage parts of
> Scotland, it has perhaps been one of the chief labours of
> the ministers to abolish stated observances, because they
> continued the remembrance of the former religion. *We
> therefore who came to hear old traditions, and see an-
> tiquated manners, should probably have found them
> amongst the Papists.* (127-128, my emphasis)

The ambiguities and ironies that surround Johnson's com-
parisons of past with present and primitive with advanced
cultures (pastoral societies are strong and simple but also barbarous; cities are commodious and complex but also meanly
commercial) give way here to an even deeper division of at-

[19] Of Raasay, Johnson says "We found nothing but civility, elegance, and
plenty" (*Journey*, p. 59), and Boswell records a perhaps more surprising
comment on its highly civilized refinements: "This is truly the patriarchal
life. This is what we came to find." See *Boswell's Journal of a Tour to the
Hebrides with Samuel Johnson, LL.D.*, ed. Frederick A. Pottle and Charles
H. Bennett (N.Y.: McGraw-Hill, 1962), p. 135.

titudes. Having come to Scotland to discover "a people of peculiar appearance, and a system of antiquated life" (or at least "to see something different from what we're accustomed to see"),[20] Johnson ascribes to a mere deficiency of "leisure" what is nothing less than a deflection from his principal goal. Since he says no more of this decision, it is difficult to fix the significance of the passage. Perhaps he had simply grown weary of travelling. Perhaps Dunvegan and Raasay, for all their civilized elegance, had satisfied his desire to view "the patriarchal life" ("I saw quite a different system of life," he was to say in 1783).[21] Yet explanations such as these ignore the insistence of Johnson's search for "primitive manners" and the frustration he records when that search is thwarted, whether by emigration and modernization or by the unreliability of Highland informants. That is, however skillfully we may assimilate this passage to the *Journey*'s structure of motivation something about it resists such assimilation,[22] for its casual dismissal of what had been a chief object of the tour stands out sharply from the surrounding context. At a certain point in the journey, it seems, Johnson chose not to seek what he had come to find.

In portraying the quest for a substantial past and the difficulties of fulfilling that quest, the *Journey to the Western Islands*, for all its Johnsonian singularity, is characteristic of its age. It is characteristic as well in its presentation of two related forms of ambivalence toward that past. First, Johnson shrewdly allows primitivist and progressive images of the past to create between them something more complex than either; the spare and the barren, the bold and the barbaric—these keep the past from being an object of simple desire or aversion. Second, Johnson seeks that past but only up to a point. Just when he claims to know where, if anywhere, it might be found,

[20] Boswell, *Journal of a Tour*, pp. 57, 408.
[21] Boswell, *The Life of Samuel Johnson*, ed. G. B. Hill, rev. L. F. Powell, 6 vols. (Oxford: Clarendon Press, 1934-1964), 4: 199.
[22] That this passage replaced a cancel is, of course, a noncritical fact about its distinctness from the surrounding paragraphs. See Johnson, *Journey*, pp. xxxiv-xxxvi, 128, n. 1.

he discontinues the search. In more than a few writers of this period the pictured past—frequently heroic, authentic, substantial—functions most effectively when it is "still out of reach, yet never out of view," a governing image or regulative fantasy as the pastoral world often is.

The closing pages of the *Journey* thus record a disengagement from much that Johnson had sought in the Highlands, for they present not an image of ancient meaningfulness but an account of modern endeavor, real, limited, and free of fantasy: Braidwood's work in educating the deaf. What expands the traveller's imagination here is not the flickering suggestiveness of second sight but the solidly remarkable abilities of Braidwood's pupils, who "know so well what is spoken, that it is an expression scarcely figurative to say, they hear with the eye" (163). The condition of Braidwood's pupils, moreover, is in a sense a final image of the primitive as well as a token of the present, and Johnson explicitly draws the parallel when he asks, "After having seen the deaf taught arithmetick, who would be afraid to cultivate the Hebrides?" (164). Like many figures of literary primitivism, these deaf children are at once under- and over-developed. Cut off from one mode of access to the world, they enjoy in another a contact singularly direct and unmediated, for to them letters are "not symbols of names, but of things; when they write they do not represent a sound, but delineate a form" (164). Johnson concludes his *Journey*, then, with a complex image of a developmentally rather than historically primitive state that fosters a preternaturally substantial contact with the things of the world. If the image suggests that the former is a necessary condition of the latter, it thus serves as a final emblem, now dehistoricized as well as unromantic, of the ambivalence that has governed Johnson's quest throughout the journey.

Like *Rasselas*, Johnson's *Journey* records a quest that does not so much attain its goal as make possible a fuller understanding of that goal and whose gently demystifications stand to the ironic fracturing of illusions in *Rasselas* as the aging and skeptical Johnson stands to the youthful and credulous Prince of Abyssinia. Moreover the pressure to participate in the substantial energies of the past is only intermittent in the *Journey*, and only one of several important themes. In writers of a more sublime and enthusiastic turn than Johnson we find a more intense concern with the recovery of the past and some striking attempts to solve the problem of one's entrapment in the present.

Collins, for example, displays a typical nostalgia for the artistic and emotional capacities of an earlier age, whether ancient Greece or Rome or the England of Shakespeare and Spenser or Milton. He wishes to "read the visions old" and "to feel" as Shakespeare once felt ("Ode to Fear"). The ancient power of music celebrated in "The Passions. An Ode for Music" is the symbol of a lost capacity for intense and meaningful emotion, even though that capacity—"Warm, energic, chaste, sublime"—could prove unpredictable and at times anarchic. The "Ode on the Poetical Character" similarly laments the loss of imaginative and prophetic force symbolized by Fancy's magic girdle. Where, asks Collins,

> is the bard, whose soul can now
> Its high presuming hopes avow?
> Where he who thinks, with rapture blind,
> This hallowed work for him designed?
> (51-54)

Collins' distance from the prophetic powers he seeks is enforced by explicit statement ("Heaven and Fancy, kindred powers,/Have now o'erturned the inspiring bowers") and by a kind of iterated mediacy, a continual strategy of attribution and, one might say, of emotive footnoting. We are usually told whence Collins derives his knowledge of the prophetic and passional, and it is usually from a source standing midway between the poet and the primeval origin of those powers. In the "Ode on the Poetical Character" he has learned of the magic girdle from Spenser, whom he hopes he has not read "with light regard"; and the origin of the girdle, Collins parenthetically tells us, is recounted in "fairy legends" (23). "The

Passions," too, begins by retelling history or legend ("once, 'tis said") and ends by reminding us that music's ancient power is known from history ("thy recording Sister's page") and story (" 'Tis said, and I believe the tale"). Unlike the poet Tasso, "whose undoubting mind," says Collins, "Believed the magic wonders which he sung" ("Popular Superstitions," 198-199), Collins himself seems to have learned of more than he can fully experience and to be continually separated from those powers he wishes would possess him. Even in the "Ode on the Popular Superstitions of the Highlands," as Patricia M. Spacks notes, Collins "removes himself one extra degree from his material by treating it not directly, not even as potential subject matter for himself, but as hypothetical poetic material for someone else."[23]

Along with these distancing strategies, however, and in part working against them, is a counterstrain of immediacy. In a number of the most interesting sublime poems the poet's distress at his own "laggard age" and his nostalgia for the past give way to a present encounter with just those forces whose passing he had mourned. The rhetoric of these moments of encounter is familiar, largely a combination of descriptive vividness, personification, present-tense narration, and invocation or apostrophe. Indeed, the ease or suddenness with which the poet moves from lament to encounter derives, in a sense, from the intrinsically ambiguous character of address or invocation themselves. Strictly speaking, we invoke figures who are absent and address those who are present. "But how," as Rousseau asks, "is one to distinguish, in writing, between a man one mentions and a man one addresses. There really is an equivocation which would be eliminated by a vocative mark."[24] In purely formal terms a single structure serves two

---

[23] Patricia Meyer Spacks, *The Insistence of Horror: Aspects of the Supernatural in Eighteenth-Century Poetry* (Cambridge, Mass.: Harvard Univ. Press, 1962), p. 70.

[24] Jean-Jacques Rousseau, *Essay on the Origin of Languages*, quoted in Jacques Derrida, *Of Grammatology*, trans. Gayatri Chakravorty Spivak (Baltimore and London: The Johns Hopkins Univ. Press, 1976), p. 107. On apostrophe see Jonathan Culler, "Apostrophe," in *The Pursuit of Signs:*

functions, and it is relatively easy to move from one rhetorical possibility of that structure to another: "Ah Fear! Ah frantic Fear! I see, I see thee near." In encounters like these the poet's present experience is for a moment charged with energies that had elsewhere seemed the exclusive property of a vanished past, or (much the same thing) he is for a moment carried back to that past.

Yet even Collins' moments of encounter are subtly pervaded by the ambiguity of presence and absence that resides in the structure of the invocation. The typical rhetorical situation of his poems is neither a pure confronting of absence nor a plenary experience of archaic powers but the calling into fuller being and substantiality of powers at once present and dim, or perceptible yet distant.[25] In "considering" the popular superstitions of the Highlands as a poetic subject, for example, Collins also makes them his own subject (95-137), much as Goldsmith, in the final lines of "The Deserted Village," apostrophizes the spirit of Poetry (last of the "rural virtues") even as it leaves the land. In those lines Goldsmith adjures Poetry to perform its proper functions in the rough new lands to which it is being driven, yet he also enumerates those functions in this very address and makes of them the moral center of the entire poem. Thus while lamenting the loss of Poetry and those other virtues that had fostered England's dignity and worth in the past, and hoping for the future life of those values in another land, Goldsmith also creates an extended present moment—the poem itself, and especially its last thirty-six lines—that is informed by precisely those values. In Collins, as in Goldsmith, the contemplation of absent powers shades at times into a partial recapturing of them, invocation becomes address, and the substantiality of an earlier time informs, for a moment, the sphere of the present.

Semiotics, Literature, Deconstruction (Ithaca: Cornell Univ. Press, 1981), pp. 135-154.

[25] See Norman Maclean, "From Action to Image: Theories of the Lyric in the Eighteenth Century," in *Critics and Criticism: Ancient and Modern*, ed. R. S. Crane (Chicago: Univ. of Chicago Press, 1952), pp. 408-460, esp. 442-443.

Yet only for a moment, and never completely. It is part of
the very nature of invocation and apostrophe as Collins uses
them to perpetuate the discontinuity they seek to bridge and
thus to implicate into confrontation itself the loss that is elsewhere explicitly lamented. In a different way than Johnson
Collins shows us that the need to participate in a substantial
past may be more durable than our ability to encounter it, or
even to document its existence. And by dramatizing the mind's
movement from invocation to address, or from cool consideration to warm responsiveness, Collins suggests that the need
itself may be sufficient, at least momentarily, to generate the
encounter. The potential for fantasy in all this is of course
large, and Johnson is particularly alert to it, in "London" and
in *Rasselas* as well as in the *Journey* itself. Yet he is equally
alert to the poverty of a life lived wholly in the present. The
unlettered, he tells us, "think but little, and of their few thoughts,
none are wasted on the past, in which they are neither interested by fear nor hope" (*Journey*, 65). And the poor lack the
freedom to contemplate the distant future since their thoughts
"are turned with incessant solicitude upon every possibility
of immediate advantage" (140). Such bondage to the present,
as Johnson makes clear at Iona, frustrates not just our speculative luxury but our very humanity:

> To abstract the mind from all local emotion would be
> impossible, if it were endeavoured, and would be foolish,
> if it were possible. *Whatever withdraws us from the power
> of the senses; whatever makes the past, the distant, or
> the future predominate over the present, advances us in
> the dignity of thinking beings.* (148, my italics)[26]

For a relentlessly self-conscious writer like Boswell who
finds even vivid present experience unstable and at times un-
substantial, the need for a past can make of memory a principal mode of apprehending the substance of personal experience. Thus he conceives of his journal as "a rich treasure

[26] See George H. Savage, " 'Roving Among the Hebrides': The Odyssey of
Samuel Johnson," *Studies in English Literature* 17 (1977): 495.

90

for my after days," moves freely between the present and the past tense in recording his life, and finds that the "scenes" of that life frequently improve when grasped through the medium of memory.[27] With Boswell we reach a particular sort of sophistication in Enlightenment conceptions of the past, for he sees not only that the discovery and even the creation of a substantial past may issue from present needs but also that the present may be lived in such a way as to defer, and thereby to ensure, the full apprehension of its substantiality. The fatal irony of such a strategy, of course, is that the full apprehension of lived experience cannot coincide with the moment of experiencing. One has the experience and misses, for a time, the meaning, or one has now the meaning of an experience already past. In Boswell past and present interpenetrate very differently than they do in Collins. Where Collins seeks to drive from the past a weight and significance otherwise lacking in the present, Boswell at times lives his present life with an eye to its future substantial recollection—indeed, sees that recollection, made possible by his written journal, as a way of genuinely possessing experiences he has otherwise only moved through. "I am fallen sadly behind in my journal," he laments in 1776. "I should live no more than I can record, as one should not have more corn growing than one can get in."[28]

Boswell's conception of the present as a time that will be fully grasped only in a future act of retrospection complicates not only the image of the past but the very nature of that present as well. The past becomes a sphere that one actively creates—often quite consciously—in the present, but since that present signifies mainly from the vantage point of the future, its very presentness is undermined. By a curious irony, then,

[27] James Boswell, *Boswell on the Grand Tour: Germany and Switzerland, 1764*, ed. Frederick A. Pottle (N.Y.: McGraw-Hill, 1953), p. 58; *Boswell's London Journal, 1762-1763*, ed. Frederick A. Pottle (London: Heinemann, 1950), p. 65; *London Journal*, p. 40; Boswell, *Journal of a Tour*, p. 329.

[28] James Boswell, Journal, 17 March 1776. Quoted in Frederick A. Pottle, *James Boswell: The Earlier Years, 1740-1769* (N.Y.: McGraw-Hill, 1966), p. 87.

of a kind that appears more than once in this period the remedy becomes a force prolonging and intensifying the disease: the present is lived so as to shape it into a past that will supply the deficiencies of a future present, but this very strategy further diminishes the substantiality of the present. This is a kind of narrative version of the ambiguities of presence and absence in Collins' use of the invocation, and it is one more sign of the seemingly inherent inadequacy of the period's efforts to substantialize the present by recourse to the past. For the turn to the past could result not just in a frustrated or incomplete encounter with the archaic, as in Johnson or Collins, but in an ontological impoverishment of the present as well.

The poetry of Gray provides a still more elaborate demonstration of this backfiring of the appeal to the past and of the complex connections of past with present. It is not surprising that Gray, whose chief imaginative difficulty was not that "he never spoke out," as Matthew Arnold asserted, but that he always saw through, should have perceived so clearly and so subtly the irony latent in those connections. Indeed his attitude toward the present itself is not simple. At times a life lived entirely in the present moment is imagined to be a life of bliss, marked by no "care beyond today."[29] Yet this bliss, if attractive, is also undesirable, for it is "ignorance," the state of thoughtless children or of birds and beasts:

> Their raptures now that wildly flow,
> No yesterday nor morrow know;
> 'Tis man alone that joy descries
> With forward and reverted eyes.[30]

Like Johnson, Gray sees the ability to recall the past and anticipate the future as characteristically human traits; for all their capacity to deceive or disappoint they are a significant part of what it means to have a fully human consciousness.

---

[29] Thomas Gray, "Ode on a Distant Prospect of Eton College," l. 54.

[30] Thomas Gray, "Ode on the Pleasure Arising from Vicissitude," ll. 21-24.

Edward I's purported murder of the Welsh bards, from which
Gray constructs "The Bard, A Pindaric Ode," was thus a crime
not simply against the bards themselves but against the imaginative scope that makes possible human fulfillment; for those
bards, according to Gray's source, used to remind the Welsh
"of the valiant deeds of their ancestors."[31]

Gray's particular concern with the human need to derive
sustenance from the past is more powerful than his interest
in the historical truth of events from that past. Aware that
Edward I "did not in fact suppress the bards but merely issued
an edict against vagrancy,"[32] he nevertheless perpetuates the
more dramatic legend, and something of his wry attitude toward questions of fact appears in a letter accompanying a
portion of "The Bard": "I annex a piece of the Prophecy;
which must be true at least, as it was wrote so many hundred
years after the events."[33] Gray's chief subject, then, is neither
a particular bygone moment, classical or medieval, nor even
his own age, but the human need for images of the past and
the complex pressures that this need exerts on the present.

For one thing, there is at times more than a single past in
his poems. Like a number of other eighteenth-century workers
in archaism, Macpherson and Chatterton for example, Gray
has an affinity for old texts that themselves recall earlier times.
Thus the bard of "The Death of Hoel" (from a sixth-century
Welsh poem) laments the passing of a heroic company of men.
Four hundred had gone to battle,

> But none from Cattraeth's vale return,
> Save Aeron brave and Conan strong,
> (Bursting through the bloody throng)
> And I, the meanest of them all,
> That live to weep and sing their fall.
>   (20-24)

---

[31] Thomas Carte, *General History of England* (1750), 2: 196. Quoted in
Lonsdale, ed., *Poems*, p. 180.

[32] Lonsdale, ed., *Poems*, p. 181.

[33] *Correspondence of Thomas Gray*, ed. Paget Toynbee and Leonard Whib-
ley, 3 vols. (Oxford: Clarendon Press, 1935), 1: 432-433.

And even the "Elegy Written in a Country Churchyard" is, so to speak, doubly memorial, since its remembering narrator is himself proleptically recalled by the "hoary-headed swain," and his own epitaph—to be read by "some kindred spirit"—takes its place among the "uncouth rhymes" of an earlier generation. If Gray, as Lord David Cecil has said, "always tends to see the contemporary world in relation to its historic past," his powerful sense of the relativity of perspective also leads him to see the contemporary world as itself a potential past and the past as a vanished present. This perspectival agility with respect to time tends to replace the imagined bedrock of a substantial past with a bottomless series of strata and, as in Boswell, to deprive the present itself of much of its customary here-and-nowness.[34]

Gray's most complete exploration of these problems is in his Pindaric ode "The Bard." The pastness of the bard's speech is established by the poet's past-tense lines (9-22, 143-144) but only after the poem itself opens with the sublime and ferocious immediacy of the bard's own utterance:

> 'Ruin seize thee, ruthless king!
> 'Confusion on thy banners wait,
> 'Though fanned by Conquest's crimson wing
> 'They mock the air with idle state.'

The dimmest region of speech in the poem is in fact the present. The poet says relatively little, and what he does say is not immediate and dramatic, like the bard's address, but narrative and descriptive. As a present utterance, then, the poem directly acquires its vocal strength from the past, from the voice of the bard who, "with a master's hand and prophet's fire,/Struck

[34] Lord David Cecil, "The Poetry of Thomas Gray," in *Eighteenth-Century English Literature: Modern Essays in Criticism*, ed. James L. Clifford (N.Y.: Oxford Univ. Press, 1959), p. 238. On page 236 Cecil notes that Gray was "acutely responsive to the imaginative appeal of past ages." On perspective as a technical device and a central theme in Gray see Frank Brady, "Structure and Meaning in Gray's *Elegy*," in *From Sensibility to Romanticism*, ed. Frederick W. Hilles and Harold Bloom (N.Y.: Oxford Univ. Press, 1965), pp. 183-184.

the deep sorrows of his lyre" (21-22). The poet's role is to celebrate that ancient prophetic fire and to record its catastrophic end: "He spoke, and headlong from the mountain's height/Deep in the roaring tide he plunged to endless night" (143-144).

Yet if the poet's present dissolves into the dark backward of the sublime past, the bard himself is also in a curious temporal location. Like the poet, he mourns vanished voices, "Dear lost companions of my tuneful art" (39):

> 'Cold is Cadwallo's tongue,
> 'That hushed the stormy main:
> 'Brave Urien sleeps upon his craggy bed.'
> (29-31)

Those companions revive in vision, however, and join the bard in "dreadful harmony" to prophesy the future of Edward's race, after which they disappear once again, leaving the bard "forlorn . . . unblessed, unpitied, here to mourn" (101-102). At this point the bard bears alone the prophetic weight of a second vision of the future: " 'Visions of glory, spare my aching sight,/'Ye unborn ages, crowd not on my soul!' " (107-108). And at the close of this second vision his fate is " 'To triumph, and to die' " (142). Gray constructs here a complex layering of planes of time. The bard's prophetic powers allow him to see the future as though it were present to him; Gray's perspective, and ours, locates that future-as-present in the past.

On the surface, then, the poem seems to offer an extraordinary temporal density, a richly substantial tissue of time. From another point of view, however, both the poet (Gray as narrator) and the bard actually lack a substantial present. Like the reader, the poet enjoys only the apparent presentness of what is actually past (the bard's utterance), and the bard himself inhabits a space between two ages of poetic power: the past (the Welsh bards put to death by Edward) and the future (Shakespeare, Milton, and the more "distant warblings" of poets after Milton). Thus while he is in one sense the poem's principal exemplar of substantial experience, the bard is nevertheless isolated from the full flourishings of heroic poetry and permitted to triumph only in memory or prospect. His suicide at the poem's close is therefore less a gesture of romantic defiance than an emblem or fulfillment of his true situation. Like more than a few writers contemporary with Gray, the bard exists, if that is the right word, in a kind of excluded middle, and he is forced to derive his present life from splendid but ontologically displaced visions of source and fulfillment, past and future. What he observes are two different ages of poetic mastery, but what he experiences in the present is observation alone.

Gray thus complicates and deepens the simpler paradigm of nostalgic sublimity familiar in later eighteenth-century poetry. His act of poetic memory, his turn toward the past, summons up a prophetic figure who is himself engaged in recalling an earlier age. The very figure who was to have lent substantiality to the present is required to derive his own present substantiality from visions of past and future. The effect of this receding of the horizon of the past is virtually to undo historical difference,[35] to undercut the quest for a substantial past by revealing a figure from that past who participates in a version of the poet's own dilemma. The poem's "argument" thus expands beyond the historical, for Gray seems to suggest that it is our fate, whatever age we inhabit, to fail to experience much that we can conceive experience to be. Such a fate, as Gray makes clear in the "Elegy," may keep us from extraordinary crimes as well as from extraordinary achievements; it is in any case not a fate restricted to Gray's own time but, in his eyes, one of the predicaments that complicate, thwart, and constitute our efforts to live. Even "the ways we miss our lives," as Randall Jarrell has said, "are life."[36]

While Gray never quite says that the substantial or heroic

[35] On the effects for autobiography of this undoing of difference (and thus of the idea of a "conversion" from an old to a new self), see Chap. 5, pp. 155-173.

[36] "A Girl in a Library," in Randall Jarrell, *The Complete Poems* (N.Y.: Farrar, Straus & Giroux, 1969), p. 18.

past is a knowing and useful fiction, he implies as much by showing us a figure from that past who is engaged in a quest much like that of the sublime poets of Enlightenment England. More precisely, the question of the historical actuality of such a past is not so much answered as subordinated to an exploration of our need for an image of such a past, the effects on present experience of that need, and the nature of the image itself. It is this attitude that governs his response to the *Fragments of Ancient Poetry* published in 1760 by James Macpherson, of whom Gray wrote: "This Man is the very Demon of Poetry, or he has lighted on a treasure hid for ages."[37] Macpherson himself, of course, claimed that his *Fragments* dated from "an aera of the most remote antiquity" and that they depicted features of "the most early state of society."[38] At the same time he took pains to render the heroic pastness of these forgeries as present and immediate as possible. His bards and heroes often shift from the past to the present tense in the act of remembering, and, indeed, much of their own discourse articulates a continuing act of memory. Armyn, for instance, recalls that "Arindel my son . . . saw fierce Earch on the shore; he seized and bound him to an oak. Thick fly the thongs of the hide around his limbs; he loads the wind with his groans" (52). These speakers are, in a sense, reader-surrogates engaged in a nostalgic reverie analogous to that in which a modern audience engages when it reads the Ossianic texts. One effect of this sustained remembering and making present of the past is of course to charge the archaic world of those texts with an immediacy like that which Collins achieves by invocation or Gray by the subordination of his own speech to the bard's. At many moments we may seem to hear the voice of the past itself and not just to hear about it.

At the same time, however, as in a great deal of literature touched by the nostalgia that is an element of epic and es-

[37] Gray to Wharton, *Correspondence* (2: 680), quoted in Lonsdale, ed., *Poems*, p. 212.

[38] James Macpherson, *Fragments of Ancient Poetry* (1760), ed. John J. Dunn (Los Angeles: Clark Memorial Library, 1966), p. iii. Subsequent references will appear by page number in the text.

pecially of romance, we are made conscious of a certain distance from the fully heroic or substantial past, a distance that we share with the bard and his audience as well. Even the members of that audience, says Thomas R. Edwards, "feel a distance between their own deeds and those of Achilles or Hector, the sense that time has diminished the possibilities of action. It is not now as it was then."[39] Working against the immediacy with which Macpherson's characters recall the past, then, is the sheer amount of time they devote to the act of recalling. Since his bards and other characters remember so insistently, genuine action and present persons are at times a kind of noumenon, mediated to us by an historical distance—or several layers of historical distance—too thick to be fully perspicuous and thus keeping heroic and substantial actuality always out of reach:

> By the side of a rock on the hill, beneath the aged trees, Old Oscian sat on the moss; the last of the race of Fingal. Sightless are his aged eyes; his beard is waving in the wind. Dull through the leafless trees he heard the voice of the north. Sorrow revived in his soul: he began and lamented the dead.
>
> How hast thou fallen like an oak, with all thy branches round thee! Where is Fingal the King? where is Oscur my son? where are all my race? Alas! in the earth they lie. I feel their tombs with my hands. I hear the river below murmuring hoarsely over the stones. What dost thou, O river, to me? Thou bringest back the memory of the past. (37)

The vividness and immediacy of a passage like this derive from the narrator's shift to present tense ("Sightless are his aged eyes") and from the direct discourse—also in the present tense—of Ossian himself. What complicates that immediacy, however, is the narrator's framing of Ossian's discourse and

[39] Thomas R. Edwards, *Imagination and Power: A Study of Poetry on Public Themes* (N.Y.: Oxford Univ. Press, 1971), p. 10.

the additional framing, by that very discourse, of the past that is Ossian's subject. We read an archaic (or archaized) text in which a narrator recalls an ancient hero ("Old Oscian . . . the last of the race of Fingal") who is himself lamenting a still more ancient time. Along with these pasts within pasts the relentless lamenting and questioning put the heroic past at a considerable distance from all, including Ossian, who seek to participate in it. Like the receding horizon that Tennyson's Ulysses seeks, or the Arthurian moment that his *Idylls* often refract through a series of narrator's minds, that "aera of the most remote antiquity" which the Ossianic fragments are alleged to depict seems at times as remote from the characters themselves as from us.

Macpherson's forgeries are not simply acts of nostalgia, then, but accounts of nostalgia as well. "A tale of the times of old!" begins the bard of *Carthon*. "The deeds of days of other years! The murmur of thy streams, O Lora! brings back the memory of the past."[40] And their narrators and characters are often, like Gray's bard, in a posture much like that of the later eighteenth-century poets themselves, a posture attentive chiefly, as Geoffrey Hartman has said, to memory, to "dying voices from the past."[41] To the degree that the past penetrates the present, then, it does so not simply to reveal a substantial past with all the immediacy of a present vision but to suggest as well a curious desubstantializing of past, present, and almost of temporal location itself. When Ossian hears the voice of the ghost of Conlath in "Conlath and Cuthona," he displays the confusion of a man who lives as much in the past as in the present and who therefore does not live fully in either. The poem opens with such confusion and closes with a wish for that release from both past and present which the hero has already begun to experience. These are his first words:

[40] "Carthon," in *Poems of Ossian*, trans. James Macpherson (Phila.: Thomas Cowperthwait, 1842), p. 157.

[41] Geoffrey H. Hartman, "Evening Star and Evening Land," in *The Fate of Reading, and Other Essays* (Chicago and London: Univ. of Chicago Press, 1975), p. 165.

Did not Ossian hear a voice? or is it the sound of days that are no more? Often does the memory of former times come, like the evening sun, on my soul. The noise of the chase is renewed. In thought, I lift the spear.

And these his last:

O that I could forget my friends: till my footsteps should cease to be seen! till I come among them with joy! and lay my aged limbs in the narrow house![42]

While lending immediacy to the past, then, principally through dramatic speech and shifts of verb tense, Macpherson also keeps that past at a distance, as though it were separated from the present by a barrier as much ontological as temporal. And as in Gray, one effect of this simultaneous immediacy and distance is to weaken the very idea of temporal locatedness and to identify a heroic or substantial past as a mode of existence that is always out of reach. From here it is only a short step to a conception of the heroic past as a time when men and women could freely *imagine* a heroic past. Collins had said that Tasso's "undoubting mind/Believed the magic wonders which he sung," but in Book IV of Cowper's *Task* the longing to inhabit a golden age is succeeded by envy for those past poets who could even dream of such an age:

> Would I had fall'n upon those happier days
> That poets celebrate; those golden times,
> And those Arcadian scenes, that Maro sings,
> And Sidney, warbler of poetic prose.
> . . . .
> Vain wish! Those days were never: airy dreams
> Sat for the picture; and the poet's hand,
> Imparting substance to an empty shade,
> Impos'd a gay delirium for a truth.
> *Grant it:—I still must envy them an age*
> *That favour'd such a dream.*
> (513-530, my emphasis)

[42] "Conlath and Cuthona," in *Poems of Ossian*, pp. 400, 403.

Ever out of reach, receding into the mists of the archaic, tied firmly to no historical era, not even unequivocally temporal, the past of large scope and real substance seems more and more to be an image intrinsically ideal and perhaps no more substantial than the uneasy present that Enlightenment writers hoped it might sustain and fortify.

In all but the most fervent eighteenth-century archaizers, then, and even in some of them, the turn to the past was countered by a strong sense of its irrecoverability, the mythopoeic cast of mind, in Peter Gay's terms, challenged by the critical.[43] This double attitude extends to their idea of the past as well as to their conception of its availability to the present. Johnson reminds us of the rudeness and barbarity that heroic images of the past frequently conceal; Macpherson shows us, in effect, a lost tribe of Gaelic elegists recalling a still earlier race of heroes; and Gray invents a bard, both elegiac and prophetic, inhabiting the interval between two eras of imaginative power. What is particularly interesting about this critical attitude is its ability to coexist with and qualify the impulse to nostalgic mythopoeia instead of crisply refusing it. That nostalgia is clear in a conversation that took place in 1763 between James Boswell and John Home, whose remarkably successful tragedy *Douglas* had appeared only a few years earlier. Boswell had argued against war "for making so much bloodshed." "True," said Home,

> "but consider by the exercise of how many virtues this bloodshed is brought about: by patience, by honour, by fortitude. And as to all the severities of a campaign, one day of the *ennui*, the low spirits of a man, in London is worse than them all."[44]

In *Douglas* itself, however, this admiration for the perilous intensities of the heroic temper is qualified by a skepticism

[43] Peter Gay, *The Enlightenment: An Interpretation*, vol. 1, *The Rise of Modern Paganism* (N.Y.: Knopf, 1966), p. 89.
[44] Boswell, *London Journal*, p. 244.

subtle enough to seem unconscious yet so pervasive as to be unmistakable.

The play's two prologues (spoken at Edinburgh and London, respectively) stress the recovery of a native past rivaling the "days of classic fame" enjoyed by ancient Greece and Rome, Persia and Carthage.[45] In that distant age "a god-like race sustained fair England's name," and "every hero was a hero's sire." That ancient continuity of heroism, moreover, persists, for the warmth of the audience's response to the plight of Douglas ("the hero of your native land!") and his mother ("your suppliant") will be an index of the survival of twelfth-century heroic generosity and compassion into the present. The spectators, Scottish and English, are to be granted a vision not just of ancient times but of their own noblest possibilities. The play's use of history is therefore what Kenneth Burke calls a "temporizing of essence," a treating of the essential or logically prior (Scottish or English character at its most authentic) as though it were temporally prior (ancient heroic Caledonia). To look backward, then, is really to look inward and to discover one's own most substantial self. It is not from preternatural vision, moreover, but from an attentive view of the past that we may derive our sense of that self. "Non ego sum vates," runs the play's epigraph, "sed prisci conscius aevi."

Like the play itself, Lady Randolph (Douglas' mother) begins by turning to the past as to the source of genuine life and significance. Having lost her husband to death, and (so she thinks) her child as well, she too lives a kind of death, her affection "buried," as she says, in the "bloody grave" of the family enemy she had loved and secretly married:

> O hapless son! of a most hapless sire!—
> But they are both at rest; and I alone

[45] John Home, *Douglas*, in *British Dramatists from Dryden to Sheridan*, ed. George H. Nettleton and Arthur E. Case, rev. George Winchester Stone (Boston: Houghton Mifflin, 1969), pp. 643-668. *Douglas* was first played in Edinburgh in 1756 and in London in 1757; it was published in 1757. References will be given by act and line number in the text.

Dwell in this world of woe, condemned to walk,
Like a guilt-troubled ghost, my painful round.
(1.234-237)

Thus her discovery that her son is alive is a recovery of the past in the present, even, in a sense, a recovery of the dead husband her son resembles in both feature and temperament:

Image of Douglas! Fruit of fatal love!
All that I owe thy sire, I pay to thee.
(4.181-182; cf. 3.264)

O Nature, Nature! what can check thy force?
Thou genuine offspring of the daring Douglas!
(5.127-128)

Past love, past happiness, past heroism—all seem to be restored by the emergence of the long-lost son of Douglas. Yet as Lady Randolph herself notes, that very past—and in particular its heroic temper—had been her undoing. "Implacable resentment" was the crime of her ancestors, she complains to Lord Randolph, and she tells her confidante, Anna, that "an ancient feud, / Hereditary evil, was the source / Of my misfortunes" (1.80, 175-177). And if she is proud that her son is a "genuine offspring of the daring Douglas," Lady Randolph also knows the unheroic side of heroic daring:

War I detest: but war with foreign foes,
Whose manners, language, and whose looks are strange,
Is not so horrid, nor to me so hateful,
As that which with our neighbors oft we wage.
A river here, there an ideal line,
By fancy drawn, divides the sister kingdoms.
On each side dwell a people similar,
As twins are to each other; valiant both;
Both for their valor famous through the world.
Yet will they not unite their kindred arms,
And, if they must have war, wage distant war,
But with each other fight in cruel conflict.
Gallant in strife, and noble in their ire,

103

The battle is their pastime. They go forth
Gay in the morning, as to summer sport;
When ev'ning comes, the glory of the morn,
The youthful warrior, is a clod of clay.
Thus fall the prime of either hapless land;
And such the fruit of Scotch and English wars.
(1.113-131)

This is a curious and complicated way to begin a play purporting to revive the illustrious heroic past.

Lord Randolph refuses to hear more of such talk; it would, he says, make a soldier "sit down and weep the conquests he has made" (1.134). Nevertheless, the play's critical perception of the ancient heroic temper is not expressed by Lady Randolph alone. To be sure, a number of the characters—Lady Randolph included—testify to the nobility of that temper. To Lord Randolph the "warlike Files" of the Scots are composed of "Brothers, that shrink not from each other's side,/And fond companions," for even "In vulgar breasts heroic ardor burns" (4.19-20, 23); and he finds a warlike countryman of his as noble as "the heroes of the ancient world":

Contemners they of indolence and gain,
But still, for love of glory and of arms,
Prone to encounter peril, and to lift
Against each strong antagonist the spear.
(4.121-125)

To young Douglas himself, the sight of troops on the march is nearly overpowering, an instance, one might say, of the martial sublime:

The setting sun
With yellow radiance lightened all the vale;
And as the warriors moved, each polished helm,
Corslet or spear, glanced back his gilded beams.
The hill they climbed, and halting at its top,
Of more than mortal size, tow'ring, they seemed
An host angelic, clad in burning arms.
(4.319-325)

Douglas first learned of war, moreover, from a venerable figure, an austere and aged hermit who had fought in the First
Crusade and "Against th' usurping infidel displayed/The cross
of Christ" (4.60-61). And just as Lord Randolph's countryman brought to life once again the spirit of "the heroes of the
ancient world," so the old hermit, discoursing of war to young
Douglas, "would shake/His years away, and act his young
encounters" (4.63-64). The heroic past, whether national or
personal, such passages seem to suggest, is both admirable
and recoverable.

It is something of a shock, then, to learn a few lines later
that the hermit had unwittingly slain his brother in a quarrel,
and now, plagued with remorse akin to Lady Randolph's,
"ruminates all day his dreadful fate" (4.90). The connection
with Lady Randolph is in fact far-reaching, for each is caught
at some time in a version of those mindless rivalries and pathetic oppositions that she had earlier bewailed. Scots against
English, Scots against Danes, Glenalvon against Douglas, Lord
Randolph (Glenalvon contrives it to seem) against Douglas—
such conflicts are not only pervasive in the world of the play
but murderous. Like Lady Randolph (the daughter of Malcolm, enemy of Douglas' father), young Douglas is in an impossible position between killing opposites, and the doublet-
like structure of Lady Randolph's speech underscores that
impossibility. She speaks of "the son of Douglas, and Sir Malcolm's heir," and she hopes to see in the young man's face
"the lineaments of Douglas, or my own" (3.208, 244). To be
the heir of both Malcolm and Douglas is to be not just the
figure in whom two strains of heroic blood converge but the
sacrificial victim of an impossible act of union.

Ambiguities like these surround the play's figures of valor
and permeate its ethic of heroic nobility. If Douglas' bosom
is filled with "that sacred fire,/Which in the breast of his fore-
fathers burned" (4.247-248), he is thereby connected with
Glenalvon, whose courage and warlike temper even Lady Randolph acknowledges:

I own thy worth, Glenalvon; none more apt
Than I to praise thine eminence in arms,
And be the echo of thy martial fame.
                    (3.317-319)

Earlier she had observed to Anna that Glenalvon is "brave
and politic in war,/And stands aloft in these unruly times"
(1.283-4). Yet Glenalvon is also selfish, cruel, ruthless, and
treacherous, and his martial aptness has about it something
of the despairingly suicidal. For him, warriors seek to "win
a country, or to lose themselves"(3.280). "The monster war,"
he says, "with her infernal brood,/Loud yelling fury, and life-
ending pain,/Are objects suited to Glenalvon's soul" (3.309-
311). The parallels suggested between Glenalvon and Douglas
by the various recitals of their martial fortitude, by their apparent rivalry for Lady Randolph's favor, and by the ill-tem-
pered quarrel into which Glenalvon lures Douglas (re-enacting
the old hermit's quarrel with a "rude and boist'rous captain"
who had turned out to be his brother) hint at a certain feral
impetuousness in the heroic character that sits uneasily with
the play's endorsements of ancient bravery and generous pride.
At times, indeed, Douglas' image of himself—and his very
readiness to make an image of himself—approaches desperate,
if splendid, excess: "The humble Norval [Douglas' assumed
name]," he boasts to Glenalvon, "is of a race who strive not
but with deeds" (4.375). He avows his homage to Lord Randolph but obeys a still higher power: "Within my bosom
reigns another lord;/Honor, sole judge and umpire of itself"
(4.400-401). We may recall Abdalla's description of Almanzor
in the first part of *The Conquest of Granada*:

> Honor's the only idol of his eyes:
> The charms of beauty like a pest he flies;
> And, raised by valor from a birth unknown,
> Acknowledges no pow'r above his own.
>   (1.i.255-258)

Finally, here is Douglas' prayer to the "glorious stars":

> Dead or alive, let me but be renowned!
> May heav'n inspire some fierce gigantic Dane,

> To give a bold defiance to our host!
> Before he speaks it out I will accept;
> Like Douglas conquer, or like Douglas die.
> (5.87-91)

Douglas is neither Glenalvon nor Almanzor, but he is a heroic figure in a play that insists on the precariousness of the heroic and on the unpredictability of the energies that sustain it. Even Lord Randolph, a figure less splendid though more stable than Douglas, is undone at the play's end. He goes off to battle, seeking death with the desperation of Glenalvon, in order to escape the shame and infamy that will—unjustly—succeed the glory and honor he has known:

> The world did once esteem Lord Randolph well—
> Sincere of heart, for spotless honor famed:
> And, in my early days, glory I gained
> Beneath the holy banner of the cross.[46]
> Now, past the noon of life, shame comes upon me;
> Reproach, and infamy, and public hate,
> Are near at hand: for all mankind will think
> That Randolph basely stabbed Sir Malcolm's heir.
> (5.230-237)

The entire ending of the play, in fact, is one of distributed sadness and unheroic loss. Glenalvon is dead; Old Norval is crushed by guilt; Lady Randolph throws herself, like Gray's bard, from a precipice; and Douglas has been stabbed in the back by Glenalvon. "O had I fall'n as my brave fathers fell," he cries as he loses both life and the possibility of heroism,

> But thus to perish by a villain's hand!
> Cut off from nature's, and from glory's course,
> Which never mortal was so fond to run.
> (5.204, 208-210)

There is a kind of absurdity here, a pathetic and deheroicizing gloom that undermines personal valor and divides the heroic burden of individual suffering into portions of guilt,

---

[46] Again, we should recall the career of the old hermit, who began as a holy crusader and ended as a fratricide.

loss, emptiness, and futility that nearly all the characters share. The effect is to cloud the image of ancient heroism as well as to lament its pastness. Much as Lady Randolph seems to regain the past but then loses more than she had possessed before, so the play itself seems to promise the recovery of a heroic, noble, and generously passionate age but then permits that age to slip, demythologized one might say, back into a past that suddenly looks no more heroic than any other. Home's effort to recover the heroic past is thus qualified by an acute and elegiac skepticism not simply about its recoverability but about its heroism, and the force of the play resides not so much in the loss of a golden age of scope and substance as in its questioning of the very possibility of such an age. The "celestial melancholy" to which *Douglas'* epilogue draws attention led eighteenth-century audiences to weep copiously at its conclusion, but if tears are to be shed they are as much for the shattering of an illusion as for the passing of an age. Perhaps it was just such a skeptical conclusion as Home embodies in his play that kept Johnson from visiting those islands most likely to have continued the ancient ways he claimed to seek.

The dream that both Home and Johnson entertain but cannot finally credit is expressed by Horace Walpole in a letter written a year after the publication of *The Castle of Otranto.* "Visions, you know," he tells George Montagu,

> Have always been my pasture; and so far from growing old enough to quarrel with their emptiness, I almost think there is no wisdom comparable to that of exchanging what is called the realities of life for dreams. Old castles, old pictures, old histories, and the babble of old people make one live back into centuries that cannot disappoint one. One holds fast and surely what is past.[47]

[47] HW to GM (5 January 1766), in *The Yale Edition of Horace Walpole's Correspondence*, ed. W. S. Lewis, 42 vols. (New Haven: Yale Univ. Press, 1941), 10: 192.

The passage is a delicate combination of credulity and skepticism; visions and dreams somehow become history, and the realm of the past is at once an actual and a visionary fabric. It is perhaps the ease of the passage that is most striking, its untroubled though sophisticated movement among diverse realms and its freedom from the pressure to sort out fact and fiction with an urgent or anxious orderliness. Dreamy nostalgia and critical alertness seem less antagonists than genial complements.

Despite the posture of shrewd modernity that Walpole affects in the preface to the first edition of *Otranto*, it is the nostalgic attitude that predominates. The book, he tells us, was found "in the library of an ancient catholic family," was printed "at Naples, in the black letter, in the year 1529," and is perhaps the work of "an artful priest" attempting "to confirm the populace in their ancient errors and superstitions."[48] *Otranto*, in short, may be doctrinally suspect but it is historically authentic, a document from the real past. Yet even here a certain temporal indefiniteness surrounds the work. It was printed in 1529, but "how much sooner it was written does not appear":

> If the story was written near the time when it is supposed to have happened, it must have been between 1095, the aera of the first crusade, and 1243, the date of the last, or not long afterwards. There is no other circumstance in the work that can lead us to guess at the period in which the scene is laid. (3)

Nevertheless, some details "seem to indicate" a rather late date and others "concur to make me think that the date of the composition was little antecedent to that of the impression." Walpole's account begins to suffer from the irony of accumulated conjecture, each "perhaps" or "must have been" serving to weaken rather than strengthen its predecessors in

[48] Horace Walpole, *The Castle of Otranto*, ed. W. S. Lewis (London: Oxford Univ. Press, 1964), p. 3. Subsequent references will appear by page number in the text.

the chain of guesswork and to dislodge the work—as at times happens in Gray and Macpherson—from any definite temporal location. While the preface to the first edition insists on the pastness of the work, then, the past it intimates is both a historical period and a nostalgic or mythic or romance era, part of the sphere to which Walpole alluded when he spoke of living back "into centuries that cannot disappoint one."

The preface to the second edition tells a different story. Here Walpole avows his authorship, explains his design in composing *Otranto*, and admits that his first preface had been a counterfeit. (From this perspective, the "artful priest" of the first preface, whom Walpole pretends to suspect of attempting to "confirm the populace in their ancient errors and superstitions," is an oblique reflection of the book's true author.) The second preface is not a simple retraction but a qualification of the first, as of *Otranto* itself, and its principal effect is to alter both our notion of the novel's author and our conception of its ontological status. The movement from the first to the second preface is a movement from one way of conceiving the romantic past to another, a movement, in Frank Kermode's sense of the terms, from myth to fiction. "Fictions," Kermode says, "can degenerate into myths whenever they are not consciously held to be fictive. . . . Myths call for absolute, fictions for conditional assent."[49] The crucial distinction for our purposes is between two kinds of assent given to the image of the past. Both, it should be noted, are indeed forms of assent; "fiction" is not a simple opposite of "myth" but a more inclusive term that adds to the elements of mythic assent a measure of detachment, of provisionality, and of sophistication.[50] Thus the second preface does not reject the trappings of "ancient romance" but argues for their incorporation into a more modern and realistic kind of story usually, and wrongly, thought to require their exclusion. *Otranto* is to combine

[49] Frank Kermode, *The Sense of an Ending: Studies in the Theory of Fiction* (N.Y.: Oxford Univ. Press, 1967), p. 39.

[50] The distinction between myth and fiction is thus very different from the mythopoeic/critical opposition earlier cited from Peter Gay (see n. 43), for Kermode's terms do not stand in a simply antithetical relation to each other.

ancient with modern romance, imagination and improbability with nature (or fancy with attention to common life), solemnity with buffoonery, and extraordinary situations with the realistic responses of men and women to those situations. The movement from the first to the second preface, then, is something like the movement from Home's two prologues to the play of *Douglas* itself, and much of the power and interest of both works results from their incorporation of a naive into a sophisticated perspective.

What is particularly significant in the case of *Otranto* is the relationship between prefaces and novel, on the one hand, which constitute together a composite literary artifact of a certain kind, and the thematic concerns, on the other hand, of the story itself: more specifically, the relationship between Walpole as author-narrator and Manfred, prince of Otranto and central figure in the novel. For while the work (as the prefaces indicate) is in a complex position with respect to historical and literary-historical continuity, its tale is about another kind of continuity: familial and dynastic succession. Manfred, to put it crudely, attempts to impose a mythic past (and thus an artificial present) on history, while Walpole dissolves an initially mythic perspective into a fictional. If Walpole is a forger or counterfeiter he is at least acknowledgedly so; but Manfred wishes to be a counterfeiter pure and simple, and this wish is his undoing. Thus the novel's prophecies of vengeance and its showing the sins of the fathers to be "*visited on their children to the third and fourth generation*" (5) have more to do with punishment for a certain ruthless attitude toward the past, toward history as such, than toward the lordship of Otranto or the line of Alfonso the Good. In a sense Manfred's myth stands to Walpole's fiction as repression to suppression, and in Walpole's novel the former ends disastrously.

Manfred's rewriting of history is an attempt to substitute an invented past, authenticating his own present and future, for the actual past. He tells the knight of the gigantic sabre (Frederic, Marquis of Vicenza, in disguise) that Alfonso had "bequeathed his estates to my grandfather Don Ricardo," when Alfonso had in fact been poisoned by Ricardo; and Manfred's lie has its precedent in Ricardo's other act of treachery, the forging of a fictitious will declaring himself to be Alfonso's heir (64, 109). Like his grandfather, Manfred attempts to bury the actual past beneath his own inventions.

Walpole insists on the bondage into which Manfred's usurpation has thrust him. Having become the heir to Otranto through Ricardo's imposition of myth on history, he must strive to extend that myth into the future—hence his anxiety about generational continuity, the theme that opens the book. He is impatient for the marriage of Conrad and Isabella, cruel to his wife for not bearing—and to his daughter for not being—a son, insanely abrupt in offering himself to Isabella just after Conrad has been killed, and prone to impassioned talk about the hopes of his "race" (22, 24). Yet Manfred's effort to continue into the future the myth he has substituted for the past results in a number of desperate actions and striking ironies. Both Friar Jerome and Isabella herself view his offer of marriage as an unnatural act, an "incestuous design" (48), since Isabella had been engaged to Conrad. But Manfred's intended "incest" is not so much a sexual as a historical or generational crime. He wishes to marry Isabella so as to father a son, yet by usurping Conrad's place he would in a sense become his own son as well as his own father. This example of willed, unnatural, and self-bound succession, like the curiously symmetrical double marriage that Manfred suggests to Frederic, is a grotesque emblem of Manfred's effort to extend into the future the mythical past he has created. He and Isabella are, one might say, thoroughly myth-matched, and the taboo Manfred violates has less to do with marriage or kinship than with a ruthlessly possessive attitude toward the past and thus toward reality itself.

The events and disclosures that eventually defeat Manfred play a series of ironic variations on the theme of generational continuity. First, his frantic fear that he will lack a male heir is not only a reality by the end of the novel but also an irrelevance, since the legitimate claimant to Otranto, Theodore (son to Jerome and the daughter of Alfonso), at last reveals his identity. The place of the son Manfred wished to father—even, symbolically, to become—has been occupied all along. Second, Manfred attempts to kill Isabella, who was to have provided him with an heir; this act, a kind of generational suicide, is rendered more cruelly ironic by the fact that it is his own daughter, Matilda, whom he actually kills, and by his subsequent effort to "dispatch himself" (104). Cursing the day he was born (106), Manfred becomes in a more than figurative sense the thwarter of his "race" as well as the destroyer of the mythical past he had attempted to perpetuate. For in *Otranto* the actual past is alive not only in Theodore but also in those Gothic effects whose supernatural appearance is an index of the deformation that past has undergone and of the remarkable strength it yet retains. In Walpole, more ironically and melodramatically than in Boswell or Gray, we are shown the cost to the present of fervid efforts to master the past.

When Walpole spoke of living back "into centuries that cannot disappoint one," he was not speaking of the sort of living back that Manfred undertakes: the effort to rewrite the past from which the present has actually proceeded, to replace fact with myth. Walpole himself replaces fact not with myth but with fiction (in Kermode's sense), for *The Castle of Otranto*, too, is a created past, an artificial ruin. Unlike Manfred, however, Walpole knows it to be a fiction, a human creation with its own kind of legitimacy and its own special status. From the candid preface introducing the second edition to the spectacular vision in its final pages (thunder, destruction of the castle, appearance of Alfonso "dilated to an immense magnitude" and then ascending to heaven where St. Nicholas receives him), Walpole insists on the fictionality of his construction of the past, maintaining a delicate mixture of sympathy and detachment, belief and skepticism. We credit *Otranto*, to paraphrase Johnson, with all the credit due a fiction, and so does its author. The result is not a vision of the past that infuses the present and future with remarkable weight or significance, or allows us to derive our own presentness from heroic and substantial origins; the novel itself has shown the

113

dangers of that mythic and delusional effort. Rather, *Otranto* enlarges the ways in which we are free to entertain a certain image of the past, and in that mixed and limited achievement, artificial but not therefore frivolous, it displays another version of the Enlightenment writers' fascination with, and deep need for, a substantial past in which they could only skeptically believe.

Yet to put it this way is perhaps to minimize their achievement, which was not the summoning of halfhearted belief in a traditional conception of the past but, at times, the imagining of a new kind of present-sustaining past and the development of a mode of apprehension appropriate to it. Just as the idea of "nature" that Johnson honors in the *Preface to Shakespeare* is not Aristotle's or Hooker's or Milton's or Pope's manqué but a different thing, so the conceptions of the past that we find in Walpole, in Gray, in Home, and in other writers roughly contemporary with Johnson are versions of a new kind of past and a new way of conceiving that past. It is a past to which a certain amount of golden age mythology clings but also a certain controlled debunking of such mythology; a past significantly more spacious and significant than the present and yet not often animated by metaphysical energies denied to that present; and it is apprehended as a sphere that is as much the product of present needs as present knowledge, as much a fictional object to be entertained by the imagination as a repository of facts to be mastered by the intellect. We greatly misinterpret the later eighteenth century if we view this complex of delicate balances and scrupulously sustained tensions as a failure of faith or imagination, for it is in fact the triumph of a partly demythologized imagination, the product of an effort to create a new realm of values and new ways of paying tribute to those values. It is an effort of great subtlety, surprising diverseness, and enormous sophistication, an effort furthered by a remarkable number of writers and expressed in a wide variety of literary forms.

In Burke's *Reflections on the Revolution in France*, for example, the past is at times simply the source from which the present has sprung and thus an object of traditional interest and respect, but at other times it is a complex fabric of substantial values requiring to be apprehended with something of the subtlety and respect for artifice that Walpole brings to his fiction of "the manners of ancient days." Burke's most general point is that the present needs the past and ignores it only at great peril. The French revolutionaries have disastrously betrayed their own past, "the age of chivalry," and as a result, "the glory of Europe is extinguished for ever."[51] The English Revolution, in contrast, was produced by a "firm but cautious and deliberate spirit," not a hysterical rejection, for the English recognized that "antient opinions and rules of life" are a "compass to govern us" (86, 172) and express "the antient permanent sense of mankind" (275). That sense is continuous with our own and with that of the future, for society is "a partnership . . . between those who are living, those who are dead, and those who are to be born" (194-195). The English thus chose to see their "most sacred rights and franchises as an *inheritance*" rather than an abstract right ("timeless," as we say, and thus for Burke bound to no time whatsoever). They see the state as the father of individual citizens and they are proud to "bear the stamp" of those earlier citizens, who are not simply their predecessors but their "forefathers" (118, 194, 181).

Even necessary change, therefore, ought to be based on a respect for the continuity of the present and future with the past. For Burke revolution is "the very last resource of the thinking and the good," but it is nevertheless sometimes necessary (117). "I would not exclude alteration," he says, "but even when I changed, it should be to preserve" (375). The English Revolution was just such an effort:

> [It] was made to preserve our *antient* indisputable laws
> and liberties, and the *antient* constitution of government

[51] Edmund Burke, *Reflections on the Revolution in France* (1790), ed. Conor Cruise O'Brien (Baltimore: Penguin, 1969), p. 170. Subsequent references will appear by page number in the text.

115

which is our only security for law and liberty. . . . We wished at the period of the Revolution, and do now wish, to derive all we possess as *an inheritance from our fore-fathers.* Upon that body and stock of inheritance we have taken care not to inoculate any cyon alien to the nature of the original plant. (117)

The French might have done the same; their constitution had "suffered waste and dilapidation," but they "possessed in some parts the walls, and in all the foundations of a noble and venerable castle," which they might have repaired and built upon (121). Instead, aggressively forgetting that inheritance, "you chose to act as if you had never been moulded into civil society, and had every thing to begin anew. You began ill, because you began by despising every thing that belonged to you" (122).

The past is necessary to us not because it is past but because it is the chief repository of that embodied circumstantiality that can alone make our experience both real and significant. It is a repository of *authority*, and there is desperate need in human life for an authority weightier than that of the individual and more substantial than that of reason and logic. Reason and logic characteristically isolate their objects, abstract them from their contexts, and this abstraction is a proper and necessary part of their operation. But not everything, and none of the most important things, can be thus isolated or made susceptible to the work of mere reason operating in an artificial "now":

> We are but too apt to consider things in the state in which we find them, without sufficiently adverting to the causes by which they have been produced, and possibly may be upheld. (173)

The purity—or nakedness—of abstract reasoning, then, must give way to the impure vestments of reality, of what Burke repeatedly calls "circumstances," as in this justly famous passage:

116

I cannot stand forward, and give praise or blame to any thing which relates to human actions, and human concerns, on a simple view of the object, as it stands stripped of every relation, in all the nakedness and solitude of metaphysical abstraction. Circumstances (which with some gentlemen pass for nothing) give in reality to every political principle its distinguishing colour, and discriminating effect. The circumstances are what render every civil and political scheme beneficial or noxious to mankind. (89-90)

Whoever refuses to take circumstances into consideration, Burke says elsewhere, is "metaphysically mad."

It is easy to misunderstand the role of the circumstantial in Burke and thus of the past as a principal locus of the authority that the circumstantial can provide. To attend to circumstances is not simply to take a wide rather than a narrow or a concrete rather than an abstract view of one's object, a nation or constitution for example. It is also to pay a kind of ontological tribute to that object, to grant it a weight and dignity that distinguish it from less substantial objects of a similar kind. Since the axis of values associated with this ontological concern does not line up exactly with those of more traditional oppositions, it is easy to misconceive the system within which Burke is operating at any given point.[52] The ancient opposition between actions (or institutions) based on principle and those based on mere expediency, for example, at times has its traditional significance in Burke's writing. But at other times abstract principle seems almost to be a form of expediency, not because the principle is being manipulated to conceal meaner motives or goals but because an intense reliance on abstract principle is itself, for Burke, the sign of a mind so eager to get on with things that it will sacrifice the very being of the institutions it moves among. Here the opposite of principle is not expediency; instead, the opposite of

[52] Such misconceiving lies at the heart of much of the controversy concerning Burke's relation to the tradition of natural law. See n. 58.

117

both is an attention to circumstances and thus an acknowledgment of substantiality.

For the difference between attending to circumstances and attending to low motives of expediency is that the latter can never amount to more than themselves. Circumstances, however, are more than cumulative; taken together, they constitute a sphere of value distinct from both the concreteness of mere fact and the abstractness of mere principle. Just as Johnson defines legal prescription as "custom continued until it has the force of law," so in Burke the circumstantial might be defined as history continued until it has the substantiality of embodied principle, though not the absoluteness—or the nakedness and fragility—of an abstract or purely metaphysical concept. It is the point of transition that is crucial. In Johnson custom, after a time, comes to possess the force of law. In Burke necessity can at times be metamorphosed into principle: "The Revolution of 1688 was obtained by a just war, in the only case in which any war, and much more a civil war, can be just. 'Justa bella quibus *necessaria*' " (116).[53] Burke insists that such a transformation is rare and difficult, hedged about with moral pitfalls and temptations to invoke imaginary exigency. And even when conditions do justify resistance or civil war, such actions are to be considered as the administering of a "critical, ambiguous, bitter portion to a distempered state." By his hesitancy and scrupulousness, then, Burke does not wish to deny that necessity may become principle but precisely to indicate the reality and weightiness of that transformation by distinguishing it from the mere effort to disguise necessity as principle.

The authority of circumstances, then, is neither that of mere fact or interest nor that of an unabashedly metaphysical principle. We can see another example of such authority in Johnson's view of the rights of kings as Boswell recounts it in the *Journal of a Tour to the Hebrides*:

> Mr. Johnson is not properly a *Jacobite*. He does not hold the *jus divinum* of kings. He founds their rights on long

[53] The quotation is adapted from Livy 9.1.10.

118

possession, which ought not to be disturbed upon slight grounds. He said to me once that he did not know but it was become necessary to remove the King at the time of the Revolution; and after the present family have had so long a possession, it appears to him that their right becomes the same that the Stuarts had.[54]

Johnson does not hold with the abstract principle (*jus divinum*), as Boswell does, nor does he consider "long possession" to be the same in kind as short possession, just longer. It is clear that for him sufficiently long possession transforms a series of ontologically comparable years into a whole that is ontologically different from any one of them yet still not animated by an a priori or abstract or metaphysical principle. This is the sphere of substantial values that is crucial to Burke's view of things, the sphere in which necessity may turn into principle, custom acquire the force of law, the sheer plod of centuries become the stately progress of tradition, and "circumstance" come to mean not just that which stands around an event or institution but that which gives it weighty and significant being at all. In Burke circumstance virtually becomes substance.

The substantial center of a political institution or other cultural structure, then, no longer resides in a metaphysical essence existing prior to its historical embodiment but precisely in the history of that circumstantial embodiment taken as a whole. The circumstantial (and traditionally secondary) thus becomes constitutive and therefore primary. Signs of this proto-Darwinian, or Lamarckian, model of cultural history and identity are quite numerous in the later eighteenth century and not confined to Burke (or Johnson). Lord Monboddo, as Lia Formigari has argued, entrusts "the construction of Homo sapiens to the vicissitudes of the historical process, without presupposing any abstract predisposition of the single consciousness to that end," and Monboddo himself, in *Of the Origin and Progress of Language*, asserts that

[54] Boswell, *Journal of a Tour*, pp. 162-163.

our nature is chiefly constituted of acquired habits, and
. . . we are much more creatures of custom and art than
of nature. It is a common saying, that habit . . . is a second
nature. I add, that it is more powerful than the first, and
in a great measure destroys and absorbs the original nature: for it is the capital and distinguishing characteristic
of our species, that we can *make* ourselves, as it were,
over again, so that the *original* nature in us can hardly
be seen; and it is with the greatest difficulty that we can
distinguish it from the *acquired*.[55]

The counterpart to such a view in the sphere of individual
identity takes the form of a new alertness to the possibility of
constructing a self from the various roles one plays, as in
Boswell or Sterne, rather than the other way round, and even,
more fancifully, of fashioning an improved moral identity
through a system of anticipatory praise such as Goldsmith
ascribes to the French: "They please, are pleased, they give
to get esteem,/Till, seeming blest, they grow to what they
seem."[56] Goldsmith is aware that such customs can give rise
to a charade of vacuous congratulation, but he sees that charade as the defect of a system far from bankrupt in itself.

As these passages suggest, to conceive of significant identity,
whether cultural or individual, as posterior to time and circumstance is to introduce a new respect for artifice and for
the possibility of actively creating that identity rather than
treating it as given.[57] This emphasis returns us to Burke, who
had, in *An Appeal from the New to the Old Whigs*, asserted
that "art is man's nature." What I wish to emphasize here is

[55] Lia Formigari, "Language and Society in the Late Eighteenth Century,"
Journal of the History of Ideas 35 (1974): 287; James Burnet, Lord Monboddo, *Of the Origin and Progress of Language*, 6 vols., 2d ed. (Edinburgh,
1774), 1: Preface, 1, 4.
[56] Oliver Goldsmith, "The Traveller" (ll. 265-266), in Lonsdale, ed., *Poems*,
pp. 622-657.
[57] On the distinction between "essential" and "rhetorical" conceptions of
the self see Richard A. Lanham, *The Motives of Eloquence: Literary Rhetoric
in the Renaissance* (New Haven and London: Yale Univ. Press, 1976), esp.
chap. 1 and the epilogue.

that Burke's embrace of artifice in the assessment of cultural institutions depends on his belief that the identity of those institutions is to a great extent constituted by circumstance and that what those circumstances constitute is to be assessed by means of a scale ranging from the substantial to the insubstantial as well as by more traditional scales of value. These three themes—the attention to circumstance (and to history as a mode of the circumstantial), the acceptance of artifice, and the recourse to substantiality and related values—are deeply intertwined, in Burke, and account for a good deal in his thought that is not fully explainable in the language of traditional morality or political theory.[58] The French rationalists, he complains in the *Reflections*, want to dissolve "pleasing illusions," tear away "the decent drapery of life," and uncover "the defects of our naked shivering nature" (171). Such ruthless reductionism destroys the substantiality that the present derives from the past and leaves us with the mere abstracted reality of the present alone. Burke is at once aware that it is by means of "pleasing illusions" that we raise our nature "to dignity in our own estimation" and yet unwilling to give up— or undervalue—the role of such illusions. This stance is closely related to Walpole's half-critical entertaining of superstition and Gothic incident. In each case something more substantial than mere truth is being sought, and it is sought, and found, in full awareness of its status as a fiction or pleasing illusion. For Burke it is characteristic of the English that (like Walpole in *Otranto*) they did not reject but built upon their "Gothic and monkish education (for such it is in the ground-work)," and that they instinctively strove for something more than abstract correctness. For "the precept given by a wise man, as well as a great critic [Horace], for the construction of poems, is equally true as to states. *Non satis est pulchra esse poemata,*

---

[58] The perennial question whether Burke is a natural law theorist or a utilitarian-positivist, for example, seems to me insoluble in these terms, for the axis running between these two positions is quite distinct from the substantiality-insubstantiality axis that constitutes one of Burke's principal evaluative scales.

dulcia sunto. . . . To make us love our country, our country ought to be lovely" (198-199, 172).

The English, in fact, cherish not just their Gothic past but their "old prejudices," and, adds Burke, "we cherish them because they are prejudices" (183). Moreover,

> Many of our men of speculation . . . employ their sagacity to discover the latent wisdom which prevails in them. If they find what they seek, and they seldom fail, they think it more wise to continue the prejudice, with the reason involved, than to cast away the coat of prejudice, and to leave nothing but the naked reason; because prejudice, with its reason, has a motive to give action to that reason, and an affection which will give it permanence. . . . Prejudice renders a man's virtue his habit; and not a series of unconnected acts. Through just prejudice, his duty becomes a part of his nature. (183)

Prejudice is the coat to naked reason and allows man's virtue to clothe his naked nature, much as the English spirit allows institutions to be "embodied . . . in persons; so as to create in us love, veneration, admiration, or attachment" (172). Similarly, "nobility is a graceful ornament to the civil order. It is the Corinthian capital of polished society. *Omnes boni nobilitati semper favemus,* was the saying of a wise and good man. . . . He feels no ennobling principle in his own heart who wishes to level all the artificial institutions which have been adopted for giving a body to opinion, and permanence to fugitive esteem" (245). Like circumstances, prejudice, artifice, and pleasing illusion are what clothe or adorn or embody naked principles and abstractions. Such imagery is of course traditional, yet Burke does not use it in a traditional way. For clothing (and "habit"), the body, ornament and pleasing artifice are, like circumstances, constitutive of their objects rather than superadded to them. When in *Rights of Man* Thomas Paine complained that Burke "pities the plumage, but forgets the dying bird," he assumed that Burke's imagery works in the traditional way (subordinating body to soul, external to internal, accident to essence, concrete to abstract) and that Burke's values, therefore, were simply inverted. One might more accurately say, however, that Burke pities the diseased limbs since they *are* the dying tree or that he pities the faded painting since it *is* the substantial form of an inspiration that without it would lack significant being. It is really Paine who is the traditional metaphysician in this encounter and Burke who, despite the apparent traditionalism of his appeal to history, develops his argument in terms of an untraditional system of values that permits the substantiality of artifice and fiction, illusion and prejudice, to displace the logicality of mere reason and the purity of mere abstraction.

It is not sufficient to call that conception of values "aesthetic," since the aesthetic is primarily, in the *Reflections*, a way of calling attention to those forms, appearances, circumstances, and imaginings that give the past and the present not just truth or beauty but substantiality, "real existence" as Johnson puts it. In Burke's sophisticated scheme of values the past bodies forth the present, circumstances help to construct essential natures, artifice and illusion yield a wholeness and truth more substantial than metaphysical principles, and beauty generates solidity of being. The substantial world that Burke projects has more in common with the "lived world" of phenomenological description than with the conceptual structure of political theory or the tabulations of empirical survey, and this emphasis leads him away from the strictly demonstrable toward the fictional, the emotive, and the artificial. But it leads him as well toward a fuller apprehension of political reality as a sphere involving not an abstract citizenry governed by timeless principles but numbers of men and women much of whose life is given to the construction and valuing of vital fictions, the experiencing of emotions, and the fashioning— as well as the finding—of their experience and their characters. The entire history of that complex human activity is what Burke means by "the past."

Burke's embrace of artifice and illusion, his belief that the meaning of the present derives from a substantial past that is

123

to a considerable extent a fictional (though not a mythic) fabric, places him at times in an uncertain posture on the border between history and story. Any more fiction, we might say, and that fabric will become a fabrication. Indeed, in one sense the element of the fictional that enters into the past as it is conceived by Burke or Walpole or Gray is a controlled version of an impulse that achieved freer expression in writers like Macpherson and Chatterton: the impulse to literary forgery, especially the forgery of works alleged to have been written in an earlier age.

Later eighteenth-century forgery is of great interest to the literary historian precisely because it is not an isolated phenomenon but, most frequently, an intensified version of the widespread effort to discover, or create, a present-sustaining past. As Hugh Kenner has noted, the counterfeiter is doing just that, for the maker of a counterfeit bill is imitating "not the bill but the moment when that bill was (we are to suppose) issued by the Treasury of the United States: not a visible thing but an invisible event."[59] There is thus a deep connection between the forging of texts and the invention of a past. The search for a significant past could of course take relatively uncomplicated forms and serve merely private ends, as in the "outbreaks of genealogical fever" that J. H. Plumb describes in *The Death of the Past*. In the Elizabethan period "most of the . . . aristocracy's true genealogies tended to disappear after a generation or so either into oblivion or, even worse, into a yeoman's family," so aristocrats "forged medieval charters, cut ancient seals and invented ancestors with panache."[60] In the eighteenth century Boswell, with a certain self-consciousness, does something similar. When he is at Auchinleck, he sometimes finds himself "in the glow of what, I am sensible, will, in a commercial age, be considered as genealogical enthusiasm," and he attempts to transmit that enthusiasm to

[59] Hugh Kenner, *The Counterfeiters: An Historical Comedy* (Garden City, N.Y.: Anchor, 1973), pp. 72-73.

[60] J. H. Plumb, *The Death of the Past* (Boston: Houghton Mifflin, 1971), pp. 31, 32-33.

others.[61] Before his brother David leaves to become a merchant in Spain, Boswell requires him to take an oath of loyalty to the "ancient family of Auchinleck." The document Boswell produces asserts that such an oath is customary when any branch of the family "is sent forth into the world," though David, on his return from Spain, "added a ratification, and explained that the custom of swearing such oaths did not go back to time immemorial but had begun with this instance."[62]

Boswell was also given to "catechizing" his son, forcing him to recite a lengthy tracing of ancestry and family lore. "I have great enjoyment in our fancied dignity," he says, and "Sandy seems to imbibe it as I could desire. . . . I shall go on with it and habituate him to think with sacred reverence and attachment of his ancestors and to hope to aggrandize the family."[63] The "fancied dignity" that is embodied in Boswell's documents and catechetical exercises achieves somewhat more permanent form in a work like Chatterton's "Extracts from Craishes Herauldry," which mingles names and details from the poet's everyday Bristol world with others that are purely invented. The goal, as Benjamin Hoover notes, is to tie those everyday characters to history by inventing both "important ancestors and the heraldic bearings which establish that importance." The whole is a kind of statement by Chatterton "that he, his friends, his town, and his preoccupations have an impressive historical past," that "he and they amount to something."[64] For Boswell and Chatterton, as for Walpole's Manfred, to counterfeit a past is also to re-create the present that is alleged to derive from it.

Such a model, however, is too simple to account for many

[61] Boswell, *Journal of a Tour*, p. 373.

[62] *Boswell in Search of a Wife, 1766-1769*, ed. Frank Brady and Frederick A. Pottle (N.Y.: McGraw-Hill, 1956), pp. 96-97.

[63] *Boswell: Laird of Auchinleck, 1778-1782*, ed. Joseph W. Reed and Frederick A. Pottle (N.Y.: McGraw-Hill, 1977), pp. 160-161.

[64] All citations from Chatterton are to *The Complete Works of Thomas Chatterton*, ed. Donald S. Taylor in assoc. with Benjamin B. Hoover, 2 vols. (Oxford: Clarendon Press, 1971). The "Extracts from Craishes Herauldry" is at 1: 44-51, and the editor's comments cited in my text are at 2: 834-835.

of the archaizings and forgeries in the later eighteenth century, for it suggests that it is possible—and desirable— to counterfeit a sphere that is exclusively past and temporally determinate. Yet as we have seen elsewhere, such an effort is neither clearly possible nor clearly desirable. The two defining features of most Enlightenment visions of the past are an intensified immediacy working to make the past present (apostrophe, present-tense emotional outburst, and the like) and a structure of redoubled remembering (or a related pattern) which suggests that the past is a sphere whose inhabitants are themselves looking to the past for significant experience. "I suppose," says Robert Lowell in our own time, "even God was born/ too late to trust the old religion."[65] In "Rowley's Heraldic Account of Bristol Artists and Writers," Chatterton's archaized creation Rowley, having lamented the scantiness of accounts of a still earlier heroic past, falls into a dream and, as he puts it, "strayt was I carry'd back to Tymes of yore" (269). On the one hand, intensified immediacy; on the other, a vast profound in which one falls from past to past, as in Gray, Macpherson, and Cowper. The first of these blurs the sharp distinction between past and present (as does the second, in a different way) and, taken together, their contrary emphases not only decompartmentalize but also detemporalize what may be called the temporal image of the works in question. Such works mingle past and present, but they also seem to exist in a curiously indeterminate temporal location, a kind of no-time neither fully past nor fully present and therefore not fully temporal at all.

These effects of rhetorical structure in the works themselves are closely related to the values embraced by critics in the "Gothic" literature that was becoming newly known and appreciated, as well as counterfeited. Both David Hume and Hugh Blair, for example, responded strongly to the Ossianic poems, Hume negatively and Blair positively, yet each principally responded to the same feature of those poems: their

[65] Robert Lowell, "Tenth Muse," in *For the Union Dead* (N.Y.: Farrar, Straus & Giroux, 1964), p. 46.

mingling of old and new, past and present. Their very style, Hume asserts, shows their inauthenticity:

> This Erse poetry has an insipid correctness, and regularity, and uniformity, which betrays a man without genius, that has been acquainted with the productions of civilized nations, and had his imagination so limited to that tract, that it was impossible for him even to mimic the character which he pretended to assume.[66]

Blair finds in that same style "the fire and the enthusiasm of the most early times, combined with an amazing degree of regularity and art." Indeed "Ossian, himself, appears to have been endowed by nature with an exquisite sensibility of heart; prone to that tender melancholy which is so often an attendant on great genius; and susceptible equally of strong and of soft emotions."[67] For Blair, Ossian was, in effect, a bard of the Age of Sensibility, as of course he was. The taste of that age only rarely favored a poetry genuinely archaic, resolute in its primitive otherness. Instead it sought a poetry sufficiently distinct from its own to suggest the bygone strengths of a primitive era yet sufficiently familiar to demonstrate the availability of those strengths to modern idiom and sensibility. Many of Percy's ballads, as René Wellek has pointed out, "had to be rehashed and refurbished to be made palatable to 'polite' taste," and this same double view appears in Thomas Warton's *History of English Poetry* in which, as Wellek says, "a recognition of classical standards and a (tempered) appreciation of Gothic picturesqueness or sublimity went hand in hand."[68] Bishop Hurd elevates this mingled taste into a principle of cultural

[66] David Hume, "Of the Authenticity of Ossian's Poems," in *Essays, Moral, Political, and Literary*, ed. T. H. Green and T. H. Grose, 2 vols. (London: Longmans, 1907), 2: 417. Compare Boswell, *Journal of a Tour*, p. 129: Johnson, says Boswell, "maintains that . . . except a few passages, there is nothing truly ancient but the names and some vague traditions."

[67] Hugh Blair, *A Critical Dissertation on the Poems of Ossian, the Son of Fingal*, 2d ed. (London, 1765), facsimile (N.Y.: Garland, 1970), pp. 20, 27-28.

[68] René Wellek, *The Rise of English Literary History* (Chapel Hill: Univ. of North Carolina Press, 1941), pp. 123, 187. See also pp. 192-193.

development that tries to do justice to both "good sense" and "fine fabling," as he puts it near the end of the *Letters on Chivalry and Romance*.[69] "There is," he writes in the third of his *Moral and Political Dialogues*

"I think, in the revolutions of taste and language, a certain point, which is more favorable to the purposes of poetry, than any other. It may be difficult to fix this point with exactness. But we shall hardly mistake in supposing it lies *somewhere between the rude essays of uncorrected fancy*, on the one hand, *and the refinements of reason and science*, on the other. And such appears to have been the condition of our language in the age of Elizabeth.[70]

Such, at any rate, was the condition of critical values in the age of Bishop Hurd, a condition finding its literary counterpart in many of the thematic and structural patterns of eighteenth-century poetry and prose. Macpherson's *Fragments* suggest a further implication of the temporal patterns these values imply. Often, as we have seen, his characters devote themselves to melancholy lament over ages and figures of the past. When they do not, however, they sometimes become curiously disembodied, deprived of immediate background and significant locatedness, even of fully determinate audience and dramatic situation. They frequently speak, as well, in a markedly repetitive and rhythmic prose (whole speeches are built on a pattern of iambic trimeter with a varying number of unstressed syllables).[71] The resulting emphasis on voice or utterance as such—since this is all that seems certainly present at times—results in an undermining of significant action, even when it

---

[69] Richard Hurd, *Letters on Chivalry and Romance*, ed. Hoyt Trowbridge (Los Angeles: Clark Memorial Library, 1963), p. 120 (the last page): "What we have gotten by this revolution," he says, which requires that fancy ally herself with truth, "is a great deal of good sense. What we have lost, is a world of fine fabling."

[70] Quoted in W. K. Wimsatt, Jr., and Cleanth Brooks, *Literary Criticism: A Short History* (N.Y.: Knopf, 1957), p. 529, my emphasis.

[71] See the speeches, for example, of Vinvela (p. 9) and Shilric (p. 10) in the *Fragments*.

is narrated, and of dramatic character as well. Dislodged, so to speak, from a fully realized situation and even personality, Macpherson's characters seem to act and speak "legendarily" rather than really (at times the actual narrative present tense is indistinguishable from the use of the present to indicate typical or habitual action), in rhythms of evocative prose rather than in psychological or emotional rhythms, as though the primary function of these characters were to signify rather than to act or speak or be.

Consider Vinvela's opening speech in Fragment I:

> My love is a son of the hill. He pursues the flying deer.
> His grey dogs are panting around him; his bow-string
> sounds in the wind. Whether by the fount of the rock,
> or by the stream of the mountain thou liest; when the
> rushes are nodding with the wind, and the mist is flying
> over thee, let me approach my love unperceived, and see
> him from the rock. Lovely I saw thee first by the aged
> oak; thou wert returning tall from the chace; the fairest
> among thy friends.

What is uncertain here is not just the audience or the setting or the time but the entire dramatic situation and thus the very referentiality of the discourse.[72] It is difficult to imagine a situation—time, place, audience—in which these words could be uttered, not because they are stylized or unrealistic or archaic, but because the very coordinates of the kind of discourse they constitute are vaguely rather than securely present in the passage. It is almost as though a particular kind of speech act were being improperly performed—as though, for example, one were promising today to do something yesterday. It is not grammar that is being violated but that implicit allusion to the contextual that is as powerful a determinant of the appropriateness of an utterance as grammar itself. At times in

---

[72] Not historical referentiality, of course, but referentiality as a feature of internal structure. Compare John Sitter's assertion that "the unfolding desire of *Grandison* is ... to make a structure of words unburdened by history" (*Literary Loneliness in Mid-Eighteenth-Century England* [Ithaca and London: Cornell Univ. Press, 1982], p. 217).

Macpherson it seems that no conceivable situation could possibly serve as the implicit referent of an utterance. Like the sentence "colorless green ideas sleep furiously," certain passages in the *Fragments* seem simply incapable of the referential.

This means that whatever their actual source, whether the pen of Macpherson or the voice of Ossian himself, they are *intrinsically* forgeries. "Counterfeit" is an accurate term for their genesis or historical status, but it is an equally accurate description of their very character. Moreover, that counterfeit status implies a paring away of external—including referential—relations and a necessary concentration on the space of the discourse itself, on the "present" in which an utterance is enacted. As a referential time and place become undermined, the metaphoric time and place of the utterance itself acquire a bold prominence. Whatever we may think of the literary value of Macpherson's forgeries, then, structurally they are the literary kin of Boswell's experiments with temporality and tense in the *London Journal*, of Tristram's movement between the effort to trace his own history *ab ovo* and the joy he experiences in the hovering present-tense of the discourse itself, and of Chatterton's creation of a realm neither past nor present but existing, as Northrop Frye has said, "in what Blake might have called a spiritual fourfold Bristol."[73] The "world of fine fabling" to which Bishop Hurd alluded near the end of the *Letters on Chivalry and Romance* becomes associated, in the later eighteenth century, not just with a real or imagined past, or with the authentic or forged literary works of that past, but with written discourse itself, with the metaphoric place of the poetic and prose utterances in which the search for an actual past had been expressed. If a substantial past could be an enabling fiction to the present, as it was for Burke, perhaps a substantial fiction could hold together past and present in a way that real time seemed never quite capable of doing.

[73] Northrop Frye, *Fearful Symmetry* (Princeton: Princeton Univ. Press, 1947), p. 176.

At such a point, of course, the embodied fiction—the text—loses some of its instrumental power and tends rather to become an end in itself. The principal locus of substantiality, in short, is neither the past nor the present, nor even the present as it is informed by the past, but the written text, and the principal medium of that substantiality is not time in the ordinary sense but the ideal temporal order of the literary work. This progression from the past to the poetic order of time as the site or theater of substantiality can help us to explain why the writers of this period developed the particularly pure form of literature as process, focusing on the moment of utterance itself, that Frye describes in "Towards Defining an Age of Sensibility." The world of fine fabling is first sought in one or another age of romance, but it comes gradually to be identified with the space of fable itself.

Characteristically, then, the later eighteenth-century writer who turned for support to the past did not seek to abandon the present in its favor but to fuse the two into an amalgam possessing weight and significance; his goal, that is, resembled a double exposure more than a journey in a time machine. To the degree that this effort succeeded, it frequently created a complex structure of time, a kind of temporal palimpsest, that generated two related but contrary effects. The first is a thickening or substantializing of time in which past and present together come to acquire more richness and scope than either is able to achieve alone and in which, therefore, the ontological longings of the period are in some measure appeased; only in some measure, however, for that very combining of past and present serves also to dehistoricize or detemporalize each and thus to weaken the very concept, and image, of temporal locatedness. Since temporal specification is a significant part of referential discourse, of that continuing allusion to certain things and events occupying certain places and times on which any mimetic or realistic rhetoric depends, to weaken temporal locatedness is to weaken referentiality itself and to strengthen, in turn, the notion of a metaphoric

131

time and place proper to the work of art. At this point the substantiality that had been sought in the past, or in a fusion of past with present, migrates to the sphere of the poem, the theater of literature itself.

The treatment of the past in the latter half of the century thus holds together, often uneasily, at least three different sorts of undertaking: the search for a genuinely historical and substantial past; the fashioning of a mythical past; the turn to the literary order of time itself. In the first half of the nineteenth century these efforts tend to separate and to appear, greatly modified in many cases, in a relatively pure form. From this point of view there is a group of interrelated connections between the Age of Sensibility and the Romantic Era rather than a mighty line of continuity or a thorough revolutionary schism.

The most obvious, perhaps, is that between the floating authorial present that Tristram Shandy inhabits and its Byronic counterpart in *Don Juan*. This connection has been most often explored in terms of comic or satiric or ironic affinities; but each is also, clearly, a work whose insistent eclipsing of narrative by narrator seems almost to recapitulate the migration of the locus of substantiality from past to poem that I have tried to describe in the preceding pages. The effects of that migration appear as well in the practice and theory, respectively, of the two Romantic poets most strongly influenced by the literature of the English Enlightenment, Blake and Coleridge. "Blake's masters in poetry," as Northrop Frye has said, "were Gray, Collins, Chatterton and Ossian, and he believed to the day of his death in the authenticity of both Ossian and Rowley. . . . He lived to read Byron and *The Recluse*, but his heart was with *Fingal* and *Aella*."[74] The mingling of past and present that appears in some of the *Poetical Sketches* (among others, "Fair Elenor" and "Gwin, King of Norway") may suggest one kind of connection with the poets of sensibility, but those poets' exploration of the present tense and their qualified evocation of a mythic past also permitted Blake, in

[74] Ibid., p. 167.

132

his major works, to develop a narrative mode adequate to his conception of permanent states through which individual characters move at different moments of history but which yet have an existence apart from those individuals. This space-time of mythic rather than historical character seems to me a remarkable though intelligible development of the dehistoricized temporality that we find in Macpherson, Gray, Smart, and others. In Blake that temporality is made fully mythical, a temporal emblem of the nature of things rather than an account of times past, and much the same can be said of Shelley in *Prometheus Unbound* and of Keats in *Hyperion* and *The Fall of Hyperion.*

Coleridge's conception of the poem as an organic unity, as a verbal structure obeying its own laws or as a created space analogous to the space of Creation itself, has obvious and well-documented links with the idealist cast of his metaphysical studies. But the influence of the literature of sensibility strengthened those links by providing concrete and literary examples of the way in which a work could begin to liberate itself from the exigencies of the historical or mimetic or referential. Between the conception of art as a mirror and that of art as a lamp, we might say, is a phase in which the chief point of interest is the character of illumination or visibility itself: its power to disclose being, or create illusion; to form a present that has proceeded from no past; to remind us that appearance and reality are not always opposites since reality frequently appears, and thus to redeem the world of appearances by translating it from an empirical to a phenomenological context. In the later eighteenth century the partly detemporalized region of the literary work is a region designed to explore and affirm those powers.

With Wordsworth and the reinvesting of experience—the experiences of "the common day" above all—with metaphysical significance, the quest for a historical past is both altered and fulfilled. Past and present are now united by a personal history and a metaphysical bond, and their relationship is firmly dialectical, an analogue to the Augustinian and

Miltonic pattern of (fortunate) fall and redemption.[75] From a generic point of view this achievement is a recovery of romance but a recovery with a difference: not a revival of marvels but a new apprehension of the marvelousness of common experience and of the redemptive powers of the mind able to reconceive experience in this way. Only from this perspective can we see how little the mere presence of elements of "the marvelous" in later eighteenth-century literature implies a full revival of romance perception and how completely the achievement of that literature depends, in fact, on resisting a conception of experience that would have dissolved the substantial into the metaphysical and loosened the Enlightenment writers' hold on unredeemed common experience.

For the turn to the past, in that period, like its other efforts to invest experience with substantiality, is not to be set against the Romantic achievement but seen as the extraordinary effort it was, an effort to perform in the experiential realm what the archaizing forgers accomplished in the literary realm: to create a space, even a stage, of meaning and value neither transcendently authoritative nor unauthored and therefore nonexistent. To say that this effort did not issue in a recovery of romance is not to criticize but to describe it, and even to suggest one of its principal achievements. For the attempt to derive present substantiality from a turn to the past coexisted with skepticism about just such an undertaking, and the pressure of those conflicting attitudes had to be met by an imaginative effort of great tentativeness and delicacy. It was an effort of role-playing and theatrics, often enough, but one that deepens our awareness of the theatrical itself as an imaginative mode of genuine value and revelatory power. It was also, at times, an effort of confusing diversity and considerable instability, for it did not arrive at a single formulation of the relation of past to present but at a variety of such formulations. To arrange these formulations in a rough series according to their degree of artifice and sophistication is to see just how diverse that

[75] I allude to the argument of M. H. Abrams in *Natural Supernaturalism: Tradition and Revolution in Romantic Literature* (N.Y.: Norton, 1971).

effort was. The substantial past is, at different moments and for different writers, a genuine historical age; an age always out of reach; a time when men and women could freely *dream* of such a past; a necessary but tentatively held fiction; and finally, a concept that is superseded by the metaphoric time and place of fictional discourse itself, of the poem. In that progess from past to poem the writers of the later eighteenth century charted a complex territory that they also helped bring into being. A heightened attention to the space of literary discourse, however, is only one part of what later eighteenth-century writers were able to create from the proliferating ambiguities of nostalgia. Embracing both that attention and the new respect for artifice that it implies is a remarkable effort to articulate, and to master, a felt impoverishment of common experience. It is a final irony of this splendid and curious era of English literature that the mastery should so frequently have been constructed from the forms of that impoverishment.

· 5 ·

THE RECOVERY OF THE
PRESENT

> Whatever withdraws us from the power of our senses; whatever
> makes the past, the distant, or the future predominate over the
> present, advances us in the dignity of thinking beings.
> —Samuel Johnson, *A Journey to the*
> *Western Islands of Scotland*

Johnson's denigration of the present is part of an ancient and traditional system of values subordinating our lower nature (physical, sensory, present-bound) to our higher (spiritual, intellectual, ranging freely in memory and anticipation). His defense of the particularly human ability to animate Iona or Marathon with their vanished histories stands, as it were, halfway between that ancient system of values and the forms of imaginative retrospection that mark the literature of the later eighteenth century. For if a concern with the past "advances us in the dignity of thinking beings" it can also add a certain weight and dignity to present experience when that experience seems more than usually threadbare or flat or insubstantial. In this sense Johnson's splendid declaration is a traditional variant of a less traditional Enlightenment concern with the power and uses of the past.

At the same time, however, the present was itself acquiring new dignity and power, partly as a result of literary experiments with different forms of presentness: the intensities of passion as experienced by Richardson's letter-writing and -reading characters, or the bardic anguish or illumination that informs the charged "now" of the sublime ode, or the continually renewed and therefore perpetually present benediction of Smart in *Jubilate Agno*. This literary activity was, if not exactly supported, at least paralleled by critical speculation of various kinds—investigations of literature and art but also of human thinking and feeling. Many of these investigations gave new and respectful attention to the character of our immediate and prereflective experience. Writers on aesthetics, for example, "spent a great deal of effort on the problem of distinguishing among the various pleasures of the imagination by trying to describe their 'feel,' "[1] and Adam Smith, writing not on aesthetics but "Of the External Senses," does much the same thing, as in this discussion of smell:

Every smell or odour is naturally felt as in the nostrils; not as pressing upon or resisting the organ, not as in any respect external to, or independent of, the organ, but as altogether in the organ, and nowhere else but in the organ, or in the principle of perception which feels in that organ.[2]

This quasi-phenomenological concern with the character of our present experiencing is extremely widespread in the second half of the century, and it is part of an investigation whose effect was not just to explore but also to value in new ways that aspect of our experience and the world it delivers. After all, writes W. K. Wimsatt of the associationists:

Association was a potent faculty for making combinations, for seeing objects, not thin and meager as they are rendered by abstraction, but in the whole richness of their concrete significance. . . . Association under this aspect might be a way of putting back together the world which had been fragmented into atoms or moments of discrete experience by the Humean *dissociation*. It might be that we ought to set less store by reason and logic, our rationalist abstractive powers, and a great deal more by our entire mental and emotional workings, our total minds, even our instincts. These might give us a world of solid and extremely valuable reality.[3]

[1] Peter Kivy, *The Seventh Sense: A Study of Francis Hutcheson's Aesthetics and Its Influence in Eighteenth-Century Britain* (N.Y.: Burt Franklin, 1976), p. 87.
[2] *Essays on Philosophical Subjects by the late Adam Smith, L.L.D.* (Dublin, 1795), p. 283.
[3] W. K. Wimsatt, Jr., and Cleanth Brooks, *Literary Criticism: A Short History* (N.Y.: Knopf, 1957), p. 304.

In his *Elements of Criticism* Lord Kames make a very different case for the role of present experience in giving us a world of solid and valuable reality, for it is upon such experience—what Kames calls "ideal presence"—that the power of both fiction and history depends.[4] "Ideal presence," as Scott Elledge says, is "Kames's term for . . . the presence of things or events before the mind's eye, produced either by the memory of the things or events or by the creation of them by words or discourse" (2: 1169). Hence, says Kames, "in a complete idea of memory there is no past nor future; a thing recalled to the mind with the accuracy I have been describing is perceived as in our view, and consequently as existing at present" (2: 839), as are the objects evoked by literary and dramatic language. But, says Kames, if "in reading, ideal presence be the means by which our passions are moved, it makes no difference whether the subject be a fable or a true history," for "even genuine history has no command over our passions but by ideal presence only, and consequently . . . in this respect it stands upon the same footing with fable. . . . Even real events entitled to our belief must be conceived present and passing in our sight before they can move us" (2: 842, 843).

Ideal presence is neither history nor fiction but it is the mode by which, and by which alone, both history and fiction are enabled to reach and affect us. Merely present and immediate, transitory, a guarantor of no truth, "What can be more slight than ideal presence?" (2: 845), Yet on it depends almost the entire power of language over our affective life. Like light, it makes possible both truth and illusion indifferently, but like light again, it delivers to us much that we value in our world. Kames does not claim that the immediate mental image has its counterpart in fact, but he does show that a significant portion of the world of fact cannot reach us except through such an image. If the immediacy that is the necessary mode of ideal presence is less likely to advance us "in the dignity of thinking beings" than our knowledge of the distant and

[4] The passage is readily available in *Eighteenth-Century Critical Essays*, ed. Scott Elledge, 2 vols. (Ithaca: Cornell Univ. Press, 1961), 2: 838-847. Subsequent references will be cited by volume and page number in the text.

heroic past, as Johnson assumes in the *Journey*, Kames reminds us that insofar as the past is emotively "known" at all it is known precisely by means of the immediate images of ideal presence.

All experiencing takes place in the present, of course, but not all ages find this a significant or generative fact. Later eighteenth-century writers, however, are particularly interested in experiences that call attention to their presentness (whether by their vividness, intensity, transitoriness, or other means) and that therefore encourage a revaluation and even a reclamation of the present in which they occur. This interest is most obvious, perhaps, in the lyric and introspective energies of forms like the ode and diary, but it is far from confined to such forms. I want to illustrate something of its range and power by showing the degree to which a family of related ideas—the present, presence, immediacy, and others—shapes three different kinds of later eighteenth-century text: aesthetic treatise (Burke's *Enquiry*), autobiography (Franklin, Gibbon, Rousseau, and others), and biography (Boswell's *Life of Samuel Johnson*). The writers of these works, whether exploring our responses to the sublime and beautiful, or the relation of the self to time and change, or a particularly elusive yet massive kind of heroism, seek in the present what other of their contemporaries, and sometimes they themselves, seek in the past: a sphere of significance and weight, of substantiality. From this point of view the recovery of the present and the appeal to the past are two parts of a single complex movement.

Burke's *Philosophical Enquiry into the Origin of our Ideas of the Sublime and Beautiful* is an "aesthetic" treatise sharply focused on the emotive and the experiential. For one thing it considers the emotions aroused by the sublime "as an end in themselves, rather than as a means to an end" such as persuasion;[5] it is thus concerned with "aesthetic (as opposed to rhetorical) categories—categories of aesthetic *experience*."[6]

[5] Samuel Holt Monk, *The Sublime: A Study of Critical Theories in xviii-Century England* (N.Y.: Modern Language Association, 1935), p. 85.

[6] Kivy, *The Seventh Sense*, p. 27.

For another, it principally conceives of the sublime not as a literary style but as "a mode of aesthetic experience found in literature and far beyond it."[7] Burke's speculations, claims Saintsbury in a sentence as remarkable for its rhythm as its enthusiasm, "almost always go directly to the effect, the result, the event, the pleasure, the trouble, the thrill."[8] Here, we might say, aesthetic experience gives way to experience as such, and experience of a particularly passionate kind.

Despite its overstatement Saintsbury's remark can remind us that it is difficult to limit the concerns of Burke's *Enquiry* to the category of the aesthetic, even in an expanded sense of the word. Burke himself, in the preface to the first edition, described his initial difficulties in terms that have little to do with aesthetics directly. He found, he says, "that he was far from having any thing like *an exact theory of our passions*, or a knowledge of their genuine sources" (1, my emphasis). He therefore imagined that "a diligent examination of our passions in our own breasts," along with a survey of the causes influencing those passions and of the laws governing that influence might allow him to derive rules applicable "to the imitative arts, and to whatever else they [the rules] concerned, without much difficulty" (1; cf. 176). The final concern here is indeed with the imitative arts, among other things, but the subject of greatest moment is clearly "our passions." In the course of the *Enquiry* this subject expands to include much of our emotive, sensory, and (especially) immediate experience, and Burke's treatment of that experience is in no sense simply expository or analytic. Alongside the *Enquiry*'s explicit argument concerning the "origin of our ideas of the Sublime and Beautiful" runs an implicit argument affirming the depth, variety, and significance of our present and immediate experience, our "Wealth of Sentiments" in all senses of that phrase.

---

[7] Edmund Burke, *A Philosophical Enquiry into the Origin of Our Ideas of the Sublime and Beautiful*, ed. James T. Boulton (Notre Dame and London: Univ. of Notre Dame Press, 1968), p. xlvii. Subsequent references appear by page number in the text.

[8] George Saintsbury, *A History of Criticism* . . . , 3 vols., 4th ed. (Edinburgh and London: Blackwood, 1923), 3: 164.

From this point of view the *Enquiry* is not simply an aesthetic treatise but a kind of secular, emotive, and experiential theodicy whose goal is the reattribution of ontological plentitude to one significant area of human experience.[9]

Like more traditional theodicies, moreover, the *Enquiry* can be understood as an answer as well as an assertion, a response to a skeptical perception of impoverishment or meaninglessness (much as one might read Hopkins' "God's Grandeur" as a response to some of Hardy's early lyrics and, except for chronology, to some of his later lyrics as well). And as in most theodicies, the perception of impoverishment is one that the author in some sense shares or imagines as sufficiently plausible to require a serious answer. In Burke that impoverishment is not theological but ontological, a recurrent and customary attenuation of concrete experience. It can appear in the excessive perspicuity or knowability of certain visual objects through which eye and mind all too readily see (lxxi); or (a metaphoric version of the same experience) in the excessive and particular-subduing neatness of abstract and metaphysical schemes such as Burke attacks in the *Reflections*; or in abstract definitions: "I have no great opinion of a definition. . . . For when we define, we seem in danger of circumscribing nature within the bounds of our own notions. . . . A definition may be very exact, and yet go but a very little way towards informing us of the nature of the thing defined" (12). In each case, visual or conceptual, what is lost is the counterpressure on eye or mind of the object's otherness, the stubborn weight and integrity of its real existence.

More disturbing still is the form of experiential impoverishment imposed on us by sheer "use," custom and habit. It is rare, Burke argues, that we find the familiar beautiful, and in the second edition of the *Enquiry* he expands this common notion into a vision of our usual state as one of perceptual and affective anesthesia:

[9] See Thomas Weiskel, *The Romantic Sublime: Studies in the Structure and Psychology of Transcendence* (Baltimore: The Johns Hopkins Univ. Press, 1976), p. 3: "In the history of literary consciousness the sublime revives as God withdraws from an immediate participation in the experience of men."

Indeed so far are use and habit from being causes of pleasure, merely as such; that *the effect of constant use is to make all things of whatever kind entirely unaffecting.* For as use at last takes off the painful effect of many things, it reduces the pleasurable effect of others in the same manner, and brings both to a sort of mediocrity and indifference. Very justly is use called a second nature; and *our natural and common state is one of absolute indifference,* equally prepared for pain or pleasure. (104, my emphasis)[10]

What has been lost, in this view, is the immediacy and presentness of immediate and present experience. Thus, whether we "see through" an object too readily and completely or fail to see it with freshness at all, the effect is much the same: we are stranded in a world of inadequate substance, otherness, and immediacy. It is this world, the surface of our present experience, that Burke seeks to redeem, principally by demonstrating the substantiality and meaningfulness of the immediate.

To escape from "our natural and common state . . . of absolute indifference" we first require not any particular experience but the very possibility of experience, and Burke appropriately begins his treatise with that characteristic, which he calls "novelty." Best translated as "noticeability," novelty is that quality in an object which allows it to register on our consciousness instead of remaining beneath "a stale unaffecting familiarity." Noticing, however, is a relationship; from the point of view of the perceiving subject rather than the perceived object "novelty" is "sensibility," which is susceptibility or the capacity to notice something. Sensibility is not the same as judgment, and it does not ensure that our judg-

[10] On the sublime as a pill to purge melancholy, to rouse us from a dullness that can be understood as a symptom of (among other things) cultural decadence or melancholia, see Angus Fletcher, *Allegory: The Theory of a Symbolic Mode* (Ithaca: Cornell Univ. Press, 1964), p. 264, and Weiskel, *The Romantic Sublime,* pp. 18, 97.

ment will be good.[11] It simply makes it possible to perceive something on which our judgment may act. It is the primitive ability to perceive, and its opposite is insensibility.

With these two terms, "novelty" and "sensibility," Burke establishes the possibility of a perceptual (and therefore present and immediate) experience. Much of the rest of the *Enquiry* recalls us to the complexity, the power, the worth and weight of such experience. One way it does so is by means of its investigative aim which is, as Walter J. Hipple has said, in part "analytical—to separate the components of complex objects."[12] At the same time, of course, the analytic method can demonstrate the complexity of what we had taken to be simple objects. In the "Introduction on Taste," added to the second edition, Burke elevates wit over judgment on the grounds that "by making resemblances we produce *new images*, we unite, we create, we enlarge our stock; but in making distinctions we offer no food at all to the imagination" (18). Judgment merely analyzes known reality; wit increases our stock of reality. For much of the *Enquiry*, however, it is as though he were attempting to demonstrate precisely the fecundity of judgment or analysis, its ability to enlarge our stock of available reality by rendering complex and multidimensional what had seemed simple and flat.

This analytic effort is at times merely numerical, a demonstration of plurality, but at other times it discloses not just a multiplication of like entities but competing or at least heterogeneous dimensions of the object under consideration. The effect is to add to the numerousness of the elements composing that object but also to the differentness of its dimensions and thus to its ontological "thickness" and complexity as well.

[11] "In the morning of our days, when the senses are unworn and tender, when the whole man is awake in every part, and the gloss of novelty fresh upon all the objects that surround us, how lively at that time are our sensations, but how false and inaccurate the judgments we form of things," p. 25.

[12] Walter J. Hipple, Jr., *The Beautiful, the Sublime, and the Picturesque in Eighteenth-Century British Aesthetic Theory* (Carbondale: Southern Illinois Univ. Press, 1957), p. 85.

Taste, for example, is "not a simple idea, but is partly made up of a perception of the primary pleasures of sense, of the secondary pleasures of the imagination, and of the conclusions of the reasoning faculty" (23). Such an analysis is not a mere matter of subdivision, for the components of taste are not homogeneous but belong to different systems. The pleasures of sense and imagination, which together constitute what Burke calls "sensibility," are one thing; the conclusions of judgment are another.

A proper diagram of taste, then, is not a uniform and multiply divided spectrum but a pair of distinct axes depicting heterogeneous values:

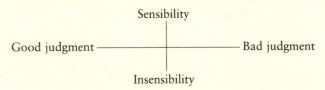

The same is true of pleasure and pain. They are distinct but not homogeneous or continuous. Thus Burke calls the cessation of pain "delight" and the cessation of pleasure (depending on the manner and degree of permanence of its cessation) either "indifference," "disappointment," or "grief." These relationships might also be represented as a pair of axes:

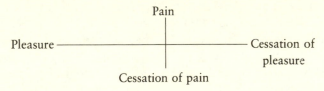

Or, if the traditional opposition of pleasure to pain compels us to place them on a continuum, that continuum must contain a discontinuity: the idea of "indifference" which is, so to speak, a border between heterogenous realms and thus a guarantor of the positive and distinct (rather than merely relative) characters of pleasure and pain:

Pleasure	Cessation of Pleasure	Indifference	Cessation of Pain	Pain

By means of such distinctions a concept or an experience is not simply subdivided (like a zoning map) but inhabited (like a region).

The *Enquiry* is, to a great extent, an exercise in the making of distinctions like these and of the simpler sort of distinction as well.[13] It distinguishes the sublime from the beautiful; the beautiful from the complete (and the ugly from the deformed or incomplete); the beautiful from the proportionate, the fit, the elegant, and the fine (or specious); the elegant from the fine or specious, and so on. The result is something like the movement from a lower to a higher level of magnification but also like the movement from silhouette to sculpture. It establishes both multiplicity of dimension and numerousness of feature and thus supplies an image of experience that is substantial as well as profuse.

It is with immediate experience, above all, that Burke is concerned: sensory appearances, sudden emotional responses—all that makes up the perceived present of our multidimensional temporal existence. As a result he ignores or sharply subordinates all but the immediate causes of that experience ("Origin," in his title, is a nonhistorical and almost an atemporal term, referring to the origin of certain ideas in our immediate experience rather than in the past, individual or collective).[14] For example: "A perpendicular has more force in forming the sublime, than an inclined plane; and the effects of a rugged and broken surface seem stronger than where it

---

[13] At times such distinctions are structurally enacted as well as argued. Thus, section 1 of Part Two tells us that "the passion caused by the great and sublime in nature, . . . is Astonishment." Only in section 2, however, do we learn that the sublime causes astonishment by means of fear ("terror"—or terrifyingness—in the object creates in us a fear whose final effect is astonishment).

[14] See Martin Kallich, "The Argument Against the Association of Ideas in Eighteenth-Century Aesthetics," *Modern Language Quarterly* 15 (1954): 126. In the *Reflections*, of course, Burke is concerned with historical origins and with the circumstances and traditions to which they give rise.

is smooth and polished. It would carry us out of our way to enter in this place into the cause of these appearances" (72). Similarly, he relies as little as possible on the testimony of subsequent reasonings about our immediate experience. Investigating the "cause" of beauty, he seeks "a primary cause acting on the senses and imagination" (92). An object of beauty possesses "powers and properties that prevent [i.e., anticipate] the understanding, and even the will," and that, "seizing upon the senses and imagination, captivate the soul before the understanding is ready either to join with them or to oppose them" (107). This emphasis on immediacy accounts for Burke's extraordinarily lengthy and apologetic effort to exclude "proportion and fitness from any share in beauty" (107), for these qualities, "the discoveries of reason, are posterior and never anterior to the perception of an object and the recognition of its beauty."[15]

Burke is not simply making a neutral distinction between two modes of apprehension, one immediate and emotive, the other discursive and rational. He is also offering a defense of the former. Indeed, in his subsequent discussion of "compounded abstract" words he insists that while such words cannot be fully understood without analysis into their individual components, yet "when you have made such a discovery of the original ideas, the effect of the composition is utterly lost" (164). He does not claim quite so much in the case of beauty and proportion, but he does insist throughout on the authority and rightness, as well as the distinctive character, of our immediate experience.

Nothing does more to focus the *Enquiry* on such experience

[15] Neal Wood, "The Aesthetic Dimension of Burke's Political Thought," *Journal of British Studies* 4 (1964): 46. Cf. Vladimir Nabokov, *Transparent Things* (N.Y.: McGraw-Hill, 1972), p. 2: "A thin veneer of immediate reality is spread over natural and artificial matter, and whoever wishes to remain in the now, with the now, on the now, should please not break its tension film." Nabokov's fable is in part about the subversion of immediate reality by the habit of historical thought. See also Wallace Jackson, *Immediacy: The Development of a Critical Concept from Addison to Coleridge* (Amsterdam: Rodopa NV, 1973), esp. chaps. 3, 4, and on the connection between immediacy and the sublime, pp. 69-70, 83.

than Burke's persistent attention to the physical body, for it is the nature of the body to experience at, and thus to serve as an emblem of, the level of the immediate. What is often taken to be an excessive reliance on implausible or outdated physiology is from another point of view an unswerving effort to remain within the sphere that the *Enquiry* as a whole seeks to reclaim, the sphere of present experiencing and immediate response. A brief anthology will serve to recall Burke's characteristic procedure in this area:

> When we go but one step beyond the immediately sensible qualities of things, we go out of our depth. (129-130)

> As these emotions [pain and terror] clear the parts, whether fine, or gross, of a dangerous and troublesome incumbrance, they are capable of producing delight. (136)

> Beauty acts by relaxing the solids of the whole system. (149-150)

Burke is often far more elaborate than this, and consequently still less convincing, in his physiological explanations, yet neither the elaborateness nor the implausibility of his accounts suffices to deter him, for "an investigation of the natural and mechanical causes of our passions, besides the curiosity of the subject, gives, if they are discovered, a double strength and lustre to any rules we deliver on such matters" (139-140).

If such rules acquire "strength and lustre" from their being grounded in the bodily, the body gains something too: an enlargement and refinement of the functions we conceive it to perform. Much as he expands our conception of the sublime by in part restricting the sphere of the beautiful, so Burke wins new powers for the body's immediate experience by limiting the role of the mind.[16] After explaining in Part Four of the *Enquiry* why darkness is terrible (because the radial fibres of the iris contract to a painful degree), Burke anticipates the objections of the skeptical reader:

[16] See Martin Price, *To the Palace of Wisdom: Studies in Order and Energy from Dryden to Blake* (Garden City, N.Y.: Doubleday, 1964), pp. 361-369.

147

It may perhaps be objected to this theory of the mechanical effect of darkness, that the ill effects of darkness or blackness seem rather mental than corporeal; and I own it is true, that they do so; and so do all those that depend on the affections of the finer parts of our system. The ill effects of bad weather appear often no otherwise, than in a melancholy and dejection of spirits, though without doubt, in this case, the bodily organs suffer first, and the mind through these organs. (146-147)

Had Burke argued that the bodily organs first perceive bad weather and the mind then suffers, he would have been on surer ground. But he wishes to affirm not just the considerable dependence of our mental on our bodily life but something close to a parity between them and thus, by extension, to attribute a fuller range of power and meaningfulness to the body's characteristic mode, the experience of the immediate. "The only difference between pain and terror," he argues elsewhere, "is, that things which cause pain operate on the mind, by the intervention of the body; whereas things that cause terror generally affect the bodily organs by the operation of the mind suggesting the danger; but both agreeing, either primarily, or secondarily, in producing a tension, contraction, or violent emotion of the nerves, they agree likewise in every thing else" (132).

In a work devoted so energetically to the making of distinctions among the emotions (the sublime versus the beautiful, pain versus pleasure, pleasure versus delight) it is at first surprising to find an insistent effort to establish the unity of the senses, but this effort too is part of Burke's unwavering elevation of the bodily and the immediate. "Sweet things," we learn, "are the smooth of taste," and thus we may call "sweetness the beautiful of the taste" (153-154, 155). Rays of light passing through a transparent glass or liquor are agreeably softened in the passage, "and the liquor reflecting all the rays of its proper colour *evenly*, it has such an effect on the eye, as smooth opaque bodies have on the eye and touch" (159). Indeed, "there is such a similitude in the pleasures of" sight and touch that those colors most pleasing to the eye might be found "likewise most grateful to the touch," Burke conjectures (121). In short, "there is a chain in all our sensations; they are all but different sorts of feeling, calculated to be affected by various sorts of objects, but all to be affected after the same manner" (120).

Such assertions perhaps foster greater awareness, as Boulton claims, "of the complexity of the aesthetic experience" (lxxiv), but they serve a more specific end as well. By insisting that the senses enjoy a primary relation not just with traditionally "higher" powers (emotions, thought) but also with each other, Burke enlarges their independence. It is as though he had granted them first names as well as patronymics and thus emphasized not just their derivation or subordination but also their own "generational" character. At such a point the senses can begin to become a "system" or a "sensory order" and the world they deliver a sphere of significant reality in its own right.[17] The senses are the body's way of knowing immediate experience, and the present they constitute is what Burke is here attempting to reclaim.

His treatment of obscurity works in an analogous way, in this case by questioning the traditional subordination of significance to intelligibility. "To make any thing very terrible," Burke argues, "obscurity seems in general to be necessary," for "it is our ignorance of things that causes all our admiration, and chiefly excites our passions" (58, 61). "A clear idea is therefore another name for a little idea" (63). Such a position is open to criticism on various grounds—aesthetic, intellectual, even moral—and it has received it, in Burke's time and later. Like the treatment of "Power" (added in the second edition) that immediately follows it, however, the account of obscurity is primarily an insistence on the otherness of the sublime object, its resistance to our energies and categories of knowing and thus its resolute ontological density as an object

---

[17] Modern research, of course, has shown the senses to be not less but far more dependent on the mind than Burke suspected.

"out there."[18] In his *London Journal* of 1762-1763 Boswell laments, "I see too far into the system of things to be much in earnest." So Burke, like Boswell, Gray, and others in this period, is extraordinarily sensitive to what might be called the dark side of lucidity and perspicuity, as though at some level there were a fundamental opposition between the knowable and the substantial. Perhaps we cannot acknowledge the full value of the being of objects or the power of words until we at least question the belief that being and power are always the congenial (and usually inferior) partners of intelligibility and meaningfulness. Just as his insistence on the unity of the senses, then, implicitly questioned their subordination to feeling and thought and thus emphasized the present of sensory experiencing, so his insistence on obscurity questions the subordination of significance to intelligibility and thus emphasizes our immediate experience of the sheer weight and power of things.

The obscure (and therefore "other"), moreover, insofar as we contemplate and seek to penetrate it, has a certain inexhaustibility that allies it with boundlessness (something evermore about to be illuminated) and that is the reflex of our effort to know it. The obscure is not just the unknown but the unknown being pressed toward knowability, even if it permanently resists that pressure. As long as it does resist, it maintains eye and mind in a present exertion without permitting them to slip into the pastness and passivity of sensory or mental possession. As a result obscurity itself draws us toward present experiencing. An intermittent light in darkness, Burke says, and an intermittent sound in silence, are more terrible than pure darkness or pure silence (84). They are so because they remind us afresh, and unpredictably (unlike a regular light or sound), of those conditions of privation. "The attention is roused by this [sudden beginning]; and the faculties driven forward, as it were, on their guard" (83). Moreover, "expectation itself causes a tension." Thus, "though

[18] On the "wholly other" see Rudolf Otto, *The Idea of the Holy*, trans. John W. Harvey, 2d ed. (N.Y.: Oxford Univ. Press, 1950), esp. pp. 26-27.

after a number of strokes, we expect still more, not being able to ascertain the exact time of their arrival, when they arrive, they produce a sort of surprise, which increases this tension yet further" (140). (That surprise is nicely caught in the shift of grammatical subject from "we" to "they.") The full perception of otherness, then, requires that the faculties be "on their guard," and this state of alertness is precisely the state in which the habitual is subordinated to the novel, past to present, reflection to sensation, self to other. What obscurity "illuminates," therefore, is not just the otherness of the sublime object but also the continually renewed present of our immediate, experiential life. It shows us with uncommon vividness our own immediate experiencing.

Just as Burke's account of the obscure object works to separate the plane of immediacy from the depths of the habitual and reflective, so his account of words insists on the gaps between signifier and signified, word and concept, sound and meaning, the affective immediacy of language use and the intellectual duration of understanding. Like poetic images (62), words—at least "compounded abstract words" like *virtue, persuasion,* and *magistrate*—enjoy their full force in the immediate present while their full intelligibility appears only on subsequent reflection. And Burke does not shrink from the ultimate consequences of this position: "In short, it is not only of those ideas which are commonly called abstract, and of which no image at all *can* be formed, but even of particular real beings, that we converse without having any idea of them excited in the imagination" (170). As Stephen K. Land has noted, Burke here moves away from the Lockean picture-theory and toward something like the conception of meaning as use that we find in Wittgenstein's *Philosophical Investigations*.[19] This leads Land to conclude that Part Five of the *Enquiry,* despite Boulton's assertions, "does not follow from Burke's general discussion of the sublime but raises new issues

[19] Stephen K. Land, *From Signs to Propositions: The Concept of Form in Eighteenth-Century Semantic Theory* (London: Longmans, 1974), pp. 46, 47. All of pp. 39-48 is relevant to Burke.

and tends away from the Lockean climate of the main argument."[20]

From another point of view, however, Part Five is an appropriate conclusion to the *Enquiry*, for Burke's modification of Locke is another instance of his attention to the reality and meaningfulness of the immediate. In Burke's scheme we do not hear a word and immediately comprehend it or receive its image, for comprehension waits upon reflection. Instead we hear it and are immediately affected by it (not by an image of its referent). Such a "superficial" model of our verbal experience, Burke argues, is perfectly adequate to account for efficient verbal intercourse. Burke was aware of the novelty of this idea (167-168), and if he had not been the reviewers of the *Enquiry* were sufficient to disclose it to him (175, n. 14). Yet he not only ends the discourse with Part Five but also ends that last part—and thus the *Enquiry* as a whole—with a bold statement of this very idea: "Words were only so far to be considered, as to shew upon what principle they were capable of being the representatives of these natural things, and *by what powers they were able to affect us often as strongly as the things they represent, and sometimes much more strongly*" (176-177, my emphasis).

Beyond the stress on the immediate, however, there is a larger sense in which the discussion of words is a proper conclusion to the *Enquiry*, for that discussion is a particularly strong example of a pattern that constitutes one of the *Enquiry's* most comprehensive implicit arguments. What is most striking about the treatment of words is its bold rejection of the traditional subordination of language to meaning and of words to things such as we find in Johnson's preface to his *Dictionary: "Words are the daughters of earth, and . . . things are the sons of heaven."* If the topic of words seriously enters the *Enquiry* only in Part Five, however, the questioning of such subordination does not, for it has pervaded the entire treatise. Time and again, Burke confronts a traditionally hierarchical relationship between two concepts (words and things,

---

[20] Ibid., p. 39. See *Enquiry*, p. lxxxi.

for example) and works either to reverse the subordination or to question it and to grant to the customarily subordinated term a new authority and at times a new dominance. The pairs can be arranged in two columns, the left being in each case the traditionally superior term:

the intellect	the senses
the mental (or spiritual)	the physical
reason	passion
reason	taste*
things	words
meaning	language
utterance	effect of utterance
things as they are	things as they are felt
clarity of expression	strength of expression
clarity (visual, intellectual)	obscurity
the internal	the external
depth	superficiality
the enduring	the immediate and momentary
social feelings	self-preservation
pleasure	anxiety, melancholy**
love	fear (dread, horror, awe)
the beautiful	the sublime

* "And indeed on the whole one may observe, that there is rather less difference upon matters of Taste among mankind, than upon most of those which depend upon the naked reason; and that men are far better agreed on the excellence of a description in Virgil, than on the truth or falsehood of a theory of Aristotle" (24). Burke elsewhere says that he wishes to "communicate to the taste a sort of philosophical solidity" (6).

** Even "positive pleasure," such as beauty provides, puts us in a posture of debilitated languor: "The head reclines something on one side; the eyelids are more closed than usual, and the eyes roll gently with an inclination to the object, the mouth is a little opened, and the breath drawn slowly, with now and then a low sigh: the whole body is composed, and the hands fall idly to the sides. All this is accompanied with an inward sense of melting and languor" (149). Such an effect is not surprising since it is a form of "relaxation," that "languid inactive state" in which the nerves are liable "to the most horrid convulsions" and which results in "melancholy, dejection, despair, and often self-murder" (135). The reader who objects that "This Can't Be Love" will discover elsewhere that "the passion excited by beauty is in fact nearer to a species of melancholy, than to jollity and mirth" (123). Such an account may betray an effort to debunk over-romanticized conceptions of love and attraction. At least there is something wonderfully shocking in Burke's summary reduction of a cherished Western tradition: "Beauty acts by relaxing the solids of the whole system" (149-150). A thing of beauty is a joy forever.

Each of these pairs recalls one or more of Burke's arguments and emphases in the *Enquiry*, and a few, taken alone, are perhaps only curious. But what looks in the individual case like an odd insistence on the effect of words without concepts, or on physiological explanation, or on the superiority of terror to "mere positive pleasure" is actually a thoroughgoing effort to revise an established structure of experience and value. In virtually every instance, the *Enquiry* ascribes new interest, new authority, new "philosophical solidity" to the right-hand term, often by restricting the force and meaning of its traditional (and traditionally superior) partner.

Years later, as we have seen, in the *Reflections on the Revolution in France* and elsewhere, Burke would do much the same with oppositions like reason and prejudice, metaphysical principles and historical tradition, the abstract and the circumstantial, essence and accident, soul and body. In both realms, aesthetics and political history, Burke's criticism rests on a careful disordering of established hierarchies of value and arises from a perception of the experiential impoverishment that those hierarchies impose. In the *Enquiry* as in the *Reflections*, this disordering amounts to an effort to revise many of the terms and metaphors by means of which we establish and indicate value—an effort, therefore, to bring into being, to establish and authenticate, the sphere of the substantial. Burke's insistence, in the *Enquiry*, on the meaningfulness of the present and the power of the immediate is a significant part of that large and complex effort.

We have seen that in the later eighteenth century the turn to the past is an imaginative act of two distinct though interrelated stages. The first involves a search for a realm (in this case, the past) ontologically distinct from what is felt to be the insubstantial present, a search that for a variety of reasons proves incomplete or only partly successful. In a sense it is a search for a traditional value in a new place. From this emerges the second stage, more successful but also successful in a different way: the discovery not of a new locus of traditional value but of a new way of valuing, and thus a way of reclaiming those objects of experience that the traditional scheme had been unable to invest with the required import and meaningfulness.

A similar pattern governs many of the period's efforts to win for present experience an adequacy of being. Here again the search for a new locus of meaning releases new criteria of meaningfulness so that what is found is not quite what had been sought. In exploring the bodily, the terrifying, and the immediate, Burke does not simply discover fresh sources of values and experiences that had been formerly found in the intellectual, the pleasing, and the deeply meditated. Rather, he develops a new system of values and valuing and, as a consequence, revises the traditional relationships between certain categories of experience (the sublime and the beautiful, pleasure and terror, and so forth). That revision does not simply retain a traditional structure of clear subordination and reverse the terms; often, rather, it puts hierarchical terms into relationships of competition, of parity, of heterogeneity, and thus works to revise a traditional pattern of ordering as well as the elements it had ordered. As a result new differences and kinds of difference emerge, but at times a certain salutary diminishing of difference as well.

Autobiography provides an extremely interesting example of such revision since it is a literary mode that traditionally depends on a movement from old to new, past to present, a movement that is often as much an ontological as a temporal progression. In the later eighteenth century, though, this movement—like the turn to the past—is almost never accomplished. What emerges is, again, a new system of valuing in which the very idea of such an ontological change is questioned and revised. The result is an illumination of the sphere of present experience different from, but closely related to, the illumination provided by Burke's enquiry into our perhaps unexpectedly substantial immediacy.

Peripeteia, or "Reversal of the Situation," says Aristotle, "is a change by which the action veers round to its opposite," while *anagnorisis*, or Recognition, "is a change from ignorance to knowledge." "The best form of recognition," he adds, "is coincident with a Reversal of the Situation, as in the Oedipus."[21] Not every great tragedy, of course, offers so devastatingly grand a coincidence of Reversal and Recognition as *Oedipus the King*, nor are such shifts of direction—large or small—restricted to tragedy. For Reversal, like Recognition, is a species of change, and change is necessary for movement. Structurally, the Aristotelian Reversal is part of a family that includes other large-scale effects, like the transformations and disclosures of comedy and romance, as well as the humbler turning points of forms like the ode, the sonnet, and the verse epistle. Such turning points, like a fulcrum, mark at once a structural division and a locus of change and movement.

The form that this turning point typically assumes in autobiography was determined over fifteen centuries ago by St. Augustine in his *Confessions*. Drawing on the life of St. Paul and on the analogies between that life and the patterns of destruction and renewal that pervade the New Testament, Augustine established the experience of conversion as a central—almost a generic—element of Western autobiography. Augustine's conversion, recorded in Book 8 of the *Confessions*, is the determining event in a narrative filled with anguish and self-division yet, like the New Testament, ultimately a history of redemption. It is an event governed by a specific conception of causality, what M. H. Abrams terms "the Christian paradigm of right-angled changed into something radically new";[22] for Augustine undergoes not just a new expe-

---

[21] S. H. Butcher, *Aristotle's Theory of Poetry and Fine Art*, 4th ed. (N.Y.: Dover, 1951), p. 41 (*Poetics* 1452a).

[22] M. H. Abrams, *Natural Supernaturalism: Tradition and Revolution in Romantic Literature* (N.Y.: Norton, 1971), p. 113. See also pp. 47-48, 83-87.

rience but a new kind of experience, and the self that is born from this moment is in crucial ways distinct from the self that had entered it. From this transforming event, moreover, Augustine begins to discover not only his true self but also his proper relation to God and to that providential order, created and sustained by God, from which a diseased will had earlier led him. As a result Augustine finally subordinates self-discovery to adoration of his Creator, autobiography to theodicy.[23]

It is not its theodicean—or even its theological—concerns that make the *Confessions* such a richly generative text in Western literature, though these concerns have shaped the pattern of spiritual autobiography to an uncommon degree. Nor, for all their brilliance and their particular interest to modern readers, are Augustine's explorations of time, of memory, of language, and of interiority the chief sources of the sheer potency of the *Confessions*. These features are all subordinate to the central event that at once transcends them and lends them their full significance: the experience of conversion itself. For Augustine has not only placed his conversion at the thematic center of his autobiography but also endowed it with such symbolic power as to make it an emblem of many kinds of spiritual uprooting, reversal, redirection, and recovery; it is this symbolic power that has made the *Confessions* something we might almost call an archetypal narrative.

Augustine records a sudden, unwilled, and radical change that takes place in a single moment whose mystery, fullness, and significance mark it as belonging to a different order of time than that of everyday life, a moment of *kairos* rather than *chronos*.[24] It is a moment in which the ordinary course of life is intersected by another dimension of experience and after which nothing can be quite as it had been before. The

[23] A point neatly obscured by some modern editions of the *Confessions* that omit the last three books, no doubt because they are less "personal" than the first ten. I have used the translation by John K. Ryan (N.Y.: Image, 1960).

[24] See Frank Kermode, *The Sense of an Ending: Studies in the Theory of Fiction* (N.Y.: Oxford Univ. Press, 1967), pp. 46-48.

ability of such a scene to shape later religious autobiography is not surprising. Augustine's is a personal account, but it is also so thoroughly imbued with the structural patterns, imagery, and ethos of the New Testament—to say nothing of its tissue of biblical allusions—that it is at least as much an account of Christian Man who, alienated from himself and his God, at last finds both through the miracle of grace. But the influence of the *Confessions* is by no means restricted to religious autobiography or to the period in which such autobiography chiefly flourished, the seventeenth and early eighteenth centuries. For if the scene of Augustine's conversion affirms the efficacy of God, in its broader outline it also affirms the very possibility of human change, qualitative change. It testifies to the perennial dream that, as Tennyson put it, "men may rise on stepping-stones/Of their dead selves to higher things."

This dream informs works as different in their aims and values as Wordworth's *Prelude* and Mill's *Autobiography* in the nineteenth century and *The Autobiography of Malcolm X* and Robert Lowell's "Life Studies" in the twentieth. For despite the distances, temporal and temperamental, that separate them, each of these writers makes a sizable imaginative commitment to the idea of conversion, and that commitment, in turn, rests upon a prior faith in the kind of experience conversion is, a faith in the reality and significance of crises, decisive and transforming moments. The *kairos*, for these as for many autobiographers, is an available category of perception, a possible and meaningful way to conceive experience.

What distinguishes the major autobiographical writers of the later eighteenth century, however—Boswell, Gibbon, Sterne, Franklin, Rousseau—is precisely the disappearance, or near disappearance, or mock appearance of such moments. Critical moments are either denied, or desired but unavailable, or multiplied to such a degree that they lose their singularity and, with it, that qualitative difference from ordinary experience that is their defining characteristic. The virtual uniformity of this phenomenon reflects a good deal more than generic inventiveness, for it suggests that the later eighteenth century had a particular way of imagining those interrelated concepts that a crisis or conversion in autobiography typically draws together: the nature of causality, of the self, of individual experience and its sources of meaning, and of temporality. In the autobiographies of this period there is a dislocation and revision of traditional values that is precisely analogous to Burke's revisionist activity in the *Enquiry*.

It is instructive, for example, to set Augustine's *Confessions* beside one of the greatest of fictional autobiographies, *The Life and Opinions of Tristram Shandy, Gentleman*. Each is a first-person narrative; each, in its own way, begins with the narrator's earliest moments (Augustine, after a prayer, with his infancy; Tristram, after a dedication, with his begetting); and each strives to recount the personal history of the narrator from those earliest moments to the present. But Augustine's autobiographical narrative, unlike Sterne's, is also a theodicy that translates the providential scheme of Christian history into the personal realm of autobiographical confession. Thus, like the historical pattern that the Bible records, Augustine's personal history is marked by a crucial determining event, a point at which the character of his life undergoes real and radical change. In *Tristram Shandy*, however, we find either a leveling of events to uniform significance—a nonepochal conception of time and causality—or multiple parodies of such critical moments grounded in mere chance and contingency: the disastrous clock winding at Tristram's conception; the corruption of "Trismegistus" to "Tristram"; the fall of the leadless window. Nor are such events re-enactments of biblical archetypes, as any number of events in the *Confessions* clearly are. The nearest approach in *Tristram Shandy* to what might be called Augustine's figural consciousness is Walter's habit of beginning impatient outbursts against the women of his household with "not since Eve. . . ." But this habit hardly presupposes that faith in the archetypal dimension of human experience which allows Augustine to warn a friend that "whether it is in a wife or a mother, it is still Eve (the temptress) that we must beware of in any woman."[25]

[25] *Ep.* 243: 10. Quoted in Peter Brown, *Augustine of Hippo* (London: Faber, 1967), p. 63. On Sterne, see Martin C. Battestin, *The Providence of*

Like his figural awareness, Augustine's belief in *kairoi* is ultimately a belief in two orders of reality, human and divine, and in the possibility that the temporal or "horizontal" continuum of human life may at any time be intersected by the hierarchical and "vertical." A special and redemptive significance derived not from experience but from the creator of that experience may at any moment manifest itself, whether in the whole of human history, as with the Incarnation, or in the life of the individual, as with Augustine's experience of grace and conversion. The last four books of the *Confessions*, in fact, turn from narrative movement to a conceptual progression that is analogous to a spiritual ascent along that vertical axis. Thus Augustine's use of particular memories in the first nine books leads to an examination of memory, and this introduces a discussion of time that, in turn, leads to a meditation on God's timelessness and on his creation of the world and of time itself. Similarly, an interpretation of the book of creation, Genesis, moves to a discussion of the principles of interpretation and from there to a recognition that the analogical structure of the universe which makes possible such interpretation was itself established at the creation. In these last books Augustine enacts a triple movement: outward from himself to the created universe; backward in time toward the moment of creation; but also "backward" toward the ontologically prior, and thus upward to an apprehension of the forever potent essences of all things. The very structure of the *Confessions* demonstrates, as one philosopher puts it, that "for Augustine, time is an invitation to participate in eternity."[26]

Time is many things for Sterne, but an invitation to participate in eternity is not one of them. In what seems an almost

---

Wit: Aspects of Form in Augustan Literature and the Arts (Oxford: Clarendon Press, 1974), pp. 242-243.

[26] Robert Jordan, "Time and Contingency in St. Augustine," in *Augustine: A Collection of Critical Essays*, ed. Robert A. Markus (Garden City, N.Y.: Anchor, 1972), p. 275. I have also made use of the treatment of the *Confessions* by Kenneth Burke in *The Rhetoric of Religion: Studies in Logology* (Boston: Beacon, 1961), pp. 43-171.

systematic subversion of Augustinian categories and assumptions *Tristram Shandy* relies exclusively on the temporal or horizontal dimension of experience. Tristram engages in no ascent like that which closes the *Confessions*—indeed, *Tristram Shandy* does not conclude but simply ceases to progress along that horizontal dimension—and Tristram's world knows nothing of that intersection of the timeless with the temporal upon which, for Augustine, the very possibility of significant experience depends. The significance of Tristram's experiences is authenticated by nothing more or less than the sentiment with which he invests them; and the nature of those experiences—accidental, comic, pathetic, externally unmomentous—simply underscores the role of the individual self as the final arbiter and chief creator of their value. For Tristram "critical moments" are multiple, subjective, and indistinguishable in kind from all other experiences.

In Rousseau's *Confessions* they are nearly indistinguishable in number as well.[27] For which shall we choose to isolate as the determining events in Rousseau's life? His being falsely accused of breaking Mlle. Lambercier's comb? Or falsely accusing Marion of stealing the ribbon he had taken himself? The meeting with Mme. de Warens—"Cette époque de ma vie a décidé de mon caractére" (48)—or the day that united him with Thérèse le Vasseur and thereby "fixa mon être moral" (413)? If, as Rousseau claims, "je dois à Mad^e de Larnage de ne pas mourir sans avoir connu le plaisir" (253), what does he continue to owe her after meeting Zulietta? "J'ai parlé de Mad^e de Larnage dans les transports que son souvenir me rend quelquefois encore; mais qu'elle étoit vieille et laide et froide auprès de ma Zulietta!" (320). Worse yet, when Mme. d'Houdetot visits, "ce fut de l'amour. . . . le prémier et l'unique en toute ma vie" (439). As every reader of the *Confessions* knows, moreover, it is with the rest of Rousseau's life as with his passion for women. Page after page reports crises,

---

[27] Jean-Jacques Rousseau, *Les Confessions*, in *Oeuvres Complètes*, tome 1, ed. Bernard Gagnebin and Marcel Raymond (Paris: Pléiade, 1959). Subsequent references appear by page number in the text.

turning points, moments after which, insists Rousseau, all is changed:

> . . . je touchois au moment funeste qui devoit trainer à sa suite la longue chaine de mes malheurs. (260)

> . . . j'étois bien éloigné de prévoir que cette jeune personne feroit un jour le destin de ma vie, et m'entraîneroit, quoique bien innocemment, dans l'abyme où je suis aujourd'hui. (346)

> Mais il est tems d'en venir à la grande revolution de ma destinée, à la catastrophe qui a partagé ma vie en deux parties si différentes, et qui d'une bien légére cause a tiré de si terribles effets. (474)

In part this tendency to see critical moments everywhere expresses a search for order, for traceable and adequate causes; it proceeds from the same cast of mind that leads Rousseau to portray himself as the target of a malign and subtle conspiracy and to speak so often of fate and destiny. More important, however, is the guide by which he, like Sterne, recovers from the past the moments of his life: "Je n'ai qu'un guide fidelle sur lequel je puisse compter; c'est la chaîne des sentimens qui ont marqué la succession de mon être. . . . je ne puis me tromper sur ce que j'ai senti, ni sur ce que mes sentimens m'ont fait faire; et voila dequoi principalement il s'agit" (278). There are so many crises in the *Confessions* because Rousseau felt so many moments to be critical, because he recalls those feelings—indeed, feels them again—as he writes, and because feelings are the only unfalsifiable standard by which to value those moments and that life. "Nous ne sommes plus," Jean Starobinski remarks, "dans le domaine de la *vérité*; nous sommes désormais dans celui de l'*authenticité*."[28]

---

[28] Jean Starobinski, *Jean-Jacques Rousseau: La Transparence et l'obstacle* (Paris: Plon, 1957), p. 247. See also Lionel Trilling, *Sincerity and Authenticity* (Cambridge, Mass.: Harvard Univ. Press, 1973), pp. 73, 93. Trilling and Starobinski usefully correct the emphasis of Georges Gusdorf and others on Rousseau's "sincerity." See Gusdorf, "Conditions et limites de l'autobiogra-

We may take as an example the moment in Book 6 when, troubled by fears of his own damnation, Rousseau has recourse "aux expédiens les plus risibles":

> Un jour rêvant à ce triste sujet je m'exerceois machinalement à lancer des pierres contre les troncs des arbres, et cela avec mon addresse ordinaire, c'est à dire, sans presque en toucher aucun. Tout au milieu de ce bel éxercice, je m'avisai de m'en faire une espéce de pronostic pour calmer mon inquiétude. Je me dis, je m'en vais jetter cette pierre contre l'arbre qui est vis à vis de moi. Si je le touche, signe de salut; si je le manque, signe de dannation. Tout en disant ainsi je jette ma pierre d'une main tremblante et avec un horrible battement de coeur, mais si heureusement qu'elle va frapper au beau milieu de l'arbre; ce qui véritablement n'étoit pas difficile; car j'avois eu soin de le choisir fort gros et fort près. Depuis lors je n'ai plus douté de mon salut. (243)

Rousseau at once calls his act laughable and asserts that it permanently allayed his fears. He can do so because of his enormous fidelity to the feeling of events rather than to later, and ontologically secondary, reasonings about that feeling. It is not that he cannot or will not reason, but that the feelings accompanying an event constitute a final, rather than just a preliminary, tribunal in which to determine its worth. Thus while the act of experiencing may in one sense be corrected by reason at a later date, in another sense it can never be. To judge emotional experience by reason is to make them comparable, to translate one mode of conscious existence into another, and this Rousseau, like Burke, steadfastly refuses to do.

This very quality of Rousseau's privileged moments, moreover, is intimately connected with their numerousness. If the heart of such moments is the authenticity of feeling with which they are experienced, it is just such authenticity that Rousseau

---

phie," in *Formen der Selbstdarstellung*, ed. Günter Reichenkron and Erich Haase (Berlin: Duncker & Humblot, 1956), p. 111.

avers to be the informing principle of the *Confessions* as a whole and that he is able to re-experience in remembering those moments. The implications of this are significant, for as Georges Poulet observes, "the memory of a deed is not the deed itself, but the memory of a feeling is still a feeling."[29] What underlies the sheer multiplication of crises in the *Confessions*, then, is that for Rousseau, as in a different way for Sterne, the moment of crisis has become ontologically indistinguishable from any other moment. Crisis or "conversion" is no longer a confrontation with a different order of reality but with a heightened version of the only reality these writers fully credit. And the temporal mode in which Augustine had experienced that confrontation, the special fullness of the *kairos*, has become displaced into an intensified successiveness, a manic *chronos*, of which Sterne's breathless prose and Rousseau's emotional peaks and valleys are the perfect literary embodiment.

This emergence into a single order of reality and a single mode of temporal experience is in many ways a liberation: from an idea of time that denigrates the immediate and momentary, for example, and from an idea of the present that overlooks the variety of which it is capable. So much Sterne, Burke, and Rousseau make clear. But it is not without its pathos for Rousseau, as at times for Sterne, Boswell, and others. "In the larger theatre of Rousseau's imagination," as Liliane Greene puts it, "any episode of the drama loses its finality. . . . For nothing can guarantee the stability of the outer object or of the changing self."[30] It is worth recalling, of course, that finality is not always an unalloyed blessing, that stabilities are of more than one kind, and that there are other names for instability. In his *Memoirs* Gibbon records the growth of a stability that would certainly have failed to satisfy Rousseau yet which entirely satisfied Gibbon. Franklin's *Autobiography* offers a complex picture of a life that

[29] Georges Poulet, *Studies in Human Time*, trans. Elliott Coleman (N.Y.: Harper Torchbook, 1959), p. 177.
[30] Liliane Greene, "Landscape in Rousseau," p. 5. Text of a paper given at the Symposium on Romanticism, Connecticut College (April 1975).

many might call mercurial and unsettled but which Franklin calls free. Both Gibbon and Franklin, that is, display that typically eighteenth-century withdrawal of faith from the idea of decisive and transforming moments that we see also in Sterne and Rousseau, but it is as though they had freely resigned such faith long ago, "nor cast one longing lingering look behind."

For one thing, Gibbon and Franklin begin their autobiographical narratives with detailed accounts of their ancestry, and Franklin, in addition, addresses his work to his son, since his "posterity may like to know" the means by which he achieved his "considerable Share of Felicity" (43).[31] The effect of this strategy is to emphasize continuity, to place the autobiographer firmly in a sequence of generations that enforces his connectedness with others rather than the identity that sets him apart. So, too, both writers powerfully generalize the self. Franklin insists that he is not so much a man of singular talents as one accustomed to recognize opportunities and make the most of them, as many others might learn to do. Gibbon seizes on what is universal or general in his experience, proceeding, for example, from "the general idea of a militia" down to "the Regiment in which I served, and to the influence of that service on my personal situation and character" (107), or speaking of himself in what might be described as the third person typical: "The miseries of a vacant life were never known to a man whose hours were insufficient to the inexhaustible pleasures of study" (140).[32] Even more than Franklin, moreover, Gibbon stresses the role of chance in his life, avoiding not simply the notions of fate and destiny that pervade Rousseau's *Confessions* but also the method of parody by which Sterne at once rejects fatality and makes us aware of the re-

[31] *The Autobiography of Benjamin Franklin*, ed. Leonard W. Labaree et al. (New Haven and London: Yale Univ. Press, 1964). See Robert F. Sayre, *The Examined Self* (Princeton: Princeton Univ. Press, 1964), pp. 18-19.

[32] Edward Gibbon, *Memoirs of My Life*, ed. Georges A. Bonnard (London: Thomas Nelson, 1966). Compare Gibbon's reluctance to describe the onset of sexual awareness since it "less properly belongs to the memoirs of an individual, than to the natural history of the species," p. 84.

jection. His first introduction to Roman history "must be ascribed to an accident" (42); and he twice asserts that greater wealth or greater poverty might have kept him from his major work (89, 153). "Our lives are in the power of chance," and he has been fortunate enough to draw "a high prize in the lottery of life" (131, 186).[33]

The ease of Franklin and Gibbon with the contingent and quotidian implies, as we might expect, a virtual absence from their autobiographies of genuinely critical moments. Franklin substitutes the steady fruits of habit for sudden transformations, and Gibbon repeatedly introduces moments that may promise to be decisive but are not: the death of his mother and father, for example, or his conversion to Catholicism ("at the age of sixteen I bewildered myself in the errors of the Church of Rome" [58]). The famous account of his entrance to Oxford is typical. It "forms a new aera in my life," he begins, for "in my fifteenth year, I felt myself suddenly raised from a boy to a man" (46). But then: "I spent fourteen months at Magdalen College: they proved the fourteen months the most idle and unprofitable of my whole life" (48). His attitude toward the militia, as toward the moment in which he completes his *History*, is the same. What is extraordinary and sudden, for Gibbon, is always later undone.[34] What endures, what makes a difference, is the result of slow and cumulative growth. "Human Felicity," as Franklin said in a Johnsonian moment, "is produc'd not so much by great Pieces of good Fortune that seldom happen, as by little Advantages that occur every Day" (207).

Both Gibbon and Franklin are finally concerned with freedom, with the intellectual freedom that Franklin expresses by

[33] John N. Morris, *Versions of the Self* (N.Y.: Basic Books, 1966), pp. 72-73. See also Martin Price, "The Inquisition of Truth: Memory and Freedom in Gibbon's Memoirs," *Philological Quarterly* 54 (1975): 396.

[34] Gibbon's nearest approach to a genuinely transforming moment is of course his view of the Forum (pp. 134-136). But even this is connected with his early attraction to history, and to Roman history (pp. 41, 42), and is an intensified confirmation of an existing direction, not a reversal or "right-angled" change.

his distrust of restrictively systematic reasoning and with the still more necessary freedom of the self from the roles through which it articulates itself in the world. "Freedom is the first wish of our heart," Gibbon declares, "freedom is the first blessing of our nature: and, unless we bind ourselves with the voluntary chains of interest or passion, we advance in freedom as we advance in years" (45). Such freedom is not conferred by a sudden transformation of one's identity; that way lie the perpetual oscillations between all and nothing that Rousseau notes in himself (332, 522) and that reach their full pathological extreme in Cowper's life as recorded in his *Memoir*: as oscillation between abject fantasies of persecution (with a longing for the release of death or madness) and the sudden shining upon him of "the full beams of the Sun of Righteousness."[35] Rather, Franklin and Gibbon attempt (to borrow Peter Gay's words on Hume) "to substitute the authentic if relative certainty of experience for the absolute but spurious certainty of metaphysics or tradition."[36] Both seek the merely and fully human, and this ideal informs the unconverted lives that they record in their autobiographies.

Boswell's journals, especially the *London Journal* of 1762 to 1763, display the full complexity of the later eighteenth century's treatment of autobiography and, in a curiously direct form, much of the sensibility from which it proceeded.[37] Boswell was no stranger to the ready adoption and discarding of roles that Franklin illustrates in his *Autobiography*—"I have discovered that we may be in some degree whatever character we choose" (47)—and his enjoyment was the keener for the passionate interest with which he watched himself perform: "The scene of being a son setting out from home for the wide world and the idea of being my own master, pleased me much"

[35] It is crucial to see that Cowper himself supplies the materials and terms for a psychological reading of his sufferings and conversion, as Augustine, for example, does not.

[36] Peter Gay, *The Enlightenment: An Interpretation*, 2 vols. (N.Y.: Knopf, 1969), 2: 306.

[37] *Boswell's London Journal, 1762-1763*, ed. Frederick A. Pottle (London: Heinemann, 1950). All citations will be given by page number in the text.

(41). It is "the scene" and "the idea" that Boswell instinctively notes and that continue to dominate his mind as he assumes the style of the Spectator or Digges-Macheath or any of the other possible selves that swarm through the pages of the *London Journal*.

Franklin's distance from the roles he adopts is different, less that of the appreciative spectator than that of a man gauging the measure of his liberty, the psychic space separating his posture at any particular moment from the free self that stands at the center of the *Autobiography*. Boswell is not so certain that a reliable self underlies his roles. As a result the fluidity of his role playing coexists with a strong and anxious wish to "fix" himself, to establish a secure and stable identity, whether as an officer of the Guards, or as a respectable lawyer, or as the next patriarch of "delightful Auchinleck, the ancient seat of a long line of worthy ancestors" (79-80). Boswell tries to bring about this reformation by himself and to externalize his own authority in the form of monitory journal entries and memoranda, but what he really seeks is an external force, a compulsion from without, that cannot be so readily resisted as the mere promptings of his own more sober self. Thus in 1761 he implores Thomas Sheridan: "My dear Sir, keep me in the right path. My Mentor! My Socrates! direct my heedless steps!" (9). In 1763 he pleads to Samuel Johnson: "Will you really take a charge of me?" (285). And when Johnson commends his keeping of a journal, Boswell is moved to apostrophize the honored journal itself: "O my journal! art thou not highly dignified? Shalt thou not flourish tenfold? No former solicitations or censures could tempt me to lay thee aside; and now is there any argument which can outweigh the sanction of Mr. Samuel Johnson?" (305).

F. A. Pottle wryly speculates that Boswell, like Gibbon, "simply read himself into a conversion" to the Roman Church at age twenty (6). What that youthful enthusiasm foreshadows is not simply Boswell's need, however ambivalent at times, to submit himself to external authority (Lord Auchinleck, Sheridan, Johnson) but also his faith, equally ambivalent, in the possibility of "conversion," of a decisive and significant transformation of the self. His journey from Edinburgh to London, for example, is ritualized with precisely such a goal in mind. Leaving home, Boswell makes triple bows at Holyrood-house—"once to the Palace itself, once to the crown of Scotland above the gate in front, and once to the venerable old Chapel"—and to Arthur's Seat, "that lofty romantic mountain on which I have so often strayed in my days of youth" (41-42). The second part of what is unmistakably a *rite de passage* occurs when Boswell sights the earthly city that his imagination invests with the power if not to save at least to transform him: "When we came upon Highgate hill and had a view of London, I was all life and joy. I repeated Cato's soliloquy on the immortality of the soul, and my soul bounded forth to a certain prospect of happy futurity. . . . I gave three huzzas, and we went briskly in" (43-44). But on the very next day, though "bold, easy, and happy," he has "a kind of uneasiness from feeling *no amazing difference* between my existence now and at Edinburgh" (45, my emphasis). Boswell is still Boswell; the ritual has failed. While it will be some time before the scheme of joining the Guards collapses entirely, it is on this day, only his second in London, that he begins to doubt the power of the city to re-create him.[38]

He can doubt because he knows that he is the sole author of the hope he feels and that the meaning which the mind so readily creates can as readily be withdrawn. He knows, even as he bows reverently to them, that Holyroodhouse may be considered "as so much stone and lime which has been put together in a certain way, and Arthur Seat as so much earth and rock raised above the neighbouring plains" (42); just as Rousseau knows, even as he derives comfort from it, that hitting a tree with a stone is not an infallible sign of salvation. Boswell, moreover, in a different way than either Rousseau or Sterne, takes to its logical conclusion the possibility that experience may at any moment be drained of its substantiality

[38] See Patricia M. Spacks, *Imagining a Self: Autobiography and Novel in Eighteenth-Century England* (Cambridge, Mass. and London: Harvard Univ. Press, 1976), p. 234.

and meaning. He feels "a thorough conviction of the vanity of all things" (150); he sees "the nothingness of all sublunary enjoyments" (214); an entire day passes away "imperceptibly, like the whole life of many a human existence" (188). This is the language of Stoic and Christian commonplace translated into a subjective and ontological context where it expresses a felt decay of the world's being. When Augustine gazes at the things of the world, they cry out their authorship: "He made us!" But for Boswell, as for Burke, "perfect simplicity and intimate knowledge of scenes takes away the pleasing sort of wonder and awe that we have for what is not clear to us" (176). To look hard at experience is not to pierce its familiar surface and discover a sacramental reality beneath; it is instead to be deprived of, to "see through," its meaning, perhaps a meaning that one has created oneself: "I see too far into the system of things," he writes, "to be much in earnest" (77).

While he wishes for a new and stable identity, then, conferred from without (or at least sponsored by a force outside himself), Boswell also knows this to be an impossible wish: a wish in direct conflict with the perception of experience that marks him as a writer of the later eighteenth century, and the later eighteenth century as the beginning of the modern era. For him there is no *kairos*, rich with the energies of transformation, no new self, born from the old in a moment of conversion, and no hidden order of reality capable of bursting in upon, and reversing, the course of ordinary human experience. Like the autobiographical writers contemporary with him, Boswell recognizes but resists the generic paradigm established by St. Augustine because he does not share the conceptions of reality, of time, and of the self that underlie it. Nor does the eighteenth-century autobiographer attempt, as the Romantics would, to recapture that paradigm by displacing it into a new context in which Nature, or another force, might replace that second level of reality—transcendent, supremely meaningful, distinct in kind from ordinary reality—that was for Augustine the sphere of divinity itself. At times, particularly for Boswell, the old conception of reality is vivid, like a dream from which one has awakened yet not fully emerged.

But at their most typical these writers balance a certain limited responsiveness to that dream with a real ease and adeptness in the very world of man-created truths that keeps it from being a reality.

The shift of sensibility that these autobiographies exemplify is, for one thing, a shift away from (though of course not an annihilation of) "essentialist" thinking, from the notion of fixed essences and determinate orders of being. We see this in Hume's stunning conclusion to the attack on substance begun in the previous century; in the remarkable generic experimentation that the poetry, prose, and drama of the period display, and even in Johnson's belief, echoed by others contemporary with him, that power of mind is simply power of mind and that a person's excelling in divinity rather than law is the result not of a particular kind of genius but of a sequence of accidental causes. And we see it of course in the fluidity of identity found in Sterne, Boswell, Franklin, and Rousseau, not to mention such fabricators of Gothic, or bardic, or exquisitely unstable characters as Gray, Collins, Macpherson, Mackenzie, and others. One temporal form of this shift away from essentialist thought is the breakdown of the *kairos*, that moment which insists upon a second order of time—and thus on the essentialist character of time—by intruding itself into the first. Somewhere between the Book of Genesis, in which fixed orders of creation are linked with determinate units of time ("And the evening and the morning were the first day"), and the books of Darwin and Lyell, in which a particular species or phenomenon or moment is only a phase in a continuum stretching back to the beginning of time, lies the later eighteenth century, in which the self is richly unstable yet not indeterminate and time is of one kind but in no sense unvarying.

The autobiographers of this era find, unlike Augustine, that the present they inhabit is not *essentially* different from the past they have known or the future they are likely to know yet that this present, scrutinized with something of the intensity that Burke brings to the immediacy of sensation and perception, can lead us to construct categories of value appro-

171

THE RECOVERY OF THE PRESENT

priate to its significance and worth. In Boswell, Sterne, and Rousseau, for example, as in Burke, there is a heightened conception of sentiment, of the number and kinds of human purpose it can serve, and an acute awareness of the ways—some histrionic in the extreme—in which we may enter into the experience of sentiment. This implies, in turn, a new interest in roles and role playing and a new relationship between these roles and what had been conceived as our "essential self." If there is no second self to spring phoenixlike from the first in a moment of spiritual rebirth, there is a remarkable range of roles and postures available to us, and their relationship to our more persistent identity may both mimic the Augustinian experience and, perhaps more important, lead to a less rigid conception of human identity than the traditional and traditionally hierarchical terms "self" and "role" imply.

Such a reclamation of the superficial (a "mere role") has its temporal counterpart in a new attention not to a second order of time but to the daily, the customary, and the momentary, whether it is the surface of a life unmarked by magnificently transforming experiences (as in Franklin or Gibbon or, as we shall see, Boswell's Johnson) or the literary counterpart of such a sequence of present moments, that hovering "now" of which we find different forms in Tristram's narration, Smart's or Richardson's immediacies, and the "Journal time" in which Boswell records the moments of his existence.[39] Here too, as in Burke, attention to the momentary and immediate is part of the reclamation of present experience as such, and this, in turn, part of the larger effort to discover in human experience the heft and meaningfulness of the substantial. In giving us the story of lives not dramatically turned, like Augustine's, toward a second order of selfhood, of temporality, and of being, but returned upon the newly appreciated significance of their common human experience, the autobiographers of the later eighteenth century give character

[39] Morris speaks of "Journal time" and remarks that "like *Clarissa*, Boswell's Journals are a book of moments" (*Versions of the Self*, pp. 181, 173).

and dimension to a particularly personal region of an extensive Enlightenment landscape.

Boswell's *Life of Samuel Johnson* is a biography of a special kind. Like the lives disclosed in later eighteenth-century autobiographies, Johnson's life is marked by no decisive dramatic turn, no conversion or secular analogue of conversion. But unlike those lives, it is the life of a hero, and in this case a hero whose very invulnerability to change is part of his heroic nature. A significant portion of Johnson's heroism is traditional, a matter of his accomplishments and efficacy, of what he manages to do. There are his principled good works, for example, his "unwillingness to leave unrighted any individual wrong that came to his attention, or individual suffering unalleviated," as Bertrand Bronson puts it.[40] There is the salutary effect of his conversation on the minds and hearts of others. "When he opens freely," Edward Dilly attests, "every one is attentive to what he says, and cannot fail of improvment as well as pleasure."[41] Dr. Adams puts it more strongly: "We had much serious talk together," he recalls of their last visit, "for which I ought to be the better as long as I live" (4:376). And Boswell himself makes the general point: "Few persons quitted his company without perceiving themselves wiser and better than they were before" (2:117). Beyond this there are the effects of Johnson's writings, whether the moral illumination of the *Rambler* essays, with their power to "brace and invigorate every manly and noble sentiment" (1:215), or the intellectual penetration of the *Lives of the Poets* in one of which, says Boswell, Johnson has "discovered to us, as it were, a new planet in the poetical hemisphere" (4:38). Finally there is the very heroism, given Johnson's character, of the effort that such accomplishments required. "The final importance

[40] Bertrand Bronson, *"Johnson Agonistes" and Other Essays* (Berkeley and Los Angeles: Univ. of Calif. Press, 1965), p. 47.
[41] James Boswell, *The Life of Samuel Johnson*, ed. G. B. Hill, rev. L. F. Powell, 6 vols. (Oxford: Clarendon Press, 1934-1964), 3: 110. Subsequent references are to volume and page.

of the *Dictionary*," as one critic says, "is not that it represents the work of an entire French or Italian academy but that it was carried on in time taken out from lethargy and despair. . . . Johnson's greatest works are not only testimony to his superiority of mind but concrete symbols of his victory over himself."[42]

At the same time that he insists on Johnson's accomplishments, however, and on his surmounting of the obstacles to those accomplishments, Boswell measures his hero according to an altogether different set of values. He portrays him as a figure whose very being and presence are themselves not only manifestations but modes of the heroic, worthy of such respect and admiration as we traditionally grant to action and achievement. "The *Life* reminds us again and again that Johnson's greatness is something that can be fully comprehended only by those who move in his presence";[43] that presence, however, is a form and not just a token of his greatness.

In this respect Boswell's effort in the *Life* is analogous to Burke's reclaiming of present experience in the *Enquiry*, for both offer us not only a new object of value but a new scheme of evaluation as well. We can see this by considering the role of Johnson's conversations, to which Boswell ascribes the "peculiar value" of the *Life*, for that conversation "was, perhaps, *more admirable than even his writings*" (1:31; 4:50, my emphasis). But admirable in what way? The ultimate Western models for this conception of the hero, Socrates and Jesus, were figures whose conversation was the discourse of another world, the realm of truth or the kingdom of God, a world that those heroes both revealed and symbolized. Something of this idea shapes the image of Johnson in the *Life*, though less than is often supposed; for in an important sense Johnson's conversation is valued not simply as teaching, or as a

[42] William C. Dowling, *The Boswellian Hero* (Athens, Ga.: Univ. of Georgia Press, 1979), p. 140. For a subtly argued exploration of themes of absence and presence, continuity and discontinuity in the *Life*, see also Dowling's *Language and Logos in Boswell's "Life of Johnson"* (Princeton: Princeton Univ. Press, 1981), esp. chaps. 3, 4.
[43] Dowling, *Boswellian Hero*, p. 141.

glimpse of or an avenue to another world, but as a token of its utterer, and Johnson himself is valued not just for what he symbolizes—intellectual penetration or moral integrity or triumph over oneself—but for what he is. To value in this way, as heroic, a character's very being, his presence and substantiality, required of Boswell an enormous imagiative effort, for he had to create both a particular image of Johnson and the terms that would permit us to see that image as heroic.

One way in which Boswell complicates the idea of Johnson as a hero of acts and accomplishments is to insist, precisely, on his inefficacy. Of Johnson's indolence little need be said. Whether he finds himself "so languid and inefficient that he could not distinguish the hour upon the townclock" (1:64); or lost in oblivion and dreamlike inaction, "thinking to write the Lives [of the Poets], and a great part of the time only thinking" (3:435); or discovering his past life to be "nothing but a barren waste of time" (3:99), Boswell's Johnson, despite his achievements, rarely allows us to forget for long his perpetual "inclination to do nothing" (1:463).

Less frequent, though common enough in the *Life*, are accounts of what Johnson did, but unsuccessfully, accounts of his failures. He provides Boswell with legal arguments, some quite lengthy, but they are far from uniformly successful (e.g., 2:373, 4:128-131). Indeed, at times they are offered as dissenting opinions after the fact: "Johnson was satisfied that the judgement was wrong, and dictated to me the following argument in confutation of it" (3:59). Nor do his direct efforts on behalf of others, or himself, always achieve their ends. His eloquent and energetic attempts to have the sentence of the forger, William Dodd, reduced from death to exile fail; Dodd is executed (3:120-122). He is, similarly, unable to obtain a diploma for the Master of Arts from Dublin or to gain permission to practice as an advocate without a doctor's degree in civil law (1:134). Boswell reminds us often, too, of what Johnson might have done had he made the attempt. In 1765 Johnson "had thoughts both of studying law and of engaging in politicks" (1:489); he more than once considers a parliamentary career (2:138-139); his edition of Bacon would have been executed "in a most masterly manner," had he but produced it (3:194).

Such failures and unattempted projects—particularly those involving "business" and public life—are important in the *Life* because they are important to Johnson himself. When Sir William Scott laments Johnson's not having followed the profession of law, by which he might have become Lord Chancellor and had the title of his native Lichfield, Johnson "seemed much agitated; and, in an angry tone exclaimed, 'Why will you vex me by suggesting this, when it is too late?' " (3:310). Throughout the *Life*, in fact, Boswell reminds us that Johnson values efficacy in the public world and that he regards that world at times as an enviable locus of action, accomplishment, and sheer reality. His own life, he tells Edwards, does not have the regularity of one who is in business; he is thus a straggler. "You," he continues, "are a lawyer, Mr. Edwards. Lawyers know life practically. A bookish man should always have them to converse with. They have what he wants" (3:306).[44] We see this "straggler's" respect for the practical world in his "bustling about, with an ink-horn and pen in his button-hole, like an excise-man" when Henry Thrale's brewery is to be sold, and in his hyperbolic assessment of its value: "We are not here to sell a parcel of boilers and vats, but the potentiality of growing rich, beyond the dreams of avarice" (4:87). Such a remark links Johnson, however surprisingly, with that authentic *"iron chieftain"* and captain of industry, Matthew Boulton, who had said to Boswell when he and Johnson visited his works in 1776: "I sell here, Sir, what all the world desires to have—POWER" (2:459). Johnson undertakes to sell only one brewery, in the *Life*, and he never sets up as a merchant of industrial power, but scenes like these confirm what Boswell elsewhere tells us: that "Johnson loved business, loved to have his wisdom actually operate on real life" (2:441), and that, in conventional ways at least, it does not often do so.

[44] It is only fair to add that Edwards turns out to have little that Johnson "wants," for he "has passed through life without experience" (3: 307).

Boswell's attention to Johnson's failures, to his unlived public lives, and to his powerful respect for "business" is of course not an effort to diminish Johnson, or to be evenhanded in depicting his character, or even to locate him in a state of philosophic abstraction transcending mere business. It is not an effort either to diminish or augment Johnson's heroic nature but to define one side of it, to distinguish between "uncommon powers" and "animated ambition" 1:131, abilities and accomplishments, presence and productivity.[45] Boswell points to this separation of abilities from achievements—ultimately, of character from action—in other ways as well. He reminds us that in a certain year Johnson was much and did little: "In 1772 he was altogether quiescent as an authour; but it will be found from the various evidences which I shall bring together, that his mind was acute, lively, and vigorous" (2:143). Or he records Johnson's effect on others, though not the actions by which he achieved that effect: "I recollect with admiration an animating blaze of eloquence, which rouzed every intellectual power in me to the highest pitch, but must have dazzled me so much, that my memory could not preserve the substance of his discourse" (1:460).

Passages such as these serve to isolate, alongside extraordinary accomplishment (the *achievement* of Samuel Johnson), another and different order of extraordinariness: Johnson as a locus of powers, a repository of being, a center of presence. In showing us this side of Johnson, Boswell is, to borrow Trilling's words, "not concerned with energy directed outward upon the world in aggression and dominance, but, rather, with such energy as contrives that the centre shall hold, that the circumference of the self keep unbroken, that the person be an integer, impenetrable, perdurable, and autonomous in being if not in action."[46] While much of Johnson's energy is

---

[45] Thus David L. Passler seems to simplify the *Life* considerably when he asserts that our main interest is in Johnson's translation of his brilliance into "lasting achievements," among which Passler numbers his conversations. See Passler, *Time, Form, and Style in "Boswell's Life of Johnson"* (New Haven and London: Yale Univ. Press, 1971), pp. 34-35.

[46] Trilling, *Sincerity and Authenticity*, p. 99.

certainly directed outward upon the world in aggression and dominance, much is not, or at least brings about little in being so directed. For Johnson does not win law cases or move assemblies or, usually, reform the hearts of the wayward by means of his chief activity in the *Life*, conversation. Rather, he confirms, and makes powerfully evident to others, his own substantiality of self, the authenticity and presence of his personal being.

It is this conception of heroism or extraordinariness that governs Boswell's emphasis on Johnson's originality and uniqueness, his sheer difference from others, including other eminent figures. We can see this in the way Boswell contrasts Johnson, particularly in conversation, with Burke and Goldsmith, two characters of great symbolic importance in the *Life*. Burke is established as a public figure, in contrast to Johnson, but like Johnson he is both genuinely extraordinary—"Yes; Burke *is* an extraordinary man," says Johnson— and a powerful conversationalist. The crucial difference between them concerns the role of conversation in their lives. For Burke conversation is neither a substitute for public life nor (as it certainly is for Johnson) an alternative mode of eminence. It is the natural " 'ebullition of his mind; he does not talk from a desire of distinction, but because his mind is full' " (4:167). Burke's talk is thus the outer and unstriven-for expression of powers that have found their chief employment elsewhere, though his "common conversation corresponds with the general fame which he has in the world" (4:19-20). Johnson himself must, and does, work at conversing powerfully, but Burke simply cannot help it. "Yes, Sir; if a man were to go by chance at the same time with Burke under a shed, to shun a shower, he would say—'this is an extraordinary man' " (4:275). This ease and power appear in the challenge Burke poses to Johnson. " 'That fellow,' " he says in 1776, " 'calls forth all my powers. Were I to see Burke now, it would kill me' " (2:450). Burke's powers, however, are always "forth," and effortlessly so. The contrast between these two giants, then, does not concern the extent of their powers but the degree to which each is identified with his conversational strength and thus the relation of conversation to the main business of an extraordinary man's life. Burke's talk confirms the greatness he exhibits in his real profession; Johnson's talk is his profession.

The treatment of Goldsmith sets in relief both the extent and the special nature of Johnson's qualities, particularly his force and presence. Like Burke, Goldsmith is an extraordinary man, a great writer, and Johnson acknowledges his eminence: "Of Dr. Goldsmith he said, 'No man was more foolish when he had not a pen in his hand, or more wise when he had' " (4:29; cf.2:235-236). Imagining himself, however, to be not just "a very great man" but a man great in the Johnsonian way, Goldsmith becomes a ludicrous parody of Johnson, striving pathetically for a conspicuousness he cannot, even by obstreperous insistence, achieve. Indeed Johnson's mere preparation to speak, his "rolling himself," manages to drown out Goldsmith's talk: "Stay, stay,—Toctor Shonson is going to say something" (2:257; cf. 1:412-414, 423).

It is crucial to see that Goldsmith is not ludicrous simply because he is eager to "shine"; Johnson too treats talk as display and combat; he too will sacrifice truth to victory in conversation; and he too, though in a different way, appears an "inspired idiot" to some (1:412 n.6; 1:147). Rather, Goldsmith fails to see what we as readers must see, that there are at least two different forms of greatness in the *Life*, one identified with writing, business, politics, and other modes by which the self is objectified in the public world, the other identified with private conversation and with sheer power of presence. (This is clear even in the contrast between their youths. Goldsmith exhibited no early signs of extraordinary powers, while Johnson was "from the beginning Ἄναξ ἀνδρῶν, a king of men" [1:411, 3:168, 1:47].)

Standing between Burke and Goldsmith, then, Johnson emerges as not only a great writer but a hero of presence by nature (unlike Goldsmith, who is not); a figure who in addition exerts himself to this end, perpetually and heroically (unlike Burke, who need not); a man for whom heroic presence is a principal mode of being, indeed *the* principal mode of being (as it cannot be for Goldsmith and need not be for Burke), and who is—mainly by virtue of that fact—unique. He is unique in a special sense distinct from the originality that the degree of his talents confers upon him. This is why Boswell insists on his utter individuality and untranslatability. Indeed there is about Johnson, as Boswell presents him, something of that mysterious and distinguishing eminence that Johnson himself ascribes to poetry. It "cannot be translated" (3:36); it towers "above the common mark"; and it is something, like light, which we immediately recognize, though "it is not easy to *tell* what it is" (3:38) Thus when Johnson dies a singular mode of being dies with him. Boswell had observed in 1773 "that few men are missed when they die. They are like trees cut down in a thick forest. We do not perceive the blank."[47] But, as an "eminent friend" says near the close of the *Life*, Johnson "has made a chasm, which not only nothing can fill up, but which nothing has a tendency to fill up.—Johnson is dead.—Let us go to the next best:—there is nobody;—no man can be said to put you in mind of Johnson" (4:420-421).

This conception of Johnson, insisting at once on his remarkable powers and on the singular mode in which they are manifested, entails a correspondingly complex biographical treatment. On the one hand, Boswell shows us those powers by a multiplicity of views and kinds of view attesting to the variousness of Johnson's nature. He "achieves complex variations in perspective," as Frank Brady puts it, "by mingling the first-person forms of the diarist (the subject seen by himself in the present) and the autobiographer (the subject seen by himself in retrospect) with third-person forms: the limited (the subject seen by contemporaries) and the quasi-omniscient (the subject seen by the biographer)."[48] In addition to these forms of narration there are other perspectives from which we see Johnson. His own writings are mentioned, described, quoted;

[47] From "Journal in London, 1773," in *Boswell for the Defence*, ed. W. K. Wimsatt and F. A. Pottle (N.Y.: McGraw-Hill, 1959), p. 164.

[48] Frank Brady, "The Strategies of Biography and Some Eighteenth-Century Examples," in *Literary Theory and Structure*, ed. Frank Brady, John Palmer, Martin Price (New Haven and London: Yale Univ. Press, 1973), p. 247.

his letters are copiously and starkly reproduced, as are the "essays" he delivers in conversation (2:209-210, 323, 372); more private expressions such as prayers, meditations, diaries—even his relatively lengthy and fragmentary Paris diary (2:389-401)—are also included, with, at times, fragments and variant readings (2:313-315). And of course, always, there is his conversation. This multiplication of perspectives, like the sheer size of the *Life*, is part of an effort to view Johnson's complex nature from many sides, to accomplish what no single view or narrative technique could hope to accomplish.

On the other hand, the very copiousness and variety of Boswell's biography remind us of what Johnson's biographer cannot do, not because Johnson is too complex or his biographer inadequate but because, as a hero of presence, Johnson can only be rightly known in the present (in his presence). Thus the multiple perspectives also compose a thematically central "failure" of sorts, a kind of splendid parody of the "Compleat Biography," since they all share a fatal mediacy that betrays Johnson's characteristic mode even as it discloses it to us. Even the accounts of Johnson's conversation, which readers since Boswell have singled out as the distinguishing feature of the *Life*, cannot escape this mediacy: "I cannot too frequently request of my readers," says Boswell, "while they peruse my account of Johnson's conversation, to endeavour to keep in mind his deliberate and strong utterance. His mode of speaking was indeed very impressive; and I wish it could be preserved as musick is written, according to the very ingenious method of Mr. Steele, who has shown how the recitation of Mr. Garrick, and other eminent speakers, might be transmitted to posterity *in score*" (2:326-327). Such a system, of course, would supply only a more detailed map of the Johnsonian landscape, not a firsthand view of it, for a score is not a performance. Thus Geoffrey Scott was exactly right to assert that Boswell's rival biographers "did not even know that biography is impossible."[49]

---

[49] Geoffrey Scott, *The Making of the Life of Johnson*, vol. 6 of *Private Papers of James Boswell* (Mount Vernon, N.Y.: Privately printed, W. E. Rudge, 1929), p. 16.

It is the particular nature of Johnson's greatness, however, not the general imperfection of life writing, that makes a *Life of Johnson* impossible. Any writer of heroic or encomiastic biography must lament the fact that posterity cannot experience at first hand the greatness of his subject, cannot enter into his or her presence. But when the greatness of the subject consists, as with Johnson, so largely in that very presence there is a special and powerful sense in which biography is "impossible," in which the *Life* must fail to bring us into the presence of the life. Boswell's portrayal of Johnson is thus something like a sublime deictic ambiguity, convincing us for long stretches that Johnson is in a sense "here" yet at the same time insisting on his essential and ungraspable thereness. From this point of view Boswell's publication of the *Life* only after Johnson's death is a symbolic fact of great importance, for that death marks the end of Johnson's power to be "here" to anyone.

Johnson's heroism of presence appears in his consistency of manner. He "talked alike to all," whether to eminent men or Strahan's poor apprentice boy (2:323), among old friends or in "the presence of a stranger" (2:438), and he talked the same, early as late (3:336). But conversation is only one part of what Boswell calls "this great man's attention to small things" (4:191). It is this trait of Johnson's, in fact, that justifies Boswell's own frequent attention to "inconsiderable" details (2:111) and "innumerable detached particulars . . . even the most minute" (1:6). For what Johnson's consistency reveals is not just fixity of opinion or moral stability but a kind of ontological plenitude. He is no less fully himself in trivial situations than in grand, with strangers than with familiars; there is never diminishment or restraint of his being and presence. The point is not that great things may be accomplished in trivial situations; his extraordinariness in such moments is not a matter of what he achieves but of how thoroughly he is, of his complete presentness to the particulars of experience, however inconsiderable. Johnson's remark in his life of Sydenham, quoted in the early pages of the *Life*, exactly describes this aspect of Boswell's hero: "There is no instance of any

182

man, whose history has been minutely related, that did not in every part of life discover the same proportion of intellectual vigour" (1:38). Indeed, Johnson's willingness to offer this extraordinary opinion as a general truth is itself testimony to his own singularity.

The theme of Johnson's ontological continuity, the virtually unbroken presentness of his being throughout his life, lends a special meaning to Boswell's professed authenticity and thoroughness. His willingness to "run half over London, in order to fix a date correctly," for example, is certainly a sign of his scrupulous concern with factual accuracy. But it is also, like much else in the *Life*, an indirect and symbolic testimony to Johnson's continuity of presence, to a figure who always, while he lived, powerfully existed. Thus every fact or moment, event or utterance that Boswell omits, every vacuity in his biographical record, threatens to misrepresent not just the authentic details of Johnson's life but the animating presentness that informed it. By each omission or error, to adapt Johnson's words on another topic, "the continuity of being is lacerated" (3:419). To get a fact wrong is here to replace something that was with something that was not, being with nonbeing. This is why minute biographical accuracy, in the *Life*, is a form of ontological tribute.

Consequently, Boswell frequently gives the impression that he is attempting to fill all gaps with, if not the facts themselves, at least something, that he wishes to provide readers of the *Life* with an analogue to the uninterrupted being that Johnson revealed during virtually every moment of his life. These gaps, in fact, would often be invisible to the reader if Boswell did not call attention to them and to his efforts to fill them with suitable material:

> During this year [1770] there was a total cessation of all correspondence between Dr. Johnson and me, without any coldness on either side, but merely from procrastination, continued from day to day; and as I was not in London, I had no opportunity of enjoying his company and recording his conversation. To supply this blank, I

shall present my readers with some *Collectanea*, obligingly furnished to me by the Rev. Dr. Maxwell. (2:116)

A more personal form of this attention to continuity of being appears in the letters Boswell writes to Johnson when they are apart for long periods. Typically, Boswell complains of Johnson's coldness, of his forgetting him or ceasing to care for him, and Johnson, as typically, is irked by this incessant need for assurances of love and regard:

> I have received two letters from you, of which the second complains of the neglect shown to the first. You must not tye your friends to such punctual correspondence. You have all possible assurances of my affection and esteem; and there ought to be no need of reiterated professions. . . . [Y]ou must not think me criminal or cold if I say nothing, when I have nothing to say. (3:362)

Boswell's wish for "reiterated professions," however, does not arise from a fear that affection has cooled but from a need for tokens of Johnson's presence. It is by this presence that Johnson principally sustains Boswell, and its attenuation or interruption is what Boswell seeks to counter by requests for avowals of love and friendship. Like readers of the *Life*, as Boswell imagines them, Boswell himself requires tokens or analogues, if not images, of the Johnsonian presence. Thus his apparently weak inability to be satisfied by professions of regard is not so much a radical insecurity of character as a logical response to the nature of Johnson's characteristic mode of greatness. Johnson's epistolary professions can appease, but they cannot satisfy, for however warm or minute, they are ontologically distinct from what Boswell needs and what Johnson can supply only to those immediately about him: his heroic, sustaining presence, the *presentness* of his presence.[50]

---

[50] "Most of Boswell's narrative concerns how Johnson's sheer presence affects his acquaintances," writes Elizabeth Bruss in *Autobiographical Acts: The Changing Situation of a Literary Genre* (Baltimore and London: The Johns Hopkins Univ. Press, 1976), p. 71 (and see also pp. 83-84). Beyond this, the *Life* shows that Johnson's presence *is* a significant mode of his greatness.

In portraying Johnson as a figure whose mighty nature must be conceived in terms of such values as power of being, presence, and substantiality (and their opposites), Boswell creates a wide-ranging scheme of values in the *Life* that serves to unify much of its diverse and circumstantial detail. In particular it clarifies a certain amount of the imagery by which Johnson is described, it adds a significant dimension to the themes of death, vacuity, and annihilation, and it establishes the unity of many sections whose organization or coherence is not otherwise very clear.[51]

First, much of the imagery describing Johnson stresses precisely his presentness, the continual evidence of powers defined enough to make him a man always strongly marked, always remarkable not just for what those powers can accomplish but for their sheer noticeability as well (what Burke, in the *Enquiry*, calls "novelty"). He turns knowledge into wisdom, animates the inert, and adds to truth itself the power of existing potently:

> His superiority over other learned men consisted chiefly in . . . a certain continual power of seizing the useful substance of all that he knew, and *exhibiting* it in a *clear* and *forcible* manner; so that knowledge, which we often see to be no better than lumber in men of dull understanding, was, in him, true, *evident*, and *actual* wisdom. (4:427-428, my emphasis)

He seizes and also exhibits; knows, and expresses forcibly; makes evident and actual what might have remained mere inert "lumber." Thus, too, as Bishop Percy observed, "the conversation of Johnson is strong and clear, and may be compared to an antique statue, where every vein and muscle is distinct and bold. Ordinary conversation resembles an inferiour cast" (3:317). Again it is not Johnson's wisdom and eloquence that are singled out but their presentness, the bold relief in which he displays the truth of which he is master.

---

[51] On the thematic organization of narrative units see the appendix to the present chapter.

What sustains and elevates others is not truth alone but that power to stand forth which Johnson confers upon it. In a sense Johnson is to others what Kames says "ideal presence" is to anyone: that means of touching—of affecting—us without which the greatest truth is powerless.

It is preeminently in his conversation that Johnson so exhibits the truth, and thus it is only when with him that one can fully experience it. The imagery of natural forces, which often works to suggest Johnson's power, also suggests spatial and temporal location and, by implication, reminds us that Johnson must be experienced to be understood, that one must be there, in his presence, to know the nature and power of the man. His company, for example, is a weather of the mind that makes Boswell forget "the influence of a moist atmosphere" that had earlier troubled him (1:426). Elsewhere Johnson is "a warm West-Indian climate, where you have a bright sun, quick vegetation, luxuriant foliage, luscious fruits; but where the same heat sometimes produces thunder, lightning, and earthquakes, in a terrible degree" (3:300). This is an image of pervading fertility and sublime power, but it is also an image of a place, and places can only be known by those who visit them. Thus when Johnson has been lax in correspondence, Boswell writes: "I must, therefore, look upon you as a fountain of wisdom, from whence few rills are communicated to a distance, and *which must be approached at its source*, to partake fully of its virtues" (2-144, my emphasis). The metaphor (a fountain of wisdom) is a cliché; what is fresh is its function in establishing not the abundance of Johnson's wisdom and influence but the degree to which these are bound to the substantial presence he creates and inhabits.

The opposite of presence is of course absence, and this large thematic category lends a special coloring to the treatment of death (and the fear of death), vacuity, and annihilation in the *Life*. Boswell's accounts of Johnson's fear of death allow us to connect it with his radical uncertainty concerning the condition of his soul and thus his fear of judgment and damnation. "The dread of annihilation," however, of nonexistence (3:295), is rather different, for it strikes not at Johnson's spiritual condition but at his very existence, and it carries a special force to a figure who has principally lived in the mode of presence and presentness. Whatever the power of Johnson's works, his examples, or (once he is gone) his memory in others' minds, on page after page of the *Life* Boswell has tied the extraordinary meaning and import of Johnson's life to his actual personal presence. The result is that whatever else death signifies, it means the end—the absence—of Johnson in a sense far beyond that in which it means the absence of any man. The *plenum* and *vacuum* that Johnson mentions early in the *Life* are, in a way, the chief symbolic coordinates of his existence in that work, more significant even than life and death since they show us how to understand life and death in Johnson's case. It is as though Johnson's life were a continuing conversion of *vacuum* into *plenum*, of absence (indolence, despair, and so forth) into presence, death into life, and as though he were capable only of these extremes, as he could not drink wine moderately, only not at all or to excess. The perpetual threat of absence makes for a presence more substantial and intense, more fully there, than other men know in their own lives. It is the final dissolving of that presence into absence that Johnson's death signifies in the *Life*: "He has made a chasm, which not only nothing can fill up, but which nothing has a tendency to fill up."

Two passages not directly concerned with Johnson illuminate this theme from other angles. In a letter to Boswell concerning Macpherson's alleged Gaelic manuscripts, Johnson says: "Where are the manuscripts? They can be shown if they exist, but they were never shown. *De non existentibus et non apparentibus*, says our law, *eadem est ratio*" (2:296). Its pertinence to Ossian aside, the legal phrase suggests the conception of character that governs Boswell's treatment of Johnson's life, especially his conversational life. Johnson fully discloses what exists in him and in so doing demonstrates his existence; not to disclose it is, in a sense, to annihilate that existence, to render it indistinguishable from nonexistence. This idea takes a different form in Langton's recollections of Johnson:

187

> Being in company with a gentleman who thought fit to maintain Dr. Berkeley's ingenious philosophy, that nothing exists but as perceived by some mind; when the gentleman was going away, Johnson said to him, "Pray, Sir, don't leave us; for we may perhaps forget to think of you, and then you will cease to exist." (4:27)

As Boswell's need for tokens of an absent Johnson suggests, Johnson's joke is, if philosophically dubious, phenomenologically true, at least in the world of the *Life* and in his own singular case. No character in Boswell's biography lives more fully in the mode of presentness and appearance than Johnson, or, to put it another way, no other character impresses his being so powerfully on the materials of immediacy and depends on their ability to take the impression. There is a sense in which what is most characteristic of Johnson is indeed lost when he is absent, not just because his presence reveals his genuine self so fully (as with many people, extraordinary or not) but because the singular nature of that self is capable of full being only in the medium of the present, and of presence. In a special though powerful sense, for Johnson, if not for his Berkeleyan antagonist, out of sight is out of existence.

This conception of Boswell's hero seems to contradict the traditional idea of Johnson as a rock of timeless principle amid a sea of whiggish and atheist flux, a figure for whom temporizing and temporality are two sides of the same coin since he has no essential connection with either. The view I am arguing for does not quite contradict this idea though it does sharply qualify it. First, the notion of Johnson as faith's Gibraltar in the dire Straits of the Enlightenment tends to confer on him something of the power, but also something of the inhuman thoughtlessness, of anachronism. While this is in fact one common notion of Johnson, Boswell's point is rather that Johnson constructs his solidity, his permanence, from the very materials of flux and momentariness that surround him—that he is less like a stone troubling the living stream than like an iceberg towering above the waves: consubstantial with his surroundings, yet of sublime strength, solidity, and definiteness. This amounts, of course, to a revision of the idea of the hero as a figure set qualitatively apart from his contemporaries and from time itself, living in something like that "state of solemn elevated abstraction" in which Boswell had "*supposed*" Johnson to live "in the immense metropolis of London" (1:384, my emphasis). But Johnson is not that kind of hero. In making him the kind of hero he is, Boswell reveals his concern not with traditionally heroic or transcendent confirmations of worth or selfhood but with what Trilling terms "the ideal of authentic personal being": the individual's experience of himself as strong, coherent, substantial, indubitably here.[52]

In the figure of Johnson Boswell creates a hero whose career subordinates action to authenticity, performance to presence. This conception of the hero entails a corresponding revaluation of the status of the event, for while things happen in the *Life*, events are primarily significant not for their causal potency but for their revelatory power. The *Life*, therefore, does not mainly concern itself with the plot of Johnson's life but with the mode of his existence, with what a phenomenologist might call his way of being in the world. Boswell's exhaustive treatment of detail helps to maintain that emphasis, as does his management of conversation, which draws on its special ability to be a potent assertion of being without becoming a deed. The chief threat to such a figure is thus not a wresting from him of traditional heroic or transcendent possibilities but a "debility of his sentiment of being," an affliction that Trilling rightly sees as equivalent to the notion of "ontological insecurity" as R. D. Laing has formulated it and that is closely related to what the eighteenth century understood by "melancholy" and "hypochrondria."[53] The chief heroic activity of such a figure is precisely the showing forth of that being in all its solidity and presentness.

[52] Trilling, *Sincerity and Authenticity*, p. 93. See also the introduction by Martin Price to *Eighteenth-Century Studies* 4 (1970): 4-5.

[53] Trilling, *Sincerity and Authenticity*, p. 160. See R. D. Laing, *The Divided Self: An Existential Study in Sanity and Madness* (Harmondsworth: Penguin, 1961), pp. 17, 39, 41-42.

THE RECOVERY OF THE PRESENT

This redefinition of the heroic is part of the age's widespread exploration of presence and presentness and part of its still larger search for modes of experience possessing greater weight and significance than common reality yet not participating in an order metaphysically distinct from that reality, for modes of the substantial. Burke's *Enquiry* attempts to liberate the sphere of the present (the emotive, the bodily, the immediate) from its traditionally subordinate status, to grant it new complexity, new meaningfulness, and new authenticity. In the case of autobiography that subordinate status has its major source in Augustine's conception of an order of time that cuts across, both interrupting and transcending, ordinary temporality. The autobiographers of the later eighteenth century discover, with responses of varied kinds, that there is no such transcendence and no second order of time. A writer like Boswell is of particular interest here because he moves with great clarity between older and newer conceptions of the self, of time, and of a life's significant structuring and because he imagines the possibilities of those newer conceptions with such power and subtlety. The *Life of Samuel Johnson*, consequently, both depends upon and goes beyond the discoveries of Burke's *Enquiry* and the explorations of the autobiographers. It depends on a reclamation of the present such as Burke performs and on the multiple rejection of transcendence (personal, temporal, ontological) that the autobiographers display. But it demonstrates, beyond these, that not just interest but greatness of a new and singular kind can be wrested from the fragility and paradoxes of presence and presentness, and that the substantial, therefore, can take the form of the authentically heroic.

APPENDIX

Boswell's conception of Johnson as a hero of presence helps to account for some structural aspects of the *Life* that trouble even sympathetic readers. While such episodes as the dinner with Wilkes and the meeting with George III display the patent coherence we expect to discover in traditional fictional scenes, many of the narrative units of the *Life* seem to disclose no principle of organization beyond the chronological. A significant number of these units, however, are unified by those themes I have been considering: modes of presence and absence, immediacy and mediacy, and related concepts. The apparent attacks on Mrs. Thrale, for example, which have often been understood as the result of ill will or biographical rivalry, are in fact elements of a thematic concern with Johnson's actuality and with the number of ways one can mistake and misinterpret that actuality.

A passage of several pages in 1778 is organized by precisely this theme (3:224-230). Wilkes opens the passage by laughing at Johnson's concern with liberty, a concern that he cannot conceive to be genuine. Boswell, surprisingly easy with Johnson, regrets that very ease, for he misses the awe and veneration with which his "superstitious love of mystery"—or simply "the cloudy darkness of my own mind"—at times surrounds the figure of Johnson. In a sense Boswell longs for a version of the prejudice that blinds Wilkes to the real Johnson. Next Boswell catches Mrs. Thrale in an error of fact and makes the connection with her general readiness "to deviate from exact authenticity of narration." Then Johnson paraphrases a sentence from Thomas à Kempis concerning the desire to make others as we wish them to be, recalls his anger at Hurd for publishing only a selection of Cowley's works, defends the publication of diaries and journals (against Mrs. Thrale) as giving "an honest picture of human nature," and, at breakfast the next morning, recommends vigorously "a strict attention to truth, even in the most minute particulars" since it is "more from carelessness about truth than from intentional lying, that there is so much falsehood in the world."

Boswell's reminder in the next paragraph that Sir John Hawkins and Mrs. Thrale have spread falsehoods about Johnson brings this heterogeneous section to a close. From first to last, however, virtually every detail has concerned not just truth but biographical truth and the temptations to stray from one's real experience of a person or to reconstruct that person according to one's wishes or views. These are problems of representation, and the apparent disorderliness of Boswell's chronological account does not conceal the single-mindedness of his thematic grouping. (A related section later in the *Life* sets a long denunciation of Mrs. Piozzi's *Anecdotes* [4:339-348] next to a still longer mass of Johnson's correspondence [4:353-370]. The contrast here is between falsehood and truth but also between the mediacy of Mrs. Piozzi's anecdotes and the relative immediacy of Johnson's epistolary presence. A related contrast of modes is that between Boswell's closing four-paragraph summary of Johnson's character and the effort to render his presence that has dominated the preceding hundreds of pages.)

The similar underlying coherence and apparent heterogeneity of an earlier section are perhaps least tediously shown in a rough outline (1:255-278):

1. Boswell can find nothing published by Johnson in 1754 except his "Life of Edward Cave."
2. Lord Chesterfield attempted, "in a courtly manner, to sooth and insinuate himself with the sage."
3. Johnson, however, "despised the honeyed words," indignant that Chesterfield had, "for many years, taken no notice of me" but has now fallen "a scribbling" about the *Dictionary*.
4. Dodsley, to whom Chesterfield admiringly read Johnson's famous letter, was taken in by the lord's apparent indifference. But such cool conduct, says Boswell, was "nothing but a specimen of that dissimulation which Lord Chesterfield inculcated as one of the most essential lessons for the conduct of life."
5. Boswell adds Johnson's remark that Chesterfield's letters to his son "teach the morals of a whore and the manners of a dancing-master."
6. On 6 March David Mallet publishes Bolingbroke's works. Johnson remarks of Bolingbroke: "Sir, he was a scoundrel, and a coward: a scoundrel for charging a blunderbuss against religion and morality; a coward, because he had not resolution to fire

it off himself, but left half a crown to a beggarly Scotchman, to draw the trigger after his death."

7. At Oxford Johnson visits the Rev. Mr. Meeke. "I used to think Meeke had excellent parts, when we were boys together at the college: but, alas!
    Lost in a convent's solitary gloom!"
   When he left Meeke, Thomas Warton recalls, Johnson said: "About the same time of life, Meeke was left behind at Oxford to feed on a Fellowship, and I went to London to get my living: now, Sir, see the difference of our literary characters!"

8. Johnson is concerned about "Poor dear Collins." "I have often been *near* his state," says Johnson, "and therefore have it in great commiseration." In another letter about Collins Johnson remarks "that understanding may make its appearance and depart, that it may blaze and expire."

9. Since his wife's death, says Johnson, "I have ever since seemed to myself broken off from mankind; a kind of solitary wanderer in the wild of life, . . . a gloomy gazer on the world to which I have little relation."

10. And immediately after, Boswell's *Life* begins a new year: "In 1755 we behold him to great advantage; his degree of Master of Arts conferred upon him, his Dictionary published, his correspondence animated, his benevolence exercised."

What connects these diverse passages is, again, the themes of presence and absence. Johnson's scanty publication in 1754, Chesterfield's dissimulations, Bolingbroke's cowardly resort to posthumous publication, Meeke's academic entombment, Collins' decline, Johnson's encompassing grief for Tetty—each is a mode of absence, a withholding of the full presence of the self from the world. It is this pervasive and multiform absentness that makes the triumphant opening of 1755—when we "behold him to great advantage," at last fully present—a thematic turn as well as a chronological boundary.

Finally, a related grouping in 1776 (2:459-3:2). Here Boswell sets Johnson's presence against the decline of Charles Congreve, a valetudinarian not drunk but "always muddy," "quite unsocial," who springs up with delighted anticipation when Johnson seems to be concluding his visit. Congreve's case is illuminated by Johnson's remark that David Garrick's brother, Peter, might have been "as brisk and lively" as his brother. "Depend upon it, Sir, vivacity is much an art, and depends greatly on habit." A further contrast to Congreve in decline is provided by Mr. Richard Green, who displays an "obliging alacrity" in showing his carefully ordered museum and whose motto is, tellingly, "*Nemo sibi vivat.*" Finally, in the course of a discussion of Johnson's use of the word "scoundrel" Boswell mentions his response to Mrs. Thrale, "who had asked him how he did." "Ready to become a scoundrel, madam," says Johnson; "with a little more spoiling you will, I think, make me a complete rascal." Recalling again the dreadful example of Congreve, Boswell explains: "He meant, easy to become a capricious and self-indulgent valetudinarian; a character for which I have heard him express great disgust."

In each of these cases what governs a mass of diverse materials is a conception of Johnson's ontological potency and of its opposite: one or another form of absence, disappearance, concealment, or attenuation of individual presence. The latency of the theme accounts, in part, for some of the *Life's* apparent diversity, yet it is a powerful organizer of much in the *Life* that may appear underorganized. That very latency, moreover, serves to establish the themes of presence and absence as not just overt concerns of Boswell or Johnson but major assumptions of the entire world of the *Life* and thus categories of value through which the dramatic audience perceives and assesses that world. In this way Boswell obliges his dramatic audience to see Johnson in the only terms that make him fully visible.

· 6 ·

AMBIGUITIES OF
OTHERNESS

The view of literary development argued in the preceding chapters at once qualifies and affirms the place of English literature and thought in the Enlightenment as a whole. The distinction between British and Continental styles of thought has been emphasized so regularly and mechanically since the seventeenth century that it has come to seem as much an anxiety-ridden fiction of national identity as a useful historical fact, a fiction that has obscured our view of the Enlightenment as often as it has saved us from facile historical generalization. Certainly there is little in English writing of the later eighteenth century that reproduces the critical headiness, the secularizing and iconoclastic energy, of the French Enlightenment. But just as certainly, English writers are themselves engaged, complicatedly and often reluctantly, in nothing less than a surrender of transcendence. What they feel themselves required to surrender takes many forms: religious experience; a second self— at times, bardic or visionary—emerging in power and coherence from the uncertainties of everyday identity; a (past) golden age of chivalry, heroism, faith, or spiritual unity; literary romance conceived as an unself-conscious singing of the marvelous by a poet "whose undoubting mind," as Collins puts it, "Believed the magic wonders which he sung"; and more. In each case what is being given up is a second level of experience both distinct from and superior to ordinary life.

This movement is not only a surrender of transcendence but also a reclamation of the nontranscendent, of common life: a fashioning of its elements into something weightier and more significant than the elements themselves, yet belonging to the same order of reality:

Pound St. Paul's Church into atoms, and consider every single atom. It is, to be sure, good for nothing. But put all these atoms together, and you have St. Paul's Church. So it is with human felicity, which is made up of many ingredients, each of which may be shown to be very insignificant.[1]

Within that single order of reality, moreover, the difference between St. Paul's Church and its individual atoms is striking—so striking, in fact, that we would not stretch the word unconscionably if we spoke of the Church as in some sense a transcendence, rather than a mere agglomeration, of its atoms. That is, there is conservation as well as change in the eighteenth century's relinquishing of transcendence, and this twofold relation accounts for many of the elegiac ironies, interminglings of achievement and loss, and shadowy doublings that mark its literary texts.

I have earlier mentioned Kierkegaard's conception of paradox as a kind of ontological bridge (as well as a blockade) "between an existing cognitive spirit and eternal truth," and the reliance of later eighteenth-century writers not on paradox but on unparadoxical forms of doubleness like dilemma, contradiction, and antiphony. It is as though Renaissance paradox were turned inside out, its terms now struggling not to unite (and by that effort of union to intimate a realm in which such union might take place) but to separate. The ontological implications of both kinds of figure can be shown by a simple diagram in which O^E represents the order of common experience and O^T an order transcending common experience:

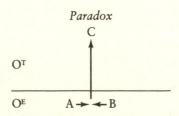

[1] Johnson, in *Boswell's London Journal, 1762-1763*, ed. Frederick A. Pottle (London: Heinemann, 1950), p. 313.

Here two contradictory terms, A and B (cold heat, dark with excessive bright), are forced into relation by syntax, and the meaningfulness of this relation is conserved by the common metaphysical assumption or interpretive convention that their absurdity gestures toward a third term, C, located in an order transcending not only terms A and B but also the laws of contradiction governing their order. Pressure inward is, so to speak, translated upward to a sphere capable of accommodating such verbal and conceptual hyperdensities or ontological plenitudes, even if that sphere can be known only by negation.

Dilemma, on the other hand, like that implied in Imlac's observation that while Rasselas is making the choice of life he neglects to live, is a kind of inversion of paradox and can be diagrammed as follows:

Dilemma

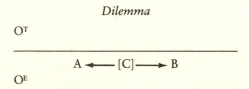

Here there is only one pertinent level of experience, one order of being. The two terms, A and B, moreover, pull apart rather than converge, and what they pull apart from, C, is not a central plenitude but an absent or merely hypothetical third term, whence the brackets surrounding C. There is no union, save in aberrant fantasy, of marriage and celibacy, of the source and the mouth of the Nile, or of making the choice of life and unself-consciously living. If the terms of paradox converge on an implied plenitude, those of dilemma strain away from a central vacuity that is the mere shadow or impress of a vanished and transcendent center.

The pattern of literary development suggested by these rhetorical and schematic forms of shorthand finds counterparts of a somewhat different kind in Earl Wasserman's contention that the centrally paradoxical metaphor of *concordia discors* loses much of its power to image and therefore master experience, in the course of the eighteenth century, and in my own claim that the century's literary development is less a movement from a literature of product to a literature of process (as Frye argues) than a movement from a fusion of these modes to purified forms of each. Both of these accounts entail a movement from paradoxical to nonparadoxical structures, a movement analogous to the proceeding of a single from a double ontology (one order of being from two), along with a simultaneous countermovement from a single complex term to a pair of simpler terms. As two orders of being give way to one, the density of the single complex term that had designated the union of those two orders generates two distinct terms both of which operate within a single ontological field. It is as though paradox or oxymoron were metamorphosed into hendiadys, "darkness visible" (conceived as a single if unconceptualizable phenomenon) becoming "the darkness and the visibility."

Insofar as a figure like paradox gestures toward the transcendent, it usually does so by virtue of the relationship between its two terms, not by virtue of the intrinsic nature of either of them. Where one of these terms itself denotes a transcendent reality, however, we come upon an ancient and traditional Western mode of imaging the entry of objects of ultimate value or plenary being into the world of human reality: the fusion of form with matter in the Aristotelian scheme, for example; of God with man in the Incarnation; of God's breath with the dust of the earth, soul with body, in the creation of man himself; and so on. Such fusions are themselves dramatic focusings of dyadic ontologies, those systems or metaphors that assume "a pair of ontological categories as the real."[2] Insofar as the terms of each pair, moreover, align themselves respectively with fixity and flux, being and becoming, as the literature of product and the literature of process do, they show themselves to be part of a particular—and pervasive—kind of two-term ontology, that which conceives of reality as a relationship between "a class of constants char-

---

[2] J. Feibleman, "History of Dyadic Ontology," *Review of Metaphysics* 6 (1952): 351.

acterized by persistence and a class of variables characterized by change."[3]

Whether transcendence is introduced into the paradoxical relationship by one of its terms or is intimated by the paradoxical structure alone, the literature of the later eighteenth century seems to do two things: it relinquishes the transcendent term itself, and it conserves a tensional relationship of some kind while divesting it of the transcendent intimations that belong to paradox. There is only one major order of being, that of common natural and human reality,[4] but within that order there arise tensional relations that recall, without reproducing, something of the tension that had formerly arisen from the yoking of ontologically heterogeneous objects. While both terms are drawn from a single order of being, the sphere of common experience, in their tension they mimic the ontological tension of paradoxes like those that lie at the heart of dyadic ontologies.

In a sense what occurs is a toppling or lateralizing of a hierarchical structure, a lateralizing that preserves the tension between elements (though that tension is no longer the tension of paradox and no longer carries the suggestion, latent in much paradox, that at another level of being the opposed terms are actually a single term) but projects it into a single ontological sphere. Schematically (1) becomes (2):

My excuse for so abstract and even diagrammatic an exposition is that I am trying to isolate a pattern that operates in a diverse and at times confusing number of contexts, a pattern that marks a change not just in the literary language and structures of the eighteenth century but in its paradigms of valuation as well. Among those single-order tensional re-

---

[3] Ibid.

[4] Although there are of course ontological distinctions within that order, as between dream and perception, tree and "tree," and so forth.

lationships whose skeletal structure is sketched above are many of the topics to which the preceding chapters have paid more concrete attention: the relation between the experiential and the metaphysical in Johnson; between mere temporal sequence and "tradition" in Burke's *Reflections*, or between pleasure and pain (and therefore attraction and repulsion) in his *Enquiry*; between two orders of time in Sterne and two or more in Gray, Ossian, and others; between two attitudes toward the past (one nostalgic, one critical) in Walpole; between self and role in Boswell and Sterne; between the world as given to and the world as constructed by consciousness (in the *London Journal*, for example, or *A Sentimental Journey*); between the frailty and the mightiness of Johnson himself in Boswell's *Life*, and (more simply) between the ordinariness of common men and women and the extraordinariness of great geniuses,[5] a relation articulated (and enacted) by Boswell's biography and celebrated by Henry Mackenzie in his essay on Burns:

> To the feeling and the susceptible there is something wonderfully pleasing in the contemplation of genius, of that supereminent reach of mind by which some men are distinguished. In the view of highly superior talents, as in that of great and stupendous natural objects, there is a sublimity which fills the soul with wonder and delight, which expands it, as it were, beyond its usual bounds, and which, investing our nature with extraordinary powers and extraordinary honors, interests our curiosity and flatters our pride.
>
> This divinity of genius, however, which admiration is fond to worship, is best arrayed in the darkness of distant and remote periods, and is not easily acknowledged in the present times or in places with which we are perfectly

[5] Or, analogously, between the Olympian detachment of both "Observation" in "The Vanity of Human Wishes" and the narrator of *Rasselas'* first paragraph, on the one hand, and the community of striving souls that the narrators of both works, at their conclusions, at last enter. On this see W. J. Bate, "Johnson and Satire Manqué," in *Eighteenth-Century Studies in Honor of Donald F. Hyde*, ed. W. H. Bond (N.Y.: Grolier Club, 1970), pp. 145-160.

acquainted. Exclusive of all the deductions which envy or jealousy may sometimes be supposed to make, there is a familiarity in the near approach of persons around us not very consistent with the lofty ideas which we wish to form of him who has led captive our imagination in the triumph of his fancy, over-powered our feelings with the tide of passion, or enlightened our reason with the investigation of hidden truths. It may be true that "in the olden time" genius had some advantages which tended to its vigor and its growth, but it is not unlikely that, even in these degenerate days, it rises much oftener than it is observed, that in "the ignorant present time" our posterity may find names which they will dignify, though we neglected, and pay to their memory those honors which their contemporaries had denied them.[6]

Genius here is both distinct from and continuous with common humanity. By its "supereminent" reach some men are "distinguished" from the rest, displaying a "divinity of genius" that properly calls forth "worship" and excites a sublime awe comparable to that excited by "great and stupendous natural objects." At the same time, however, what genius invests with "extraordinary powers" is "our nature" and what its presence expands "beyond its usual bounds" is precisely "the [generic human] soul." There is, in short, an obvious and even overwhelming sense in which the person of genius transcends common humanity, yet there are at the same time connections, filiations, even intimacies that tie together what our perception of the sublimity of genius had so astonishedly distinguished. The genius, one might say, is St. Paul's Church to the atoms of common humanity, and the ontological continuity in both cases is as significant as the more striking and sublime otherness. (I explore the implications of this ontological internalizing of difference and discontinuity later in the chapter.)

[6] Henry Mackenzie, *The Lounger* No. 97 (9 December 1786), quoted in *Eighteenth-Century Critical Essays*, ed. Scott Elledge, 2 vols. (Ithaca: Cornell Univ. Press, 1961), 2: 979.

In such structures as these, which only mimic paradoxical relations involving a transcendent order, the relationship itself acquires a new importance. For in direct proportion as the terms themselves are divested of genuinely transcendent status, the mimicking of that status derives purely from the relationship and from the intensity of difference it can generate between two nontranscendent terms. This is an abstract way of approaching the familiar fact that various kinds of disharmony, tension, disturbance, and disruption become sources of value in the later eighteenth century even when their effect is distinctly not pleasurable. From one point of view, of course, the valuing of such tensions is an effort of intensification, part of a search for potent and even overpowering experience. But from another point of view that very search (with the tensions it discovers) is the result of a still larger effort to insist on significant differences between things and thus to conserve the category of "the other" at a time when the classical locus of that category and producer of those differences, the concept of a transcendent order, is growing less and less available.[7]

Seen as a strategy for the disengagement from transcendence, then, the main thrust of later eighteenth-century literature can be understood in terms of several interrelated models: as a turning inside out of paradox; as a lateralizing of the hierarchical; and as a displacement, in Frye's sense, of tensional structures involving transcendence by tensional structures that only mimic such involvement. What each of these models emphasizes, in its own way, is the movement from a two-level to a one-level structure of experience and the compensatory activity of putting together elements from the latter in imitation of the former.

Seen as a reclamation of common experience, however, the thrust of that literature looks very different: not a combining

[7] See Neil Hertz, "The Notion of Blockage in the Literature of the Sublime," in Geoffrey H. Hartman, ed., *Psychoanalysis and the Question of the Text* (Baltimore and London: The Johns Hopkins Univ. Press, 1978), pp. 68-70.

202

but a dividing, even a desynonymizing, the generation of various kinds of difference within a single but not uniform or homogeneous order of experience. The conclusion of *Rasselas*, for example, can certainly be seen as a combining of (among other things) hope and skepticism, wishful fantasy and critical awareness, the impulse to conclude and the drift of ongoingness, each of these pairs constituting an unstable amalgam that reflects, for Johnson, the conditions of our existence.[8] But it may also be seen, *must* also be seen, I want to say, as a dividing rather than a combining, an insertion of difference into a unitary scheme or consciousness, a "fall" that is not at all simply negative and that recapitulates, in different terms, Rasselas' much earlier fall from innocent oneness with his "world" (the Happy Valley) into discontent, self-consciousness, self-division, and a larger world (chapter 2). In the same way, the nostalgic and primitivist impulse we have traced in Gray, Ossian, Walpole, and others, like the distinct but related work with multiple temporal experience that Boswell and Sterne perform, is in one sense a combining of two or more orders of time but in another a dividing of one-dimensional temporal experience (our inhabiting of the present moment, or of our own time and era conceived as temporally uniform, and so on) into two or more layers or kinds, an introduction of difference into temporal identity. Much the same could be said of Burke's dividing and complicating of present experience in the *Enquiry* and of his introduction of discontinuities into what had been taken as continuous spectra of emotions (from pleasure to pain, from the beautiful to the sublime, and so on). And that central resource of the Age of Sensibility, personification, especially in its most striking and critically least tractable form, the apostrophe, is equally susceptible of interpretation in terms of each of the models I am discussing. When

[8] See Johnson's *Idler* No. 58: "Yet it is necessary to hope, tho' hope should always be deluded, for hope itself is happiness, and its frustrations, however frequent, are yet less dreadful than its extinction." In Samuel Johnson, *"The Idler" and "The Adventurer,"* ed. W. J. Bate, John M. Bullitt, L. F. Powell, vol. 2 of The Yale Edition of the Works of Samuel Johnson (New Haven and London: Yale Univ. Press, 1963), p. 182.

Collins exclaims, "Ah Fear! Ah frantic Fear!/I see, I see thee near," does the poem dramatize the confrontation of two independent entities, the poet and Fear, or the dividing of the unitary poet (and of that simple notion of independence) into a double and difficult structure? What Collins calls the "shadowy tribes of mind" are uncertainly or ambiguously located; as a result the individual unity and strict separation of self and other become deeply problematic and, in their difficulty, thematically prominent.

From this point of view the movement from a two-level to a one-level ontological scheme—and thus from relationships between levels to relationships within one level—is a shift of concern from differences between to differences within, a shift that has two opposite but inseparable consequences.[9] First, there is a multiplication of kinds of available experience and terms for that experience. When attention is redirected from the relationship between ordinary and transcendent experience to ordinary experience itself, the latter becomes more complex, multifarious, and subtly discriminated than it had hitherto seemed to be. But, second, it also begins to display an intrinsic dividedness that it had not disclosed when distinguished, as a whole, from a transcendent level of experience. From this perspective, that of wholeness rather than numerosity or complexity, there is loss rather than gain, diminution rather than expansion. Over against the creation of additional "realities" within reality itself, then, is a fissuring or crazing of the unity and stability—the identity—of that very reality.

It is this two-sidedness of what seems to me a fundamental imaginative gesture of the later eighteenth century, a fundamental mode of conceiving reality, that lies behind the nearly overwhelming number of ways in which its literature affirms not merely the copresence but something like the consubstantiality of assertion, mastery, triumph, on the one hand, and questioning, loss of control, and defeat, on the other, as though

[9] See Barbara Johnson, *The Critical Difference: Essays in The Contemporary Rhetoric of Reading* (Baltimore and London: The Johns Hopkins Univ. Press, 1980), pp. ix-xi, 105-106.

there were only emptiness from which to conjure weight and only the collapsible from which to make structures.[10] This sense that the negative doubles or shadows of things are somehow within them, and connected to them by links more intimate and compromising than simple opposition or antithesis, has a specifically literary bearing, focused most sharply perhaps in the riven unities of a work like *Jubilate Agno*, or in the uncertainty of invocation/address in Gray and Collins, or in Boswell's attempt to live prospectively so as to reap experience in recall (yet thereby blighting the present that is to be garnered). But it has a more extensive sweep as well, calling attention to the inherent precariousness of experiential as well as literary ventures: the effort to make "the *choice of life*" or to find happiness; to remain (or become) sound of mind or simply stable; to rejoice in God's connection with the visible world; to seek strength in the past or the present; to tell the story of another's life or one's own. The opening of Boswell's *London Journal* is touching in its youthful (and rhetorically uncertain) faith that efforts like these can be successful:

> The ancient philosopher certainly gave a wise counsel when he said, "Know thyself." For surely this knowledge is of all the most important. I might enlarge upon this. But grave and serious declamation is not what I intend at present. A man cannot know himself better than by attending to the feelings of his heart and to his external actions, from which he may with tolerable certainty judge "what manner of person he is." [James 1:24][11]

The keeping of his journal is to give Boswell "a habit of application" and improve his powers of expression, but it is also to provide him with a regular tribunal to whose approval he can shape his conduct. And, as these opening lines make clear, it is to acquaint him with his own nature, with the

[10] See W. K. Wimsatt, Jr., *The Prose Style of Samuel Johnson* (New Haven: Yale Univ. Press, 1941), p. 96.
[11] Boswell, *London Journal*, p. 39.

"manner of person he is." That the journal's relation to his life may symbolize, and even exacerbate, an actual division rather than promote a desired unity does not yet trouble him. Boswell here believes that he is a *certain* "manner of person" and that this person's nature is both adequately knowable and fundamentally unitary rather than ungraspable because never single. But a more apt quotation from the New Testament epistle whose name he bears occurs just a few verses earlier: "A double-minded man is unstable in all his ways" (James 1:8).[12] This doubleness is internal, a relation within oneself rather than between oneself and another person or force, and it is at once generative of internal complexity and destructive of "identity" as such. Simultaneously remedy and prolongation of ill, such strategies as Boswell's enlarge the self's possibilities while diminishing its selfness; inevitably, therefore, they render equally problematic the relationally defined concept of otherness.

> Taken in the religious sense, that which is "mysterious" is—to give it perhaps the most striking expression—the "wholly other" (θάτεϱον, *anyad, alienum*), that which is quite beyond the sphere of the usual, the intelligible, and the familiar, which therefore falls quite outside the limits of the "canny," and is contrasted with it, filling the mind with blank wonder and astonishment.[13]

To the degree that the later eighteenth century's relation to the transcendent was one of readjustment—complex, inven-

---

[12] Several features of this first chapter of James underline the instability that Boswell neatly excises. First, James distinguishes a man who "does" the word from one who only hears it, and he then compares the latter to "a man beholding his natural face in a glass: For he beholdeth himself, and goeth his way, and straightway forgetteth what manner of man he was" (1: 23-24). That Boswell's journal may be a mirror which he regards but upon whose "image" he does not act is never suggested in his own text; nor does he hint that the image of a person's own nature—"what manner of person he is"—is exactly what is being forgotten or avoided, not discovered, by the figure in James's epistle.

[13] Rudolf Otto, *The Idea of the Holy*, trans. John W. Harvey, fifth impression revised with additions (London: Humphrey Milford, 1928), p. 26.

tive, often reluctant—rather than simple relinquishing we should
expect the same of its relation to the principal defining feature
of the transcendent, that in which its transcendence or be-
yondness consists and which Rudolf Otto terms the character
of the "wholly other." What we find, in fact, is again a process
of double aspect: 1) a search for otherness in spheres distinct
from the transcendent, that is, in various areas of common
experience (other people, the past, the present newly examined, exotic or unfamiliar locales, experiences whose obscurity
or awesomeness excludes us from full participation in or comprehension of them, even the enigmas of oneself); and 2) a
recognition that, while these areas of experience may indeed
be "other" in some sense, they are not *wholly* so, as of course
they cannot be. Something of this straddling or softening of
the line between self and other appears in the exuberant
transgressions of Sterne. The desert that would flower for
Yorick in *A Sentimental Journey* does so because he would
carry to it a bouquet, both adornment and love-token; and
the "Dear Sensibility" and "great SENSORIUM of the world"
that is the source of such generous feeling itself vibrates between the externality of the Newtonian universe and the in-
most reaches of the feeling heart.[14]

An analogous uncertainty is part of the meaning of figures
like invocation, apostrophe, and personification. It is often
difficult and at times impossible to decide which sense of
"figure" most adequately describes a particular eighteenth-
century example of personification, for many seem to be as
much figure of speech (and thus a projection of the poet's self)
as encounterable figure or personage (and thus really "out
there"). Powers or presences within the self are in some sense
made other, though not in the way that a god or a muse, to
a believer in gods and muses, is other. In one sense such
personifications exemplify a taming of the other, a partial
withdrawing of metaphysical commitments, but in another
sense they represent, like Johnson's adjective-derived abstract

[14] Laurence Sterne, *A Sentimental Journey Through France and Italy*, ed.
Gardner D. Stout, Jr. (Berkeley and Los Angeles: Univ. of California Press,
1967), pp. 115-116, 277-278; and see Appendix E, pp. 353-355.

nouns ("equinity"), the conferring of a certain independence and substantiality on qualities, on the contingent. As Martin Price says, "the personification is achieved only by the mind at the limits of its power, exploring dim realms or even creating its own fictions. . . . If the sublime is the art of transcendence, the personification is among its characteristic works."[15] (The emphasis on "art" in this account recalls Burke's acknowledgement that "there are scarce any things which can become the objects of our senses that are really, and in their own nature infinite," although a "sucession and *uniformity* of parts," as in a row of pillars, can "constitute the artificial infinite."[16] As "infinite," the artificial infinite is other, always "there"; as "artificial," a product of human art, it is of course "here.")

The minor characters in Boswell's *London Journal* have a curiously close connection to this two-sided or uncertain kind of personification for they are at times both inside and outside Boswell's consciousness and identity, as much self as other; they thus enlarge and complicate that identity even as they half erase its boundaries and thus its very nature as an identity. If anything in the Age of Sensibility is, in recent critical jargon, a site traversed by codes rather than a system of stable and determinate significance it is Boswell in this journal. Here is part of his memorandum for 31 December 1762: "Then Louisa; be warm and press home, and talk gently and Digges-like. Acquire an easy dignity and black liveliness of behaviour like him. . . . At six, Sheridan's. Be like Sir Richard Steele."[17]

Even more striking than the role-playing impulse are Boswell's imperatives to himself, especially the curiously infeli-

---

[15] Martin Price, *To the Palace of Wisdom: Studies in Order and Energy from Dryden to Blake* (Garden City, N.Y.: Doubleday, 1964), p. 368. See also his brilliantly suggestive essay, "The Sublime Poem: Pictures and Powers," *The Yale Review* 58 (1968): 194-213.

[16] Edmund Burke, *A Philosophical Enquiry into the Origin of Our Ideas of the Sublime and Beautiful*, ed. James T. Boulton (Notre Dame and London: Univ. of Notre Dame Press, 1968), pp. 73-75 (my emphasis on "artificial"). See Neal Wood's interesting extension of this notion to political succession in "The Aesthetic Dimension of Burke's Political Thought," *Journal of British Studies* 4 (1964): 60.

[17] Boswell, *London Journal*, p. 113, n. 5.

citous "Acquire," for they reveal an effort not just to move
beyond the self by assuming others' identities (Digges-Macheath, Steele, and so on) but to lend to the self a commanding
authority by externalizing—uttering, in the form of the memorandum—a part of it. It is not clear what an entirely successful externalizing of this kind would look like: a delusional
system, perhaps, or the history of religion as Blake views it
in the eleventh plate of *The Marriage of Heaven and Hell*.
For Boswell, however, these monitory presences are not over-
but underexternalized, inadequately other, and he is driven
to various expedients for intensifying their otherness, such as
binding himself to figures of authority in a kind of grafting
experiment in which they play the stock of otherness to Boswell's scion of self:

> For heaven's sake, think now that if you don't care, you're
> gone for ever. Sit in all morning and bring up journal
> well, so as to have week clear with its warm transactions.
> At two call Temple, confess errors, *and not only resolve
> but promise. So as to be under his power.*[18]

There are eighteenth-century writers for whom these are
not interesting problems or significant solutions, who do not
doubt the stability and determinateness of the self, or for
whom self and role exist in such easy mutual intercourse as
to create no anxiety at the boundaries. Franklin's presentation
of his life, for example, as a book—marked by some few
errata—whose story is one of progressively widening influence, cool acquisition of (or entering into) roles, and growing
identification of the individual self with the nation, can tempt
one at times to interpret the maxim "honesty is the best pol-
icy" as a denial that there is a (Boswellian) problem at all:
"Self is the best other," as one might rephrase it. But Franklin
is one of several interesting exceptions to the larger effort that
Boswell exemplifies, an effort to conserve the category of the
other while surrendering its transcendent import or diminish-

[18] Ibid., p. 265, n. 2 (from Boswell's memorandum for 21 May 1763), my
emphasis. Passages like this suggest that when Boswell speaks elsewhere of
journal writing as "making another self" there is a sense in which he may
also mean "making an other [into one-] self."

ing its distance from oneself and one's common experience, as the previous chapters have suggested. Such an effort inescapably intensifies loss while resisting it. For to locate the other within the self is to give what is "there" a "here-ing," to grant otherness a fuller representation only by eroding its essential nature.

We have, so far, a relinquishing of the transcendent, an action central to that pervasive experience of loss which stamps so many literary forms in the later eighteenth century with features of the elegiac mode. We have as well a variety of compensatory actions that at once mimic and terminate the waning relation to a transcendent order. These actions in turn introduce a particular kind of problematic complexity into the differences—and therefore the relationships—between the transcendent and the ordinary, other and self, solution and problem (or cure and affliction), and they also introduce doubleness and division into what had seemed the univocal solidity of many of these terms and concepts taken alone. If we add to this swiftly summarized group of elements another, familiar to every student of the period—the widespread appearance in life as in art of the melancholic or depressive or "hypochondriack" state of mind—we find a constellation of features significantly resembling the symptoms outlined by Freud in "Mourning and Melancholia" (and in the later *The Ego and the Id*).[19]

Mourning and melancholia are both responses—one normal, the other pathological—to loss, "loss of a loved person, or . . . of some abstraction which has taken the place of one, such as one's country, liberty, an ideal, and so on" (14:243). Both are characterized by painful dejection, loss of interest in the outside world, loss of the capacity to love, and inhibition

[19] Sigmund Freud, "Mourning and Melancholia," in *The Standard Edition of the Complete Pyschological Works of Sigmund Freud*, trans. James Strachey et al., 24 vols. (London: The Hogarth Press, 1957), 14: 239-258. Subsequent references will appear in the text by volume and page number. See also pp. 28-29 of *The Ego and the Id* in vol. 19 of the *Standard Edition*.

of activity. But the melancholic character also displays, often prominently and insistently, a severely diminished sense of his own worth that may be expressed in self-reproach, self-reviling, and the delusional expectation of punishment. This "disturbance of self-regard is absent in mourning" (14:244). Thus "in mourning it is the world which has become poor and empty; in melancholia it is the ego itself" (14:246). What impoverishes the ego is the judgment passed on it by another part of the ego as the result of the following process. Unlike the mourner, who painfully (and often lengthily) withdraws his libido from attachment to the lost object by means of a hypercathexis that psychically prolongs the object's existence so as to permit disengagement from it, the melancholic does not attach elsewhere the libido he withdraws from the object but withdraws it into the ego itself to establish an *identification* (rather than an object-relation) with that object. Since the relation was originally ambivalent, the conflict between ego and object is now internalized as a cleavage between the critical activity of the ego and the ego as altered by identification with the object: "Thus the shadow of the object fell upon the ego, and the latter could henceforth be judged by a special agency, as though it were an object, the forsaken object. In this way an object-loss was transformed into an ego-loss" (14:249).

What is conserved by the mechanism of melancholia is, in a sense, the object itself, for by means of identification the ego internalizes the object and transforms the hostility directed against it (part of the originally ambivalent relation) into aggression directed against the ego, aggression that can now be openly and vigorously expressed in what is at times an "insistent communicativeness which finds satisfaction in self-exposure" (14:247). (Indeed it was precisely to avoid expressing that hostility openly that the subject "resorted to" the illness of melancholia.) What is lost, on the other hand, is, first, the object as part of an object-relation rather than a narcissistic identification (the otherness of the object, one might loosely say) and, second, the ego as a relatively coherent, unimpoverished whole different from and in relation to the object (the unity and identity or selfness of the ego).

Let me point out the obvious parallels between Freud's model and the literature of the later eighteenth century before raising the question of the status, and usefulness, of the analogy itself. To the sense of loss in both mourning and melancholia there corresponds the pervasiveness of the elegiac in the Literature of Sensibility, whether focused on vanished poetic powers or ages of heroic or romance sensibility, the fragile innocence of youth, lost unions of God and man, or (more generally) the possibility of substantial experience adequate to the desires of consciousness. To the extent that these and other lost or unavailable objects are dwelt on with a concertedness at times obsessive we may find an analogue to that hypercathexis which prolongs the lost object's existence so as to be able to release it, the whole procedure constituting a kind of rapt parting stare or valedictory apostrophe. The specifically melancholic depletion of the sense of self scarcely needs more documentation than the presence of the elegiac, for it is one of the main rhetorical stances of the age, whether expressed in Cowper's savage self-revilings and expectations of punishment, Smart's convictions of unworthiness, the Man of Feeling's resolute denial of substance and satisfaction to his spectral selfhood, the sublime poets' sense of themselves as dwindled and diminished beings, or Boswell's particularized and Johnson's generalized expressions of moral, spiritual, and psychic inadequacy.

The economy of loss and conservation that is maintained in melancholia by means of an identification replacing object-loss with ego-loss also has a rather precise counterpart in the strategies outlined in the present chapter. The withdrawal of libido into the ego (or introjection of the object), the consequent splitting of the ego, and the resultingly problematic status of both ego and object (or "other") are analogues in the individual melancholic psyche to the relinquishing and conserving of transcendence, the re-installing within a single order of a tensional relationship miming the relationship between two orders (from difference between to difference within), and the problematizing of the very notions of self and other. In both cases, moreover, melancholic psyche and Literature of Sensibility, a conservative or curative strategy introduces a more resistant strain of the original illness: neurosis, for example, where there had been loss or grief or ambivalence. A strategy to circumvent or palliate loss establishes loss of another kind, a kind more diffuse, subtle, and inward, and one that—in shadowing with uncertainty such primary categories as self and other, possession and loss, past and present—generalizes a particular and finite deprivation into a proneness to erosion that seems to haunt the entire terrain of experience.

What are the objects of loss for these writers and to what particular forms of self-division does the internalization of those objects give rise? In a sense the first part of this question concerns the nature of each writer's Edenic image, that which he both values most highly and judges to be lost to common experience. For Smart a union of earth and heaven, and poet and God, is introjected as judged and judger, or errant self and redeemer, much as common experience seems both to clash and fuse with its sacramental significance. Cowper's related vision of oneness, of connection with and secure locatedness in a joyful creation, issues in the harsh polarities that set others against the self, the rescued against the castaway, heaven against earth, the judging against the judged self.[20] For Collins, Walpole, and others it is a romance past and the imaginative and emotional powers associated with it. What Walpole terms "living back into centuries that cannot disappoint one" results finally in the self-division emblem-

[20] The opening of the manuscript of "The Cast-away" is dated March 20. In the left margin at the end of the poem are three letters and two numbers that Charles Ryskamp transcribes as "Mar. 25," i.e., "presumably when Cowper wrote out the poem—March 25." To my eye, however, that "r" looks more like a "t." If Mat. 25 is short for Matthew 25, which contains the parable of the talents, whose concluding words (Matthew 25: 30) include "cast the unprofitable servant into outer darkness," then Cowper's marginal note supplies the biblical text to which his poem is a gloss or narrative expansion. See William Cowper, *The Cast-away*, ed. Charles Ryskamp (Princeton: Princeton Univ. Library, 1963), p. 12.

atized by the two prefaces—believing and skeptical, respectively—to *Otranto*, and something similar could be said of the way Collins' poetic speakers tend both to champion, and to pronounce lost, romance causes of various kinds. In Boswell the lost Edenic image is associated with stability of character, responsibility, and maturity, and it becomes more or less incarnate in a series of figures that can be (and have been) called paternal or patriarchal, figures of heroic stability: Lord Auchinleck, Paoli, Johnson, and others. Such stability, however, is continually confronted with impulses, energies, ambiguities, and alternative definitions of self that call attention to its rigidity at least as powerfully as to their own uncertainty (if Boswell's memoranda show up the impulsiveness of his behavior, impulse itself makes the memoranda at last still more ludicrous) and that—in the *Life of Johnson*—infiltrate the central figure of Johnson and not just the counterpointed character of Boswell. As for the Edenic image in Johnson's own writings it is nothing less than happiness itself, the correct "choice of life," a world adequate to the imagination and stably filling the mind. Such a world, introjected, generates perpetual strife between an unquenchable sentiment of hope and an unblinking vision of vanity, the seductive whispers of Fancy and the critical pronouncements of Observation.

These few examples will suffice. The point is that a striking number of the works treated in the preceding chapters conform to the Freudian pattern of melancholia in which a particularly acute form of loss leads to an identification with the lost object and a splitting of the ego, a splitting that reproduces inwardly the ambivalence of the original relation with the object and thus converts criticism of the object into criticism (by the ego) of the ego as altered by identification with that object. Taken only this far the analogy with melancholia is casually illustrative, providing a terminology, calling attention to the power and diversity of the elegiac mode in the Age of Sensibility, and placing a sharply focused set of literary phenomena in a larger context of human efforts to come to terms with, and to avoid coming to terms with, loss.

Two considerations, however, suggest that the Freudian model may have an illustrative power of more than casual pertinence: the role of identification in later eighteenth-century literature, and the nature and status of the lost "objects" in that literature. Identification is, of course, crucial to the development of melancholia since it is what permits the reproaches directed at the object to find uninhibited expression as critical activity aimed at oneself. Or, alternatively, it is what ensures the continuing presence of the object that those reproaches threaten to drive away. In "Towards Defining an Age of Sensibility," Frye shows the degree to which various forms of fusion and identification mark the literature of this period. Pity and fear, for example, become "moods which are common to the work of art and the reader, and which bind them together psychologically instead of separating them aesthetically."[21] More particularly Frye focuses on the trope of identification *par excellence*, metaphor, and he contrasts the classical and Augustan critics' view of metaphor (as condensed simile) and the Romantic critics' view (as an ideal identification of one thing with another in "the mind of the creating poet") with its particular form in the Age of Sensibility:

> Where metaphor is conceived as part of an oracular and half-ecstatic process, there is a direct identification in which the poet himself is involved. To use another phrase of Rimbaud's, the poet feels not "je pense," but "on me pense." In the age of sensibility some of the identifications involving the poet seem manic, like Blake's with Druidic bards or Smart's with Hebrew prophets, or depressive, like Cowper's with a scapegoat figure, a stricken deer or castaway, or merely bizarre, like Macpherson's with Ossian or Chatterton's with Rowley. But it is in this psychological self-identification that the central "primitive" quality of this age really emerges. (318)

Metaphor is here an identification of two terms, one of which is the poet himself. With respect to Freud's essay this would suggest (what Freud says has "not yet been confirmed

[21] Northrop Frye, "Towards Defining an Age of Sensibility," in *Eighteenth-Century English Literature: Modern Essays in Criticism*, ed. James L. Clifford (N.Y.: Oxford Univ. Press, 1959), p. 316.

by observation") that "the disposition to fall ill of melancholia (or some part of that disposition) lies in the predominance of the narcissistic type of object-choice" (14:250). It makes no sense simply to apply such an hypothesis to the Age of Sensibility, but we can say that in this literature there is a tendency to base primary acts of self-definition and choices of poetic subject (what one writes about, what it is important and even compelling to write about) on a fundamentally identificatory model of relationship. Such a connection sharpens the analogy with melancholia while insisting precisely on the analogical character of the relationship.

A consideration of the status of what is "lost" in the Literature of Sensibility—what is presented or acknowledged by that literature itself as lost—works to much the same end. In melancholia once the relationship uniting object and ego is shattered and the object is lost, that object is nevertheless reconstituted inwardly through a process of identification and thus continues to exist in a different mode: as part of a narcissistic identification rather than an object-relation, an aspect of the ego rather than an inhabitant of the object world. But what if there had been no "regression" from object-relation to identification but only identification from the very first? Then, if we rigorously avoid positing the prior state that the term "regression" entails, we should have to surrender the object as well, allowing it existence *only* as a modification of ego or self, as something never known by the subject outside of the mechanism of identification. The "object," then, would be inescapably colored by a certain kind of interiority or ideality, and the loss of the object would need to be either acknowledged as itself a fantasy (since there had been no prior relationship to the object) or redefined as not a movement from one state to another, possession to nonpossession, but a characteristic or attribute of just such an object, of an object having this kind of ontological status. In this case loss would be not relational but intrinsic, an attribute of a certain class of objects intrinsically "perdital."

This is precisely the status of the lost object in much of the Literature of Sensibility. Whether we look to the bardic pow-

ers that for Collins, Gray, and others both inhabit and articulate a romance past; to the image of heroic and paternal
stability that is for Boswell, much of the time, the very definition of character; to the conception of happiness, in Johnson, as plenary and abiding "agreeable consciousness," or
elsewhere, what we find is a lament for or a reaching after
objects that have never been immediately experienced either
because they lie in the irrecoverable past or because they are
by nature incapable of being experienced—objects that are,
in fact, modifications of the ego, aspects of self, constructions
of consciousness. Though such objects are not the result of a
regression from object-relations to narcissistic identification,
their ideality (including their intrinsically lost or perdital nature) removes them from actual out-thereness as effectively as
identification removes the object in melancholia.

There are (at least) three objections to this pursuit of the
analogy between melancholia and the Literature of Sensibility.
First melancholia involves an object-loss "which is withdrawn
from consciousness" (14:245), as, in a larger sense, neurosis
involves the enactment of patterns whose existence or significance (or both) is obscure to the subject. There are many
indications, however, even apart from the difficulties of drawing analogies between psyches and texts, that writers in the
later eighteenth century know very well what they are up to
and what the ironies and ambiguities of their nostalgic (and
other) projects are. Second, to draw a connection between the
internalization of the object through identification and the
generation of the object by means of imagination (the link
being a common ideality, and thus a shared apartness from
real experience of external objects) is to ignore the fact that
imagination is itself a kind of possession, a kind of experiencing, and even (following Kames) that the external cannot
be experienced until it achieves precisely that status—"ideal
presence"—which gives to the originally external and the originally internal a common mode of representation. Third (really
an explication of assumptions implicit in the first two objections), the analogy with melancholia tends to erode the distinction between imagination and fantasy, artistic illusion and

neurotic delusion. What begins as an analogy, that is, ends as an assimilation of one term to another, imagination to fantasy, art to pathology.

The difficult distinction between imagination and fantasy (to take up these objections in reverse order) is important, and not only to modern criticism but to later eighteenth-century poetry. In a sense it is the nonhistorical form of the concern with a romance or bardic past, with the possibility of an imagination unclouded by guilt about its powers: by uncertainty, for example, whether an energetic exercise of modern imagining can be distinguished from the wilfullness of mere fancy or the vain projection of neurotic fantasy. Can "false themes" authentically engage the "gentle mind," as Collins hopes, or can scenes that dare "to depart/From sober truth" be "still to nature true"? The typical response of the poets of sensibility is "Yes and no," or "We hope so." The question, that is, is not definitively answered but posed, reposed, explored, and itself taken as a major theme. Thus, the uncertainty introduced by the analogy with melancholia, provided it is allowed to remain an uncertainty, is from a critical point of view an argument in its favor.

Second, as the mention of Lord Kames may have suggested, the objection that insisting on an ideality common to the products of fantasy and imagination obscures the difference between them (and ignores the ability of imagination in some sense to take possession of external reality)—this objection is best answered by being restated as a description. The notion of "ideal presence" does not, for Kames, undo the distinction between the real and the imaginary or between imagination and fantasy; rather, in its insistence that they share a common mode of presentation it permits us, as the analogy with melancholia permits us, to see those distinctions as problematic and, again, thematically important. Insofar as those distinctions are bound up with oppositions between self and world, the internal and the external (personification, say, as figure of speech and as reference to a "figure"), the same response applies. Worrying, and worrying about, distinctions like these is a significant part of the meaning of the later eighteenth-century literary venture.

It will have become clear that these two objections and the responses to them conform to a single pattern in which the objection argues that the analogy with melancholia encourages conceptual fuzziness while the response terms that fuzziness a pertinent exploration of a distinction intrinsically problematic. A different response is required by the first objection. How can we accommodate the unknowingness of melancholia, in which ambivalence and aggression are kept from consciousness until they can be turned against the ego rather than the object, without implying that later eighteenth-century writers characteristically functioned in what might be called a sublimely unconscious state?

In fact, that unknowingness need not, and should not, be accommodated but judged irrelevant. The crucial point at which the pattern of melancholia differs from the later eighteenth-century schema is at the very beginning (their relationship is thus one of dissimilarity followed by convergence rather than similarity followed by divergence). For in that literature, as we have seen, there is no original object-relation capable of regressing to identification and thus no original ambivalence, with its component of aggression, toward an object. As a consequence there is simply no need for "the subject" to fall ill of melancholia or—and this is the heart of the first objection and, in a sense, of all three—for the critic to introduce the notion of the unconscious. It is to the work of melancholia and to the effects of that work, not to its inaugurating cause or its initial strategy of introjection, that the Literature of Sensibility supplies a parallel.

Why, then, draw the parallel at all? To ask this question is, I think, to assume that melancholia is the larger category of which the eighteenth-century experience is a particular case and to question the usefulness of merely adducing an historical and confusingly literary example. This assumption carries with it the implication that melancholia is only a response to the loss of an object one had possessed, and that it is the work of melancholia which then problematizes the categories of loss, possession, other, and self. But it is possible to see that problematizing as the initial or generative condition and its derivation from loss as itself only a special case. The difference

219

is that from this point of view the presumed initial security and distinctness of those categories is given up and their problematic or compromised status is understood not as a response to a particular loss but as part of a set of existential givens that a portion of the Freudian paradigm maps in a limited but accurate way. No particular object need have been lost (that is, once—but no longer—securely possessed), in this formulation.

What is assumed, however, is that lostness, absence, and deep uncertainty about the distinctions between self and other, the inner and the outer, the present and the past may, at various times, be experienced not just as the endpoints of a regressive or degenerative process, individual or cultural, but also as categories no less primordial and no more escapable than the clearcut fixities and sharp demarcations that a degenerative explanation views them as subverting. "We are long before we are convinced that happiness is never to be found," says Imlac.[22] But the tardiness of our discovery need not be projected into a myth of initially possessible happiness fractured by later loss; the pattern of discovery must not be taken for the structure of reality. What Johnson and his age show us in this connection, as often by resisting as by seeking such knowledge, is that the absence or otherness of happiness may be a condition of its being and thus of its presence to us; that loss may be an inescapable category of our experience, or of our perception of our experience, rather than a mode of relation to portions of our experience; and that recognitions such as these need not disable or destroy us, although they are capable of doing so. "The ways we miss our lives," to quote Randall Jarrell's melancholically echoic phrase once more, "are life."

[22] Johnson, *Rasselas*, chap. 16.

INDEX

Abrams, M. H., 156
apostrophe, 88-90, 97, 203-204, 205, 207-208. *See also* personification
Aquinas, Saint Thomas, 32
Aristotle, 30, 156
Arnold, Matthew, 92
Auerbach, Erich, 19n
Augustan literature, 3-23 passim, 36, 38, 42-43, 45-46
Augustine, Saint, 31, 35; *Confessions*, 156-161, 164, 170, 171
autobiography, 68-69, 155-173, 180, 190

Bacon, Francis, *Wisdom of the Ancients*, 77, 84
Barth, Karl, 28
Basney, Lionel, 62
Bate, W. J., 76; on satire manqué, 14, 43
Becker, Carl L., 33, 74
Benjamin, Walter, 22
Berkeley, George, 30, 188
biography, 68; and Boswell's *Life of Samuel Johnson*, 173-194
Blair, Hugh, 126, 127
Blake, William, 17, 130, 132-133; "Epigram," 21-22; *Marriage of Heaven and Hell*, 209; *Poetical Sketches*, 132
Bolingbroke, Henry St. John, Lord, 30, 78
Bonaventure, Saint, 32
Boswell, James, 12, 48, 51, 54, 56, 63, 68, 70, 120, 164, 214; *Hypochondriack*, 42; *Journal* (1764), 91; *Journal* (1766-1769), 125; *Journal* (1776), 91; *Journal* (1778-1782), 125; *Journal of a Tour to the Hebrides*, 84n, 118-

119, 124-125; *Life of Samuel Johnson*, 173-194, 200, 214; *London Journal, 1762-1763*, 16, 24, 26-27, 39, 42, 43, 91, 101, 130, 150, 167-171, 200, 205-206, 208-210
Boulton, James T., 149
Boyd, D. V., 24n, 60
Brady, Frank, 68n, 94n, 180
Bronson, Bertrand, 173
Bruss, Elizabeth, 184n
Burke, Edmund, 17, 24, 47, 54, 74, 130, 163, 164, 170; *Appeal from the New to the Old Whigs*, 120; in Boswell's *Life of Johnson*, 179-180; *A Philosophical Enquiry into the Origin of Our Ideas of the Sublime and Beautiful*, 47n, 139-154, 155, 156, 159, 171, 174, 185, 190, 200, 203, 208; *Reflections on the Revolution in France*, 27, 114-124, 154
Burke, Kenneth, 102
Burnet, James, *see* Monboddo, James Burnet, Lord
Burns, Robert, 24, 69-70, 200
Byron, George Gordon, Lord, *Don Juan*, 132

Carlyle, Thomas, 32, 77
Cecil, Lord David, 94
Chatterton, Thomas, 24, 93, 124, 130, 132; "Extracts from Craishes Herauldry," 125; "Rowley's Heraldic Account of Bristol Artists and Writers," 126
Churchill, Charles, 69
circumstances, Burke's redefinition of, 116-119, 121-123, 154
Cohen, Murray, 11-12

221

94-97; "The Death of Hoel," 93; *Elegy Written in a Country Churchyard*, 13, 41, 43, 94, 96; "Ode on a Distant Prospect of Eton College," 13, 16, 41-42, 74, 92; "Ode on the Pleasure Arising from Vicissitude," 92; "Sonnet [On the death of Mr. Richard West]," 43

Greene, Donald, 34, 63

Greene, Liliane, 164

Hagstrum, Jean, 66

Hardy, Thomas, 141

Hartman, Geoffrey, 99

Hegel, G.W.F., 15

Hemingway, Ernest, 55

Herbert, George, 51

heroism, 36, 105-108, 139, 174-175, 177-190, 194, 214

Hertz, Neil, 202n

Hipple, Walter J., 143

Hollander, John, 22

Home, Henry, *see* Kames, Henry Home, Lord

Home, John, 101; *Douglas*, 101-108, 111

Homer, 13

Hoover, Benjamin, 125

Hopkins, Gerard Manley, 141

Hume, David, 28-29, 30, 48, 51, 56, 71, 126-127, 167, 171

Hurd, Richard: *Letters on Chivalry and Romance*, 127-128, 130; *Moral and Political Dialogues*, 128

hypochondria, *see* melancholia

ideal presence, *see* Kames, Henry Home, Lord

immediacy, *see* presence and the present

invocation, *see* apostrophe

irony, 17-18, 91-92, 109, 112-113

James, Henry, 78

Jarrell, Randall, "A Girl in a Library," 96, 220

Jaynes, Julian, 78

Johnson, Barbara, 204n

Johnson, Samuel, 4, 6, 28, 46, 49, 50, 51, 54, 57-58, 63, 68, 71, 74, 101, 108, 118, 119, 171, 200, 214; *Adventurer* No. 99, 65; *Dictionary of the English Language*, 45, 55; *Idler* No. 58, 6, 203n; *Journey to the Western Islands of Scotland*, 23, 37, 59-60, 74, 78, 81-87, 90, 136, 139; *Life of Cowley*, 65; *Life of Sydenham*, 182-183; "London: A Poem," 58-62, 90; "On the Death of Dr. Robert Levet," 43, 48; *Preface to A Dictionary of the English Language*, 152; *Preface to Shakespeare*, 64-65; *Rambler* No. 8, 22; *Rambler* No. 59, 42-43, 61; *Rambler* No. 125, 65; *Rasselas*, 13, 16, 17, 24, 25-26, 37, 39-40, 43, 45, 58, 59, 65, 86-87, 90, 197, 203, 220; *Vanity of Human Wishes*, 12-13, 17-18, 21-22, 24

Kames, Henry Home, Lord, *Elements of Criticism*, 137-139, 186, 217, 218

Kant, Immanuel, 66

Keats, John, 8, 51; *The Fall of Hyperion*, 133; *Hyperion*, 133

Kenner, Hugh, 124

Kermode, Frank, 110, 113n

Kierkegaard, Søren, 15, 36, 196

Kivy, Peter, 137n

knowledge: in Augustan literature, 4, 5-6, 8-10, 15, 21; in later eighteenth-century literature, 16, 17, 18, 40-42, 43, 45, 220

Krieger, Murray, 67

LIBRARY OF CONGRESS CATALOGING IN PUBLICATION DATA

Bogel, Frederic V., 1943-
Literature and insubstantiality in later eighteenth-century England.

Includes index.
1. English literature—18th century—History and
criticism.   2. Philosophy in literature.   3. Substance
(Philosophy)   I. Title.
PR449.P48B64 1984   820'.9'006   83-43060
ISBN 0-691-06597-7